D1882657

LANDSCAPES IN INDIA

LANDSCAPES IN INDIA

FORMS AND MEANINGS

AMITA SINHA

GYAN

Published by

Gyan Publishing House
5, Ansari Road
Daryaganj, New Delhi-110002
Phone: 011-47034999, 9811692060
E-mail: books@gyanbooks.com

Distribution Network
gyanbooks.com
India, USA, Canada, UK, Australia, France

© Author

All rights reserved. No part of this work may be reproduced, stored, adapted, or transmitted in any form or by any means, electronic, mechanical, photocopying, micro-filming recording or otherwise, or translated in any language, without the prior written permission of the copyright owner and the publisher. The book is sold subject to the condition that it shall not, by way of trade or otherwise, be lent, resold, hired out, or otherwise circulated without the prior publisher's written consent in any form of binding or cover other than that in which it is published.

ISBN: 978-81-212-6473-0

First Published, 2023

Printed at: Gyan Press, Delhi.

The views and opinions expressed in this book are author(s) own and the facts reported by them have been verified to the extent possible, and the publishers are not in any way liable for the same.

LANDSCAPES IN INDIA
Author: AMITA SINHA

In loving memory of my late parents,
Pramila and Rudra Pal Sinha

Contents

Acknowledgments

This book would never have been written had I not—a little to my own surprise considering that I had no formal training in the discipline—joined the Department of Landscape Architecture at the University of Illinois at Urbana-Champaign in 1989. I immediately became involved with an ongoing conservation and tourism development project in Sarnath. Visiting the site, studying its history, and imagining its future brought home to me the crucial role of landscape in the making of a sacred complex. I thank Vincent Bellafiore, then head of landscape architecture, for the opportunity to become involved in the project. Teaching Social and Cultural Issues in Landscape Design for over fifteen years, and more recently Cultural Landscapes of South Asia, has helped me research and write about landscapes from a humanistic point of view.

I am grateful to the Research Board at the University of Illinois at Urbana-Champaign for research grants that allowed me to travel to India, and for a semester's release from teaching that allowed me to complete the manuscript. I acknowledge the help of my research assistants—Deepa Raman, Nilay Deshmukh, Arun George, Yuthika Sharma, and Raghavendran Rajagopalan. I thank Kathryn Anthony for her consistent support and Rajat Kant for the trip to Ayodhya and Shravasti. Ghanshyam Joshi of Heritage Trust, Baroda, was instrumental in data collection at Pavagadh. Becca Gollnick and Sue Chapman helped to put the illustrations together.

My teacher, Clare Cooper Marcus, first introduced me to archetypes; for this and many other insights into meaning and symbolism, I am grateful. Galen Cranz revealed to me the riches of ethnography, and Michael Southworth, the delights and complexities of cities. Muni Chakravorty, my teacher many years ago when I was an undergraduate architecture student at the Indian Institute of Technology, Kharagpur, taught me the virtues of a sustainable approach toward design. I thank my editors, Sandy Crooms and Laura Furney, of the University Press of Colorado for their enthusiastic support of the project. Laura's careful editing has improved the readability of the text considerably, and Daniel Pratt has designed a very attractive layout.

The chapters in this book have been published in various journals. I gratefully acknowledge permission to use the following material:

Introduction from "Sacred Landscapes in India: Forms and Meanings," *Geographical Review of India* 65:3 (September 2003): 241–250; Chapter 1 from "Natural Archetypes," *Geographical Review of India* 62:1 (March 2000): 26–38; Chapter 2 from "Nature in Hindu Art, Architecture and Landscape," *Landscape Research,* UK 20:1 (Spring 1995): 3–10, and "Nature in Hindu Mythology, Art, and Architecture," in *Environmental Ethics: Discourses and Cultural Traditions,* ed. Rana P. Singh, pub. 40, Vol. 39 (Varanasi, India: The National Geographical Society of India, 1993), 131–140; Chapter 3 from "Landscape of Ramayana," *Geographical Review of India* 60:1 (March 1998): 18–25; Chapter 4 from "Landscapes and the Ramayana Legend," *Geographical Review of India* 61:2 (1999): 97–111; Chapter 5 from "Pilgrimage—Journey to the Sacred Landscape of Braj," in *The Spirit and Power and Place, Varanasi, India,* ed. Rana P.B. Singh, pub. 41, Vol. 40 (Varanasi, India: The National Geographical Society of India, 1994), 239–248; Chapter 6 drawn from "The Cosmic Tree in Buddhist Landscapes," *Geographical Review of India* 63:1 (March 2001): 1–15; Chapter 8 from "Design of Settlements in Vaastu-Shastras," *Journal of Cultural Geography,* USA, 17:2 (1998): 27– 42; Chapter 9 from "Social and Spatial Order in Villages in India," *Landscape Research,* UK, 15:3 (Winter 1990): 12–20; Chapter 10 from "Courtyard Dwellings in India," *Geographical Review of India* 55:2 (June 1993): 36–47, and "The Centre as Void—Courtyard Dwellings in India," *Open House International,* UK, 19:4 (1994): 28–35; Chapter 11 drawn from "Designing Pilgrimage Sites," *LA: Journal of Landscape Architecture,* India, 1:2 (2001): 14–17; Chapter 13 from "Designing with Archetypes," *Architecture+Design,* India 17:5 (September–October 2000): 33–37.

Chapter 6 was written with the help of Rudra Pal Sinha and I acknowledge his input in every other chapter as well. Pramila Sinha's faith in my abilities to write and her unwavering support were a tremendous source of encouragement. She was an ideal mother, an understanding friend, and an inspiring teacher who taught me to seek goals and achieve them. She exemplified tradition and Indian womanhood at its best in her capacity to sacrifice herself for others and uphold the values of *dharma.* My mother told me the fascinating myths of India as bed time stories and from her I understood their true meanings, not in an intellectual sense but in their emotional impact and in revealing the hidden needs of the psyche. It was her love of nature and gardening that inspired me to write about the complex, multifaceted relationship between nature and culture. Her untimely death as I was completing this book has caused me great sadness and grief but steeled my determination to continue my explorations. I dedicate this book to my late parents Pramila and Rudra Pal Sinha.

List of Illustrations

PART ONE

INTRODUCTION

"As I define the word, a landscape is more than an area of attractive or natural scenery. It is a space or a collection of spaces made by a group of people who modify the natural environment to survive, to create order and to produce a just and lasting society."

—J. B. Jackson,
"In Search of the Proto-Landscape"[1]

The landscape of the Indian subcontinent, much of it continuously inhabited over three millennia, is an enigma in the diverse images it presents to its viewer. Amidst the great rivers, mountains, hilly plateaus, and plains exist an unchanging rural landscape nurturing a timeless way of life, fast-paced teeming metropolises of colonial origin, and medieval cities exhibiting schizophrenic personalities as they grapple with modernity. There may be no such entity as the Indian landscape, considering the tremendous plurality in topography, flora, fauna, and cultural traditions. Yet an unmistakable thread of continuity in landscapes of different regions is instantly recognizable. This thread weaves through regions with diverse ecological systems, linguistic communities, and cultural groups, drawing them into distinct landscape patterns. These patterns are best recognised in places that are venerated as sacred sites, attracting temple building and pilgrimage on local and regional scales.

In the midst of busy thoroughfares in Indian cities, large shady trees shelter impromptu shrines around which teeming traffic readily distributes itself. On crowded sidewalks mendicants sitting with framed images of gods and goddesses are likely to interrupt the pedestrian flow. No matter where the gods are housed—in wayside shrines or monumental temples—they attract devotees who visit them regularly and tend them with loving care. These spaces are an inescapable and meaningful part of the public realm. If large and significant, they become sites of annual festivals and public processions, contributing to the civic realm of the Indian city.

As the city gives way to countryside, and urban chaos to rural order, the changing landscape reflects even more forcefully the interweaving of the sacred in everyday life. The village temple is often at the edge of a pond or large water tank, a little away from the main settlement. Small shrines guard the main paths to the village and, as elsewhere, can be found under trees, at crossroads, or in the midst of forest groves. But tractors and tube wells are as much a feature of this landscape as are cattle fairs and sacred tanks.

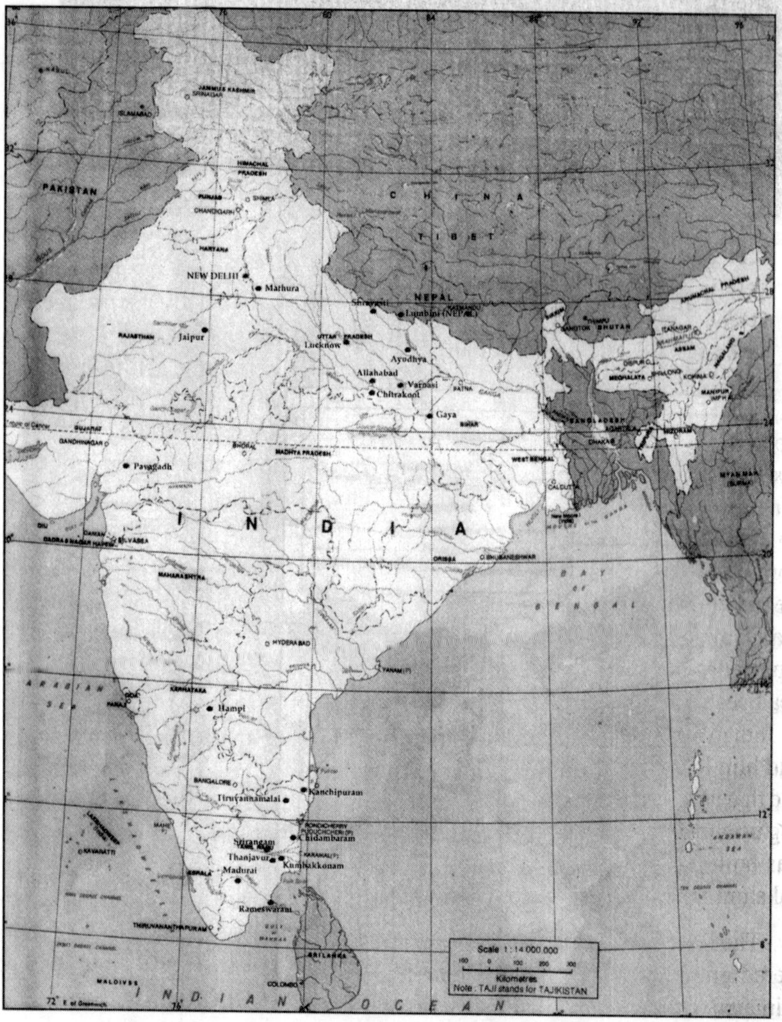

Map 1. Sacred Sites in India

0.1: Rural hamlets in northern India are scattered between the yellow mustard fields, giving the feel of a gardenesque landscape (Department of Landscape Architecture, University of Illinois at Urbana Champaign collection).

That Internet cafes rub shoulders with places of worship and machines are worked in factories with annual obeisance to god Viswakarma shows a curious juxta position of modernity and tradition. The roots of this seeming paradox can be traced to the uniquely Indian way of resolving cultural contradictions by slow adaptation of the new without necessarily overthrowing the old. Popular myths abound of how the building of infrastructure that ushered the subcontinent into the modern era was accompanied by propitiation of India's ancient gods and goddesses. In 1890, when European engineers were repeatedly unsuccessful in building a causeway at Mumbai on the Arabian Sea because the sea would rush in and destroy the causeway's foundations, an Indian labourer suggested a solution to the problem. Goddess Lakshmi told him in a dream that she was buried where the causeway was to be built and that he should a build a temple for her. The next day the Lakshmi idol was dug up and duly installed in a new temple. After this was done, the causeway was built without further problems. That temple is the now famous Maha Lakshmi temple in Mumbai.[2]

The reverence for genius loci can take different forms, from preserving sacred groves to building grand temples. Traditionally the landscape was animated with beliefs; to trace their continuity in time is an exercise analogous to landscape archaeology in which the further one digs, the more likely one is to make interesting and unexpected discoveries. The well-known holiday destinations where nature is most spectacular—the hill stations of yesterday—are not the original discoveries of the picturesque movement a century and a half ago, but were already claimed by a host of divine characters from the mythic past. The sites of great Islamic monuments of the medieval era that today form a large part of India's architectural heritage are likely to have an older hoary past, chosen deliberately to co-opt their religious value into a new system of beliefs. Yet somehow the submergence of the older way of thinking and its relics is never complete. This layering and mosaic patterning present a challenge in reading cultural landscapes.

DEFINING LANDSCAPES

Western scholars have traced the trajectory of meanings of *landscape,* but there has been no discussion of the term in the South Asian context. As J. B. Jackson points out, when the term was first introduced in English, it meant a picture of a view, an artist's interpretation. The word's meaning gradually changed to represent the view itself.[3] English-to-Sanskrit dictionaries offer the following words as translations of *landscape*: *bhu, bhumi, bhubhag, sthalam, kshetra, kshetrabhumi.* None of these terms means a view; they connote land and demarcated area.[4] They imply not aesthetic pleasure but land measured and appropriated for divine and human purposes.

The idea of landscapes as visual representations has dominated Western scholarship; however, recent writings have begun to focus on their materiality and phenomenological experience.[5] The term has undergone change in its connotation from attractive natural scenery to any humanly ordered modification of the natural environment. Landscape studies seek to understand cultural and ecological forces shaping the land. It is now recognised that these forces constitute a complex web in modifying the natural terrain and building upon it.

Landscapes are more than physical settings as containers and go beyond merely facilitating human activities. They can be read, that is, observed and interpreted as representations—signs and symbols—that encode meanings. They represent cultural narratives, communicating central tenets of culture and ways of life. They are also experienced through the senses and are far richer and more complex than linguistic texts.[6] They are dynamic entities, evolving and transforming with time. Unless landscapes are frozen in time or undergo a radical rupture with the past caused by natural or human disasters, they may be considered as palimpsests with traces of the past visible under new human interventions.

0.2: The street scene in Hazratganj, Lucknow, is typical of most Indian cities. Lively and vibrant, it has a mix of pedestrians, bicyclists, autorickshaws, cars and buses with hawkers and vendors clogging the sidewalks.

FORMS AND MEANINGS

I use the word *landscape* in an inclusive sense—open spaces and structures ranging in scale from a grove of trees to a region, from a building to a city. A landscape can be read by looking for consistent patterns of forms and meanings. These patterns are like a formal language that is understood by looking for basic forms, their origins, and their evolution and transformation across time and space. As forms evolve and mutate, their classification and rules of combination present a challenging task, particularly at the large scale of settlements. From where do forms originate? It is widely recognised that nature provides their original template. What gives meaning to forms is an intriguing question. The conjunction of forms with meanings is always slippery, presenting problematic aspects to those who seek a steadfast correlation. Although landscapes embody both personal and collective meanings, I am interested in the latter as social constructions that are apt to shift with social change.

The quest for meaningful forms, despite such caveats, need not be in vain. The history of Indian art and architecture is replete with recurring formal patterns with diverse and pluralistic expressions in different epochs and regions. Their recurrence is in part the result of strong conservative currents in Indian society that hold tradition dear as well as a cultural propensity to experiment and innovate within a timetested format. They offer a starting point for the study of how the larger cultural landscape is patterned.

TYPE AND ARCHETYPE

Design theory abounds with typological studies within which building types are classified according to form and function. Form is studied as schematic layouts and shapes of individual elements that together make up the volumetric space. Building types represent the outcome of ideological, economic, and social forces that are actualised in a building's physical form. This analysis, however, often ignores existential meanings that strike a deep chord in those who use them. Landscape studies will no doubt benefit from typological studies, but the inherent open-endedness of landscapes in accommodating functions and in their reception of cultural meanings, as well as their continual evolution and transformation over time, makes conclusive research of the kind prevalent in architectural studies difficult.

I argue that cultural landscapes, created from the natural world and shaped by human societies, are constituted by archetypal symbols. These symbols act as building blocks of an edifice that is unique despite sharing many common characteristics with other structures. The concept of archetype, going back to Plato who used it in the sense of an ideal form, can be usefully employed in discussing landscapes of profound cultural significance. *Type* is associated with formal qualities and pragmatic functions, but *archetype,* although ambiguous with regard to precise form and overt function, offers the possibility of tapping into existential meanings. If landscapes can be read in the same way one deciphers a language, archetypal forms are the roots of words. They evolve with time, assuming definite stylistic expressions, and are influenced by local conditions. These forms at the basic level can be taken apart analytically and reassembled in myriad ways just as we do with words in a language.[7]

Carl Jung's writings on the collective unconscious and archetypes offer an approach to explore psychological meanings expressed in symbols. In the Jungian perspective, the human psyche has in its collective unconscious a phylogenetic base in which the earliest human experiences are biologically encoded. An individual's psyche is determined not only by his personal history but also by the collective history of the human species.[8] The collective unconscious is shared by members of a culture and, in the ultimate degree, by all humankind. Archetypes reside in the collective unconscious and are manifested as iconic images and symbols in the physical world. They are psychic structures of the collective unconscious and constitute the archaic heritage of humanity. Jung defined archetypes as "active living dispositions, ideas in the Platonic sense, that preform and continually influence our thoughts and feelings and actions."[9] They can be compared to templates giving shape and meaning to human behaviour, nodes or centers in the central nervous system, and genetically determined releasing or inhibiting mechanisms. They function at a level below the threshold of consciousness and are understood only through symbols.

Jung's discovery of archetypes and the collective unconscious in the early twentieth century stemmed from images he encountered in his own and his patients' dreams and in the mythology and folklore of many cultures. At first he called these representations "primordial images," but later distinguished the image from the archetype, which was more like its model or schema.[10] Although the archetypal pattern is genetically transmitted, it is fleshed out in images only in specific situations whose particular details and traits vary with different cultures and geographical regions. Each culture has its own unique symbols of universal archetypes commonly found in its religious or folkloric myths. The memory of archetypes may be buried deep in the psychic substratum, yet these archetypes never fail to produce a "charge" or resonance when encountered in the outside world.[11]

The Jungian approach has been criticized for focusing on essences and ignoring social and cultural changes based on new ideas and technologies and encounters with the "other." Such criticism assumes that archetypes are constant and fixed in their meanings, ignoring their dynamic aspect in the ways that they compensate for the deficiencies of consciousness.[12] Furthermore, it ignores persistence in habits of thinking and behaviour, unconsciously reproduced over generations. Another widespread but mistaken criticism of Jung's framework has centered on its supposedly racial origins, particularly the volkish antecedents of Aryan superman-thinking in Nazi ideology in Germany prior to World War II, which led to such catastrophic results. As Jung's defenders have pointed out, Jung was hostile to all mass movements because they suppressed the individual psyche.[13] The dangers of conflating race with nationalism are only too real if the concept of collective unconscious is applied in a restricted sense, such as to a particular ethnic group. The Indian subcontinent, with its polyglot population and many intertwined ethnic strands, certainly could not use race as a basis for national identity. But ideologues, particularly fundamentalists, often have manipulated nature symbolism to their own ends, as seen in the twentieth century.[14] I would urge caution in placing too much credence on the racial origins of archetypes and would instead focus on how psychic structures, universally shared in an abstract sense, have acquired substance within the geographic and cultural milieu of South Asia. Archetypes are the universal heritage of humankind, and it is their particular expression in Indic religions and their impact upon the shape of the Indian landscape that I explore in this book. I argue that the physical reality of the natural environment in South Asia provided the raw material that Indic cultures shaped into patterns of landscape symbols. Depth psychology treats archetypes as psychic nodes manifested in image types, such as the wise old man, the great mother, the hero, and the child. I use the term broadly, going beyond psychic dispositions, to describe physical symbols—natural elements and spatial patterns. These symbols are physical manifestations of concepts that have held a central position within the cultural corpus of Indic religions and, as such, are capable of conveying profound meanings.

Archetypal symbols may be recognised at an abstract level, clothed in local materials, fashioned by local technology, and given visible shape by local imagination. The strength of tradition and the lack of separation between the sacred and secular realms in Indian culture have resulted in sustained transmission of archetypal symbols across time and space. They are shared between the religious world and the everyday life it inspires. The symbols, however, are not reproduced in toto or imitated across regions without adaptation to local climate, topography, and building traditions. I divide them into natural and spatial archetypes—the former found in the natural world and the latter a human creation inspired by natural forms and their dynamic processes.

NATURAL ARCHETYPES

In nature are found archetypal forms that have inspired human creation since the beginning of time and have thus become the loci of meanings projected by the human mind. The most spectacular natural landscapes possess the attributes of charge, that is, they inspire profound feelings of wonderment and awe. Nature affords sublimity and beauty, solace and fear, mystery and resolution. The forest, the grove or bosque, the single magnificent tree, expansive sheets of water, the overarching sky—inspiring artists, poets, thinkers, and ordinary folks—can be considered examples of archetypal forms. Designers have always been sensitive to the evocative power of nature and have drawn upon the rich vein of her forms. Landscapes are the medium through which feelings that form dialectical pairs of meanings, such as contentment and aspiration, nurturance and risk, can be expressed. These feelings stem from the deep unconscious and are experienced with one's whole being, so that the natural and built forms evoking them make up a natural language for place-making.[15] Designed landscapes are often based upon natural archetypes such as the natural forest and the natural clearing.[16]

Indic religions place an immense value on nature in their belief that natural elements communicate sacred energies that lead to realisation of divinity within. Natural elements—mountains, caves, water, vegetation, and their combination—hold the potential for becoming *axis mundi,* center of the known world, a point of rupture where communication with the non-human and godly realms is possible. The river Ganga, Mount Kailash, and the Bodhi tree are all examples of visible axes between the earth, heavens, and underworld. They are valorised as such in Indic religions and play a crucial role in cultural narratives of mythology and literature. Their representation in art and literature makes them into cultural icons. Rivers, mountains, and trees found in other parts of the sub-continent are named after them. Their presence creates a sacred landscape and encourages a secular one to evolve around it. Hills and rivers, or combinations of hills and bodies of water and forest groves, are found in every sacred site in the Indian sub-continent. They are also loci of ordinary settlements, gathering religious sentiment and community functions around them.

SPATIAL ARCHETYPES

In contrast to pre-existing natural archetypes, spatial archetypes are human creations, forming the basis of spatial organisation of settlement and buildings and representing human efforts. Building elements act as spatial archetypes in that their forms are suggestive of placidity and dynamism, tension and release, monumentality and intimacy, expanse and constriction. These feelings, triggered by perception of space and volume created by the structure, are experienced by the individual and could be described as instantaneous responses that may or may not be culturally mediated. Thomas ThiisEvenson explores the existential expressions of architecture by studying building elements mediating between the inside and the outside—roof, floor, and wall. The formal qualities of these elements can induce varying perceptions of motion, weight, and substance in which inputs from different senses are combined together and projected sympathetically into the physical environment. A roof can therefore soar or sag, a floor can float or sink, and steps can cascade or totter.[17]

As Mimi Lobell defines spatial archetypes, they are spatial expressions of the human psyche and all that it considers significant. Since the human mind has a propensity to translate almost anything into spatial terms, concepts most significant to human existence—such as the origin of cosmos, heaven, and hell; social structure; collective and individual identities; myths, rituals, and fantasies; economic exchanges; and political power—can be expressed in built form. Spatial archetypes therefore are potent carriers of meanings; for example, the pyramid and its many variations across cultures have been the sites of temples, royal tombs, and sacred reliquaries, where the relationship between earthly and heavenly realms was negotiated. Whether stepped, planar, or hemispherical, the pyramid's ascending form signifies aspiration toward the heavenly realm, a reaching to the skies, an attempt to escape the earthly and ordinary and their temporality.[18]

The great art historian Ananda Coomaraswamy, in his many writings on the theory of Indian art, pronounced India's art to be a "likeness," by which he meant an "equality as to the whichness and whatness—or form and force—of the archetype." He derived this concept from the writings of Plato for whom "equality" and "likeness" signified a real kinship and analogy, qualities that make it possible for an image to "interpret" or "deduce" its archetype. In other words, art is an imitation of an archetype that is "[n]ature in her manner of operation" of an "intelligible, not a perceptible[,] model."[19] Although cultural landscapes are not as deliberately and self-consciously produced as works of art, they are products of human design and intentions and, as such, merit close attention as to what they may be modeled after.

The most widely recognised symbol in Indian art is the figure of man—*purusha.* Art historian Kapila Vatsyayan has attempted to synthesize the fundamental principles of Indian art and architecture by drawing attention to this "figure of man in a circumscribed space" as the basic motif. This primordial human being, *purusha,* is the ancient Indo-Aryan's archetypal symbol for the cosmos. In ancient and medieval theaters for the performance of dance dramas, in sculptures of deities, and in plans and elevations of temples, this anthropomorphic figure within the basic forms of circle, square, triangle, and rectangle has been a recurring motif. Vatsyayan traces the form to geometric plans of sacrificial structures where the periodic dissolution and self-renewing beginning of the cosmos were celebrated. Here *purusha,* as a symbol of the cosmos, was symbolically immolated in a sacrificial fire.

Sacred landscapes too are conceived metaphorically as *purusha* fitted with a mandala. The understanding of landscapes as *bhu-mandalas* is reinforced through ritual circumambulations by pilgrims around natural features. Space is generated, physically and cognitively, by this act of inscription in the landscape. The conception of space as a circle/great round evolves into square/rectangular forms when cardinal directions are brought into the picture. Space is thus created from movement around a center, orientation to cardinal directions, and delimitation of sacred from profane. It is given shape in the mandala, the spatial archetype endowed with great meaning, and read metonymically as the symbol of cosmos.

The widespread use to this day of the symbol of the cosmic man fitted within the square, known as the *vaastu purusha mandala,* in temple and house-building is intriguing and points to a steadfastly held concept of a site's genius loci as an anthropomorphic figure.[20] Could the *vaastu purusha mandala* be the symbol of a psychological archetype, that of "self," a center where one could be whole, totally at home in this world, and yet transcend it? Jung used the Sanskrit word *mandala* for symbolic representations of the wholeness or totality communicated through a circle motif and quaternity (such as a cross or a square) in medieval alchemy and his patients' drawings.[21] His studies, however, did not extend to art and architecture of the Indian subcontinent. The mandala is a powerful concept in Indic religions and, as a spatial archetype, governs the layout of pilgrim complexes, cities and villages, temples, forts, palaces, and ordinary dwellings. Considerable scholarship exists on mandala and mandala-based temple architecture, with a rising number of publications on pilgrim studies as well as increasing interest in sacred space on the part of geographers and anthropologists. But extending this esoteric concept to landscapes is new.[22]

How natural and spatial archetypes function as building blocks of cultural landscapes can perhaps best be explained by the structural process of mimesis (the imitation of natural forms) and the design principle of self-similarity. The genesis of architectural space and form can be traced to mimesis. The consistent employment of the design principle of self-similarity has resulted in sustained transmission of natural and spatial archetypes across time and space on the Indian subcontinent. Mimesis and self-similarity represent a deliberate and self-conscious human effort and are useful in understanding how the language of cultural landscapes evolved.

MIMESIS

Mimesis is undertaken with a cultural understanding of what the forms mean. The transformation of natural into spatial archetypes—from nature into art and architecture and discerned in the cultural landscape as well—involves imitating visible forms and using geometry to express the concept of nature and its dynamic processes. A few wellknown examples demonstrate how this process is relevant to deciphering the language of cultural landscapes in India. Modeling a building element after a form found in nature to achieve a sympathetic correspondence between the two occurred in ancient India when the cult of the tree paved the way to worshipping freestanding pillars. The meanings shifted from the "tree of life" to the "tree of wisdom" as the cult evolved from its animistic origins into philosophical views. The reification of the tree into the axial pillar gathered up the meanings into the concept of *axis mundi,* thereby becoming the cosmic center and bridging the earth and cosmos. Similarly, the superstructure of the Hindu temple is modeled after Mount Meru, the mythic world mountain that rises from the center of the earth into the heavens; thus, the natural and the built share both form and meaning.

In addition to formal imitation, the ancient Hindus sought to give visible form to the dynamic life principle in nature as they understood it. Art historian Stella Kramrisch, in her monumental work on the Hindu temple, elucidates the principle of periodic destruction and cosmogony that is reenacted in the temple's site selection, plan, construction, and consecration. The temple and especially its plan, the *vaastu purusha mandala,* thus, become mimetic symbols of both cosmic form and process, the dynamic aspects represented in the formal design vocabulary and building rituals.[23]

The temple inspires the humble dwelling and the palatial mansion alike. Primarily a place of worship, the temple is also a social and cultural institution that promotes the performing arts, harbors fine arts and crafts, and serves as an educational center. We do not see a cleavage between the public and domestic arenas, but rather a continuation of form and meaning. The traditional courtyard house is based upon the *vaastu purusha mandala,* as the temple is, and accommodates the daily private life of the family, in which religion plays a significant role. The use of *vaastu shastra* ("wisdom of place") in house-building shows the widely held concept of the house as an auspicious structure consecrated by rituals. If the temple is a microcosm, so is the house in its own fashion.

SELF-SIMILARITY

Cultural landscapes in India may be traced to the widespread prevalence of natural and spatial archetypes and their regional manifestations through long periods of history. Cultural diffusion as the Indian subcontinent was settled over centuries was accompanied by the creation of new landscapes and modifications of pre-existing ones. Settlement occurred primarily by finding or creating new sacred sites around which towns, cities, and capitals were established. The principle of self-similarity is useful in exploring how this happens. Astronomer McKim Malville has drawn attention to self-organised patterns in time and space in pilgrim centers. An important characteristic of these patterns is self-similarity, meaning that similar patterns are repeated at different sizes. Like forest and ocean ecosystems, pilgrim sites, with their large-scale, self-organised human activities, can develop repeating constellations of fractal patterns over time, suggesting that cultural landscapes can mimic nature.[24]

One of the ways by which self-similarity is demonstrated is in the naming and remaking of local sites in the likeness of natural archetypes. Religious historian Diana Eck draws attention to the generation of symbolic landscape through the processes of spatial transposition and duplication. These processes constitute the grammar of signification in the "imagined landscape" of India, characterised by polycentricity and pluralism.[25] For example, the divine river Ganga, believed to have descended from the heavens, is a natural archetype for other rivers named after her and with similar myths of descent. There is also the transformation of the natural

0.3: Gateway to Minakshi temple in Madurai is a soaring *gopuram* with many gods and goddesses housed in niches, a veritable Mount Meru (photograph by Deepa Raman, Department of Landscape Architecture, University of Illinois at Urbana-Champaign collection).

into spatial forms, such as with built temple tanks and wells, believed to be linked directly through underground streams with the Ganga. Not only are natural archetypes such as the Ganga and Himalayas duplicated across regions, sacred sites can be transposed as when, during festivals celebrating the birth of a god, all *tirthas* (pilgrim complexes) are believed to congregate at that spot.

Self-similarity involves mimesis and duplication at a smaller scale, that is, the whole is contained in the parts. The Hindu temple is an excellent example of the principle of self-similarity employed repeatedly over the last 1,400 years in various regional styles across the country. As Adam Hardy points out:

> Indian temple architecture does follow a kind of "grand scheme," both synchronic and diachronic, and also concerning meaning. The kind of pattern underlying the complex rhythmic compositions of individual temples can also be found in the evolutionary transformations that architectural forms undergo in the course of a tradition. This pattern is congruent with archetypal ideas in Indian thought, to the extent that the architecture can be said to have an intrinsic meaning. Formal structure and meaning are both rooted in a world-view, which the temples, almost by definition, must reflect, being conceived as microcosms or images of the universe.[26]

The temple exterior is a matrix of interconnected shrine images or aedicules at various scales, from small minor niches to primary components of the structure, symbolising the dynamic, centrifugal growth of cosmos. The proliferation and fragmentation of aedicular forms through staggering and splitting convey the idea of manifestation and dissolution of multiple entities. Movement is represented through formal devices such as projection, progressive multiplication, bursting of boundaries, expanding repetition, and gyration of aedicular forms.

Thus, we see that the larger site and the individual structures contained within it are considered microcosmic replicas of the universe created with the aim of gathering its positive energies. Temple architecture attempts to give visible expression to the dynamic quality of the universe. The beholder perceives movement in a static structure, an effect achieved through careful manipulation of forms. In settlement design too is the idea that each dwelling is a self-contained replica of the larger society. The four *varnas,* emerging from the *purusha* at the beginning of time according to one myth of cosmogony, find a home in the four quarters assigned to them in the *vaastu shastras.* In house design, the spirit of the site is evoked in the *vaastu purusha,* a metaphoric representation of the entire universe manifested at the local level.

THE LANGUAGE OF LANDSCAPE

Landscapes in India offer the possibility of transcendent experiences, their cultural meaning going beyond views or the visual composition of forms. Most sacred sites offer a striking visual composition but are more than aesthetically pleasing settings. Indeed they are considered to be the homes of gods, where mortal humans can be in divine presence and derive earthly and other worldly benefits. They are places where normal perceptions of time and space are suspended, one feels whole, and moral order reigns. They are existential centers for the psyche, anchor points of orientation to help us lead a rich, spiritually satisfying life.

The remarkable cultural continuity of the idea of sacred landscape can be traced to humans' experiences with nature internalised over eons and abstracted in built form. A heightened experience of the physical environment can trigger emotions from the deep unconscious that recognize what is meaningful. Landscape symbols define for the individual all that the culture holds dear. They help to externalise deeply felt emotions related to security, kinship, and the divine world. Not every individual may have such an experience, although cultural precepts combined with the immediate experience of the site's magnificence are extraordinarily suggestive. Natural and spatial archetypes valued and revered over centuries by succeeding generations become part of the cultural and genetic memory, offering the possibility of a strong charge when encountered in real life.

Landscape meanings, complex and shifting as they are, are built upon this possibility of charge afforded by place. Oral place traditions—local, regional, and pan-Indian—aid considerably in constructing personal and collective meanings around the natural topography of sacred sites. The founding myths of settlements often revolve around miraculous events associated with a natural feature, and these events consecrate the space for the founder. In building a house, the householder's enactment of rituals honors the spirit of the site and reinforces the identity of house and self.

Each pilgrim site is different, with its own myths and landscape structure, yet contains similar natural and spatial archetypes. The Hindu temple has evolved over centuries, exhibiting many regional variations in its family of forms, while sharing a common basis in the *vaastu purusha mandala.* In house form and settlement design are regional variations caused by adjustment to local climate and topography, but the emphasis on courtyards, directionality, center, and boundaries is remarkably consistent.

Thus, across the variety of landscapes in India, one can engage in a deep reading of their similar patterns without reducing them to essences. Reading landscapes can involve a number of approaches—textual decoding, interpretation of visual representations, analysis of quantitative data on natural phenomena and human behaviour, or simply insightful observation. I draw upon epic mythology, medieval texts, my own fieldwork, and contemporary architecture to read landscapes as patterns of symbols.

CONCLUSION

The recent spate of books on the pilgrim experience and sacred geography provide examples of shared beliefs and customs regarding rivers, groves, and land.[27] Writings on the sacrality of nature as well as observations on the pervasive sacred character of the land abound.[28] Their focus is not, however, landscapes as representations, and they do not offer prescriptions on how landscapes may be conserved and made legible and accessible to pilgrims. Although occasionally symbolic meanings are the theme of these writings, there is seldom any attempt to trace the meanings to a common pattern of symbols. Vernacular landscapes of housing and open spaces are only now receiving attention. The notion that there may be a similar vocabulary of forms employed in sacred and secular architecture and open spaces has only been hinted at.[29]

The first section of the book describes natural archetypes, traces them to a transcendentalist view of nature, and introduces the reader to the reading of significant sacred and secular landscapes, landscapes that have exercised a great pull on the Indian imagination over centuries. Indic cultures exhibit a strong influence of the sacred upon the ordinary realm of thought and behaviour, which is paralleled in the physical environment as well. Sacred sites offered a prototype upon which ordinary landscapes were modeled in premodern India. They provided the template for nature veneration, its integration into the domestic and public arenas, and spatial organisation to facilitate a meaningful pattern of daily activities and civic rituals.

In this book I link new and old scholarship in disparate areas of art and architectural history and cultural geography to develop an approach to landscape studies that should be of interest to environmental designers and anyone curious about the past and future of Indian landscapes. Landscapes in India, as elsewhere, represent cultural identity, mirror social order, and inspire built forms. They are represented as such in epic texts, medieval manuals on design, oral legends, and the minds of the populace who visits and inhabits them. This book collects some of their manifold meanings and relates them to natural and spatial archetypes.

To extend the scholarship on art and architectural history into landscape studies I examine the constellation of meanings projected into the natural archetype of the tree in Hindu and Buddhist narratives and its reification into the spatial archetype of the cosmic pillar. I consider the river-mountain dyad as a natural archetype, the presence of which in the landscape allows for myths to take root and flourish. Such is the case with several pilgrim centers—Ayodhya, Chitrakuta, Braj, Kishkindha, and Pavagadh—discussed in the book. Since there is already a wide corpus of writings on the architecture of the Hindu temple, I do not focus on the temple but explore the influence of spatial archetypes on the vernacular landscapes of courtyard housing and human settlements.

The second section situates them in the grand narratives of Indic cultures so that they can be read not just as cultural ideals but as real places, historically (re)constructed at various points in time with the aid of myths. I have used Hindu and Buddhist examples of ancient sites and seemingly timeless legends that have had the greatest impact on the landscape of the Indian subcontinent. Jainism, a religion as old as Buddhism, and Sikhism, a more recent development in the history of Indic religions, deserve lengthy treatments that unfortunately cannot be attempted within this book's limited space. The introduction of Islam and Christianity has had a tremendous impact on the landscape of India, especially Islam, which claims more than a tenth of India's population as its followers. Although the aesthetic language of their art and architecture is derived from sources outside of South Asia, on the subcontinent it has evolved through a process of continuous adaptation and assimilation of indigenous design patterns and ways of building and now possesses an Indian identity. Because this long historical process deserves a book-length treatment of its own, I have not included Islamic landscapes in this book.

The third section discusses their abstraction into spatial design, which underlies settlement form and vernacular dwellings. In the fourth section, which traces continuities and discontinuities in expression of natural and spatial archetypes in contemporary landscapes and offers a design vocabulary based upon archetypal symbols to architects and landscape architects, I extend description and interpretation of landscape symbols to suggest why and how they may be incorporated into future design. As an Indian teaching landscape architecture in the United States, I have often puzzled over cross-cultural meanings of the physical environment. I am very often struck by similarities and differences in the ways that landscapes are perceived, understood, and valued across cultures. I often have found design students and professional designers to be curious about the relationships between culture and physical environment. There is widespread agreement in the design community that design is a quest for meaningful forms. Cultural meanings, however, are often elusive because they are taken for granted, hard to define, and difficult to generalise. Psychosocial meanings, such as identity and status, relationship with the divine, gender roles, and the concept of community, are visible in the physical environment—houses, gardens, neighbourhoods, and civic spaces—if only one knows how to read them. If these meanings are ignored and the language of symbols and icons is not understood, creation of new forms and shapes becomes an arbitrary aesthetic play. Sensitive designers recognize the importance of understanding these psychosocial meanings and design for not only comfort and convenience but also cultural relevance.

I write this book with the hope that reading landscapes will allow a richer understanding of society and the culture that sustains them and will give a direction to those involved in designing landscapes of the future. Traditional forms have the virtue of being rooted in place and culture. Untangling their meanings affords the opportunity for creative adaptation of forms to contemporary needs. Traditional design principles offer an excellent example of how the artificial chasm between building and landscape design, largely a creation of modernity, can be bridged.

NOTES

1. J. B. Jackson, "In Search of the Proto-Landscape," in *Landscape in America,* ed. George Thompson (Austin: University of Texas Press, 1995), 43.
2. This legend is told in "Patron Goddess of Mumbai," in *Devi 2003* (Mumbai: The Indian Express Group Newspapers), 38–45.
3. J. B. Jackson, "The Word Itself," in *Discovering the Vernacular Landscape* (New Haven, CT: Yale University Press, 1984), 3–8.
4. Anundoram Borooah, *English Sanskrit Dictionary* (Gauhati, India. Publication Board Assam, 1971 [reprint]); V. S. Apte, *The Student's English-Sanskrit Dictionary* (Delhi: Motilal Banarasidass, 1972 [reprint]).
5. See Alan Gussow, "Beauty in the Landscape: An Ecological Viewpoint," and John Gamble, "Landscape in Motion," both in *Landscape in America,* ed. George Thompson (Austin: University of Texas Press, 1995).
6. There are of course other approaches to landscape studies. Meing's ten categories of how landscapes are viewed do not include landscape as text. They are landscape as nature, habitat, artifact, system, problem, wealth, ideology, history, place, and aesthetic. See his "The Beholding Eye: Ten Versions of the Same Scene" in his edited volume *The Interpretation of Ordinary Landscapes* (New York: Oxford University Press, 1979).
7. Laurie Olin argues convincingly that landscape forms are derived from nature and its processes and are abstracted in design. Designed landscapes are based

upon archetypal settings developed in one culture and place after another, thereby affording extraordinary visual and sensory interest and stimulation. See his "Form, Meaning, and Expression in Landscape Architecture," *Landscape Journal* 10:2 (Fall 1991), 149–168.

8. Anthony Stevens, *Archetypes: A Natural History of the Self* (New York: William Morrow & Co., 1982).

9. *Ibid*, 39.

10. Elie Humbert, "Archetypes," in *Carl Gustav Jung: Critical Assessments. Vol. 2: The Structure and the Dynamics of the Psyche*, ed. Renos K. Papadopoulos (London: Routledge, 1992), 307– 317.

11. Clare Cooper Marcus's *House as a Mirror of Self: Exploring the Deeper Meaning of Home* (Berkeley, CA: Conari Press, 1995) is the best known example of the Jungian archetype of self understood through positive and negative relationships with one's house. Marcus believes that if the home is the symbol of ego-self, the garden can be the symbol of the higher or transpersonal self. She has based her research on Carl Jung's writings, particularly his reflections on the house he built for himself, and his dreams, which allowed his access to his unconscious. She quotes extensively from his autobiography *Memories, Dreams, Reflections* (London: Fontana Library, 1969).

12. As Christine Gallant observes, Jungian archetypes are different from Platonic archetypes in that they are derived from eons of human experience and are not transcendent ideals. They cannot have fixed meanings, since they are bipolar by nature, assuming a positive or a negative aspect depending on a person's attitude toward his unconscious. See her *Tabooed Jung: Marginality as Power* (New York: New York University Press, 1996). She makes a good case for the Jungian approach in literary criticism, especially its potential for highlighting the suppressed voices of the marginalised and advocating the feminist position. Jung's theories have application beyond psychology and cultural studies in the ways these disciplines interact with the physical environment.

13. See "Jung's Alleged Anti-Semitism" in *Jung*, Anthony Stevens (New York: Oxford University Press, 1994), 113–122.

14. See Joachim Wolschke-Bulmahn, "The Nationalisation of Nature and the Naturalisation of the German Nation: 'Teutonic' Trends in the Early Twentieth-Century Landscape Design," in *Nature and Ideology: Natural Garden Design in the Twentieth Century*, ed. Joachim Wolschke-Bulmahn (Washington, DC: Dumbarton Oaks Research Library and Collection, 1997), 187–219.

15. See Mike Brill, "Archetypes as a 'Natural' Language for Place-making," in *Ordering Space—Types in Architecture and Design*, ed. Karen Frank and Lynda Schneekloth (New York: Van Nostrand Reinhold, 1994), 61–78.

16. See Patrick Condon, "A Built Landscape Typology: The Language of the Land We Live In," in *Ordering Space*, 79–94.

17. Thomas Thiis-Evensen, *Archetypes in Architecture* (Oslo: Norwegian University Press, 1987).

18. Mimi Lobell, "Spatial Archetypes," *Re-Vision: A Journal of Consciousness and Change* 6:2 (Fall 1983): 69–82. Lobell identifies six prime spatial archetypes—

the sensitive chaos, the great round, the four quarters, the pyramid, the radiant axes, and the grid—that symbolize and generate the worldview of the culture, giving coherence to belief systems, actions, and forms of expression. In a profile of each archetype, she groups their features under civilisation, psyche, and space, linking sociocultural phenomena with personality development, religious beliefs, cosmological concepts, mythic images and rites, and concepts of spatial organisation.

19. See Ananda Coomaraswamy, "A Figure of Speech or a Figure of Thought," in *The Door in the Sky: Coomaraswamy on Myth and Meaning,* selected and with a preface by Rama P. Coomaraswamy (Princeton, NJ: Princeton University Press, 1997), 113–142.
20. Kapila Vatsyayan, *The Square and the Circle of the Indian Arts* (New Delhi: Roli Books International, 1983).
21. C. G. Jung, *Mandala Symbolism,* trans. R.F.C. Hull (Princeton, NJ: Princeton University Press, 1973). See also Violet de Laszlo (ed.), *Psyche and Symbol: A Selection from the Writings of G. Jung* (Garden City, NY: Anchor Books, 1958).
22. See Jose and Miriam Arguelles, *Mandala* (Boston: Shambhala Books, 1995); Giuseppe Tucci, *The Theory and Practice of Mandala* (London: Rider, 1960); A. W. MacDonald (ed.), *Mandala and Landscape* (New Delhi: D. K. Printworld, 1997); Denise Leidy, *Mandala: The Architecture of Enlightenment* (Boston: Shambhala, 1997). On Mandalas in temple architecture, *see* Stella Kramrisch, *The Hindu Temple* (Calcutta: University of Calcutta, 1946; Motilal Banarsidass, 1980 [reprint]); George Michell, *The Hindu Temple* (Chicago: University of Chicago, 1988); and Michael Meister (ed.), *Encyclopaedia of Indian Temple Architecture,* 12 vols. (Philadelphia: University of Pennsylvania, 1983–2001).
23. Stella Kramrisch, *The Hindu Temple,* 2 vols. (Calcutta: University of Calcutta, 1946).
24. The sizes of similar patterns are governed by a power-law distribution; that is, the frequency of occurrence of a particular size decreases as a power of the size of the patterns or of the structures within it. There are many more small self-organised patterns than large ones; examples include sizes of fords of Norway and other coastlines and forest fires in power-law distributions. Malville found a power law in the frequency distribution of 54 shrines along the pilgrimage circuit of Mount Kailash in Tibet and 108 shrines along the circuit in Varanasi. These patterns emerge from multiple interconnections of spontaneously self-interacting entities that are not dominated by processes striving to maintain permanence and equilibrium. See McKim Malville, "Pilgrims to Kashi—Self-Organised Patterns in Space and Time" (Beckman Lecture delivered at University of Illinois at Urbana-Champaign, 2001).
25. Diana Eck, "The Imagined Landscape: Patterns in the Construction of Hindu Sacred Geography," *Contributions to Indian Sociology* 32:2 (1998), 165–188.
26. Adam Hardy, "Form, Transformation and Meaning in Indian Temple Architecture," in *Paradigms of Indian Architecture: Space and Time in Representation and Design,* ed. G.H.R. Tillotson (Collected Papers on South Asia, no. 13, School of Oriental and African Studies, University of London, 1998), 107–135.

27. See Ann Gold, *Fruitful Journeys: The Ways of Rajasthani Pilgrims* (Berkeley: University of California Press, 1988); David Haberman, *Journey Through the Twelve Forests: An Encounter with Krishna* (New York: Oxford University Press, 1994); John Stratton Hawley, *At Play with Krishna: Pilgrimage Drams from Brindaban* (Princeton, NJ: Princeton University Press, 1981); Alan Morinis, *Pilgrimage in the Hindu Tradition: A Case Study of West Bengal* (Delhi: Oxford University Press, 1984); William Sax, *Mountain Goddess: Gender and Politics in a Himalayan Pilgrimage* (New York: Oxford University Press, 1991).
28. Kapila Vatsyayan is the general editor of the five-volume series *Prakriti: The Integral Vision* (New Delhi: Indira Gandhi National Centre for the Arts, 1994–1996); See Diana Eck, *Banaras: City of Light* (Princeton, NJ: Princeton University Press, 1982), and *Darshan: Seeing the Divine Image in India* (Chambersburg, PA: Anima Books, 1985); Anne Feldhaus, *Water and Womanhood: Religious Meanings of Rivers in Maharashtra* (New York: Oxford University Press, 1995); Stephen Huyler, *Meeting God: Elements of Hindu Devotion* (New Haven: Yale University Press, 1999); Roger Housden, *Travels Through Sacred India* (New York: Harper Collins, 1996).
29. See B. Smith and H. B. Reynolds, *The City as a Sacred Center: Essays on Six Asian Contexts* (Leiden, the Netherlands: E. J. Brill, 1987); Allen Noble and Ashok Dutt (eds.), *India: Cultural Patterns and Processes* (Boulder, CO: Westview Press, 1982); Howard Spodeck and Doris Srinivisan, *Urban Form and Meaning in South Asia: The Shaping of Cities from Prehistoric to Precolonial Times* (Washington, DC: National Gallery of Art, 1993); Francis Wacziarg and Aman Nath, *Rajasthan: The Painted Walls of Shekhavati* (New Delhi: Vikas Publishing House, 1982); V. S. Pramar, *Haveli: Wooden Houses and Mansions of Gujarat, Ahmedabad, India* (Ahmedabad, India: Mapin Publishing, 1989); Kulbushan Jain and Minakshi Jain, *Indian City in the Arid West* (Ahmedabad, India: AADI Centre, 1994).

Chapter One

Landscape Archetypes

"Thus, we confront the central problem: any landscape is composed of not only what lies before our eyes but what lies within our heads."

—**D. W. Meinig,** "The Beholding Eye"[1]

"Reading the landscape is a humane art, unrestricted to any profession, unbounded by any field, unlimited in its challenges and pleasures."

—**D. W. Meinig,** "Reading the Landscape"[2]

"The language of landscape is our native language. Landscape was the original dwelling; humans evolved among plants and animals, under the sky, upon the earth, near water. Everyone carries that legacy in body and mind. Humans touched, saw, heard, smelled, tasted, lived in, and shaped landscapes before the species had words to describe what it did. Landscapes were the first human texts, read before the invention of other signs and symbols. Clouds, wind, and sun were clues to weather; ripples and eddies signs of rock and life under water; caves and ledges promise of shelter; leaves guide to food; birdcalls warning of predators."

—**Anne Whiston Spirn,** *The Language of Landscape*[3]

The expression of built landscape, to a large extent, rests upon a culturally shaped view of nature held by society.[4] The formation of landscapes from the raw material of nature, through the agency of human culture, reflects human values— the most profound of which is nature veneration. There is no singular view of nature within a culture, let alone one shared between cultures.[5] The universal human tendencies to ascribe meanings to nature and derive inspiration from its forms have resulted in rich taxonomies of conceptual categories. A few years ago when writing an introduction to a set of readings on landscape perception, I recognised five basic categories of nature views—transcendentalist, evolutionary, utilitarian, ecological, and idealist-romantic.[6] The transcendentalist sees nature as divine; the evolutionary view stresses those aspects of nature that have aided human survival; in the utilitarian perspective nature is seen as apart from God and humankind and open to subjugation and exploitation; the ecological view is the emerging scientific paradigm, stressing the interdependence of human and natural systems; and the idealist-romantic view is an aesthetic perspective in which the guiding metaphors are based upon rationality or intuition. These views may coexist in a society, or over time a prevailing one may be supplanted by another in the course of social and cultural change.[7]

Hindus view nature as a symbol of divinity and natural surroundings as sites of hierophany where a glimpse of divinity is possible. Riverbanks, hilltops, and tree groves are sacred sites in mythology and attract pilgrims. Hindus are not unique in venerating nature; most prehistoric societies did the same in their animistic religious systems. If compared with world religions such as Judaism, Christianity, and Islam, Hinduism is far more localised or place-bound. The land is considered fundamentally sacred, sustaining myths, legends, and traditions over millennia. The transcendentalist view of nature reigns supreme in Hindu religious beliefs as in Buddhism and Jainism, the other Indic religions. India's scientific community also subscribes to the ecological view of nature, while others believe that nature may be perceived solely for its utility (the utilitarian view). These views can be widely and simultaneously held by individuals and groups.

Some evolutionary psychologists and sociobiologists believe that optimal conditions in the natural environment that aided survival during the long evolutionary span have become hard-wired in the human brain, eliciting genetically transmitted responses. Exposure to natural elements elicits positive psychological and physiological reactions; for example, the universal attractiveness of parklands or lawns is traced to the savannah, man's earliest habitat. Here the spatial arrangement of the natural environment allowed an opportunity to simultaneously see and hide, enabling visual access to prey and a retreat to safety. Hence prospect and refuge symbols found in nature, designed spaces, and art have a universal drawing power.[8] A perceptually rich and complex environment holding promise of further information (mystery) will be preferred over one that has neither; for example, winding paths and secondary vistas are deemed innately attractive. An environment that is too complex (lacking coherence) or too bland (such as flat, open ground with no perceptual cues for finding one's way about) will provoke dislike.[9] This information processing approach predicts that those natural habitats (and their built surrogates) that allowed hunting and foraging and helped in the evolutionary struggle will be preferred. What is lacking in this explanation of nature as a primordial image related to human survival is early man's psychological and spiritual experience. That nature could have a meaning beyond its potential for human survival is completely overlooked.

EARTH SPIRIT

Natural elements and landscapes function as not only encoded templates but also signals, vividly recalling the primary experience of nature.[10] The numinosity with which natural elements were experienced during the long stretch of human evolution invested them with highly symbolic significance. Terror, fascination, and mystery made up the numinous charge with which nature affected human consciousness. Natural elements—trees, hills, rivers—individually and collectively impressed themselves on the developing human psyche not only for their survival value but also for their sensory and kinesthetic stimulation of body and spirit. The physical environment is felt with one's full being and this feeling is grounded in the body. Enclosure-openness, movement-stasis, verticality-horizontality, darkness-light, and other place attributes are experienced kinesthetically, setting feelings in motion. As the human capacity for forming symbols grew with the evolution of consciousness, nature was associated with life and death mysteries. Natural elements evoked awe and reverence and were believed to reveal divinity.

Nature was deified by prehistoric societies, and its components, such as rocks, trees, wells, and springs, were recognised as receptacles for spirits. Nature was the primordial mother archetype, in time leading to the worship of the great mother goddess.[11] The great mother goddess is a primordial archetype, appearing in the early phase of human consciousness. John Mitchell describes it as the universal female earth spirit; her various aspects were personified in local gods who had therapeutic and oracular powers, and she shared or withheld bounties of nature from human beings.[12] We have material evidence of this veneration of earth spirits in the mute archaeological remains of Upper Paleolithic and Neolithic cultures at the onset of agriculture and domestication of animals. Mimi Lobell calls them "buried treasure" of women's ancient cultural heritage.[13] This heritage stems from cultures that practiced mother-goddess worship and were female-centered; that is, they had matrilineal descent and inheritance patterns, did not engage in prolonged warfare, and did not have powerful male figures as chieftains or gods. Their shrines consist of gynaecomorphic (shaped like the female body) megalithic structures, earthworks, shrines, sacred caves, springs and wells, and ritual baths.

Archaeological evidence exists on the Indian subcontinent as well. The seals of the Indus Valley civilisation show the goddess as a composite of plant, animal, and human forms. In one Harappan seal, a plant grows out of a womb, in another a woman stands between the foliage of a *pipal* tree and a tiger, and as the spirit of the tree, she engages in dialogue with the tiger.[14] D. D. Koshambi has drawn attention to the megalithic remains of the western Deccan plateau (in the present state of Mahrashtra). Here goddesses abound in caves, hillcrests, and Neolithic track crossings.[15] Excavations of Buddhist sites in the Krishna river valley (Nagarjunakonda, Yeleswaram) and Kondapur in the Medak district in Andhra Pradesh have yielded mother-goddess figurines and megalithic structures signifying the body of the goddess. In fact, the earliest Buddhist stupas in brick and plaster imitated the prehistoric megalithic tombs.[16]

The earth spirit was believed to reside in mountain caves; waters of ponds, springs, lakes, and rivers; and vegetation; and these places became her cult sites. Eric Neumann suggests that the "great round" was the primary symbol of the primordial goddess.[17] In it lay the potential for differentiating the consciousness into positive and negative aspects. In its elementary aspect, it signified containment as well as shelter and nurturance. Earth was viewed anthropomorphically as the great goddess herself—a cave easily could be imagined as her womb, containing the waters of life. And nature's ceaseless regeneration in vegetation was a manifestation of the goddess's powers of fertility.

The earliest man-made structures gathered the energies of the earth goddess into built form, bringing the sacred landscape into existence. First cult spots and resting places of nomadic tribes of hunter-gatherers, these locations subsequently became village shrines of agricultural communities. The Indian landscape contains many examples of sacred places with primeval origins. Their remarkable continuity over millennia can only be explained by landscapes functioning as symbols of natural archetypes. Let us examine meanings of significant landscape symbols, particularly those encapsulated in the archetype of center.

CENTER

Religious historian Mircea Eliade has analyzed the symbolism of center in traditional societies.[18] The center could be the point of cosmogony, a site of hierophany, or simply a spot where other worlds can be accessed. Its meaning derives from the existential experience it affords of communion with higher powers. A sense of wholeness and a feeling of well-being flow from that experience. Often center is considered an *axis mundi,* holding the cosmos together, where penetration to other worldly realms is possible. In his writings Eliade drew from an overwhelming number of archaic myths to illustrate the phenomenology of sacred and its near universality as a perceptual category. Like Jung he believed that modern man's quest for meaning could benefit from knowledge and transformation of older myths and rituals to fit contemporary culture. Like Jung he too was criticized for being an essentialist, for taking myths out of their cultural contexts and emphasizing universal meanings at the expense of their cultural specificity.[19] His contribution to the history of religions lay in his ability to take a cross-cultural, comparative stance and demonstrate common patterns of thought and experience. His most profound insights were on nature symbolism.

Many sacred sites in India can be interpreted in terms of natural archetypes— trees, mountains and caves, and rivers—evoking meanings encapsulated in the symbolism of center. The mysteries of life and death, of fertility and extinction, evolved into transcendent meanings for Indian culture, such as origin of the cosmos and its oblivion, conception of passing time and eternity, chaos and order, and the belief in a higher omniscient, omnipotent spirit. Nature was the primary signifier of these meanings. It offered a model for human efforts to find order in the landscape. The materiality of vegetation, earth, and water provided the sensory content to which meanings were attached. The vertical ascendance of trees—their branches reaching to the skies and their roots growing deep into the earth—was a symbol of aspiration, and their ever-changing foliage symbolised regeneration. Mountains reached toward the skies while containing within themselves the means to reach the substratum through caves. Although formless itself, water was nevertheless a reservoir containing all possibilities of existence. It could take form from its container or act as a solvent. It sensuality invited touch while its reflective capacity suggested distance. Prehistoric evidence of nature worship is lost in the mists of time, but the veneration of places in Hinduism and Buddhism unambiguously demonstrates archetypes at work. Their meanings can be assembled from mythology and rituals. Natural elements and their built surrogates comprising landscapes act as center. To the religious mind, they function not metaphorically but literally as places where the cosmos was born and the possibility of encountering divinity exists. As such they are pregnant with sacred energy (*numen*) and evoke feelings of *majestas, mysterium tremendum*, and *fascinas*.[20]

The transformation of a natural archetype into a built one reifies the center and accentuates its effect. This transformation marks the evolution of spatial archetype from great round to four quarters, as Lobell defines patterns in civilisations.[21] The great round is an archetypal form characteristic of the Neolithic and early Bronze Age's self-sufficient farming communities when the world was perceived as encircling the individual in a nurturing matrix and as centered in the great mother whose womb-cavern encompassed the cosmos. The four quarters, in contrast, is the world of the hero; its symbol, a cross within the square. It is characteristic of hierarchical chiefdoms of the Bronze and Iron Ages with caste systems and oral traditions glorifying the epic feats of heroes. Cosmos is perceived as a quartered universe around an *omphalos,* or "navel of the world," representing the ego in the psyche, chieftain in society, and Lord of the Four Quarters in mythology.[22]

In India, this evolution is marked by the tree becoming axis of the universe and the cave a site of enlightenment. Reification of natural archetypes occurred in transforming the tree into a pillar and the cave into a *garbha-griha* (womb) in the temple. These changes accompanied the settlement of Indo-Aryans and their patriarchal values on the subcontinent. As the cultural ideal of a sacred landscape containing river valleys and hilly plataeus and ringed by tall mountains and coastline emerged, prehistoric cult sites were subsumed into this ideal.

THE COSMIC TREE

The cult of trees as mother goddess in the archaic period evolved into the cosmic tree (*akshaya vata*) of Hinduism and Buddhism (the Bodhi tree). The new symbolic meaning of tree on the mound can be traced to the Vedic myth of the god Indra slaying the serpent demon Vrtra and thereby releasing the life-giving waters. The great round appears in the guise of the primordial mound floating in the watery chaos of the cosmic ocean, which contains the potential of the universe. Tightly coiled around it is Vrtra, guarding the waters of life. These waters are released by when he slays the demon and separates heaven and earth, holding them apart with the world pillar and thus fixing the floating mound to the bottom of the ocean. Space and time are created when the sun is released, bringing with it seasons. This myth represents a paradigmatic act of cosmogony and is repeated whenever space has to be consecrated. Thus, a natural site consisting of hilly mounds rising from a vast expanse of water possesses sacred potential because of its congruence with the mythic image.

John Irwin has brilliantly demonstrated that the origin of the holiest site in India—the *sangam* landscape of Prayaga, where the rivers Ganga and Yamuna meet—lies in its topography, reflecting the image of the mythic archetype of creation.[23] The banyan tree (*akshaya vata*) on the promontory at the confluence of the two rivers was conceived as the archetypal tree of cosmogony, making it so sacred that pilgrims since ancient times have jumped to their deaths from its branches, believing that the tree led to heaven. The tree is one of the four principal shrines that make up the Prayaga mandala, which pilgrims are obliged to visit. The cosmogonic associations of the site are strengthened by a temple to the serpent Vasuki (synonymous with the primordial serpent-demon Vrtra) and an ancient well called samudra-kup, which leads down to the waters of the underworld.

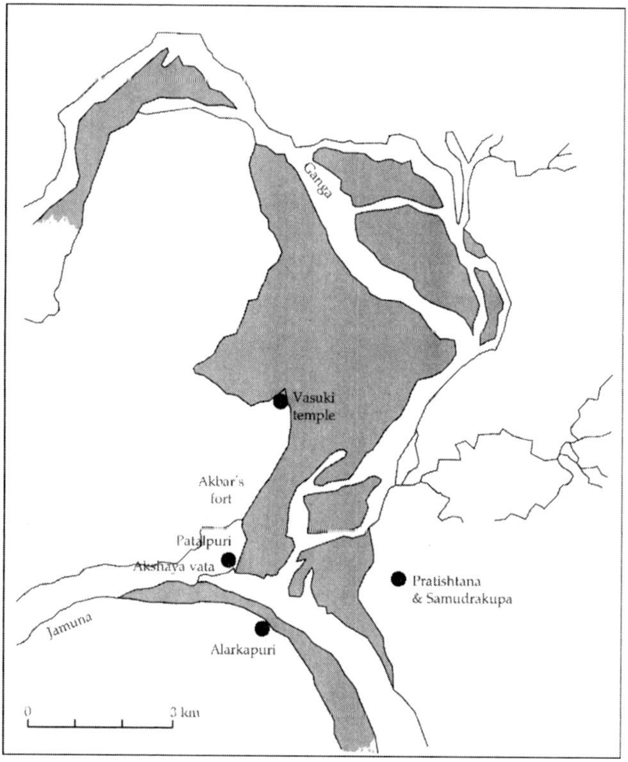

1.1: Indra *Akshaya vata* on the promontory at the confluence of the rivers Ganga and Yamuna at Prayaga symbolises the primal tree at the beginning of time and space (redrawn after Irwin 1983).

The landscape of Gaya, where an *akshaya vata* is present, is yet another center and shares several features with Prayaga *sangam*. This plain is marked by the confluence of rivers—the Ganga, Son, and Gandak, and their tributaries, the Punpun and Phalgu (dividing into Lilajan and Mohana farther south)—and five hills. On the left bank of Phalgu is Vishnupada temple, enshrining Vishnu's footprint on a rocky spur. The sacredness of this site goes back to antiquity; Rigvedic hymns describe the triple stride of Savitra (Vishnu)—on earth, in firmament, and in the sky—as symbolising the sun's rising, ascendance, and setting; the epic *Mahabharata* refers to

Savitra-pada on Udyanta hill at Gaya.[24] Because the sun was released from the primordial mound in the cosmogonic act, it is probable that the hilly landscape of Gaya with its numerous river tributaries provided a physical model for substantiation of the myth. Not too far from the Vishnupada temple is the eternal banyan tree (*akshaya vata*), survivor of cosmic floods, as the epic *Mahabharata* and several Puranas testify.

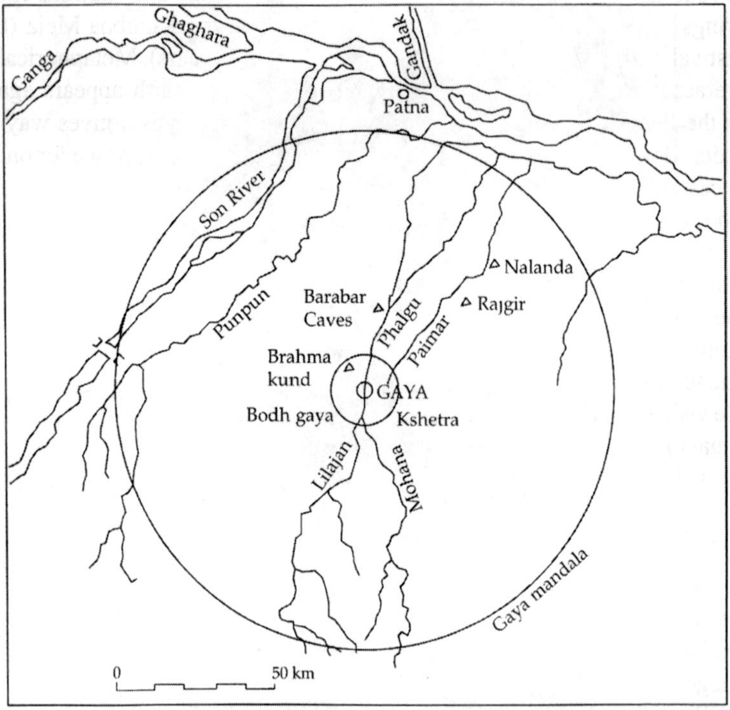

1.2: Gaya mandala, formed by three rivers and five hills, is a sacred landscape marking the release of sun from the primeval waters and arrival of life (redrawn after Marshall, Singh, and Malville 1999).

Scholars speculate that at both sites a bid was made to duplicate and concretize the symbolism of the tree of life in the form of iron pillars. Not only did the cosmic pillar hold heaven and earth apart, marking the spot where proliferation of life began, but here cosmic forces could be channeled in support of a new doctrine. At Prayaga, the pillar was surmounted by a bull and was erected not too far from the tree before the Mauryan king Ashoka came to the throne in 272 BCE and inscribed his edict on it. Seventeen hundred years later, the Mughal emperor Akbar chose the site as his fort and the pillar stood on a stone terrace until it was dismantled by the East India Company in 1798.[25] It is probable that an iron pillar also was erected at Gaya.[26]

Prayaga and Gaya are two of the holiest sites in present times. For the devout Hindu, bathing in the waters where the Ganga and Yamuna meet brings merit and washes away sins, especially during Kumbha Mela (the festival of the water pot, which is held every twelve years). Metaphorically the act is akin to periodic cosmic renewal when the earth appears again as the floods recede, and the chaos of *pralaya* (apocalypse) gives way to order. Gaya is the preeminent site for rituals ensuring eternal peace for one's ancestors. These could very well have evolved from archaic sun worship.[27] The sun, as source of all life and as the fire of final conflagration, is an apt symbol for the passage of human life from one realm to another. Viewed from a spur east of Vishnupada hill, itself rising out of the waters of Phalgu, the sun rises at winter solstice over Ramgaya hill and sets over Kapildhara. Homage to the sun takes place in tanks (Surya kunda and Uttara Manasa), and temples at Brahmani ghat on Phalgu river and nine more in the district are visited by pilgrims during festivals.[28] Gaya's landscape and the funerary rituals prescribed for every Hindu symbolize the dynamic duality in the eternal cycle of life and death at individual and cosmogonic levels.

CAVE

Caves were the earliest sites of goddess worship, dating back to late Paleolithic times in Europe. Their physical attributes—all embracing enclosure, darkness, tactile sensation of hardness and heaviness of rock—suggest a descent into the underworld. The earliest burials (prior to 30,000 BCE) took place in caves, such as the cave of La Ferrassie in the Dordogne where the body of a Neanderthal child was found buried under a stone slab.[29] The cave's physical configuration also suggests a womb because of its protective enclosure, frequent presence of water, and absence of light. The cave's symbolism encompasses the dichotomy of womb and tomb, serving as a physical representation of man's refusal to accept that death is the annihilation of existence, particularly with regard to the spirit. Thus, the place of death is also linked to rebirth. That caves became shrines of female-centered religion, one that was connected to the earth, is therefore not surprising.[30]

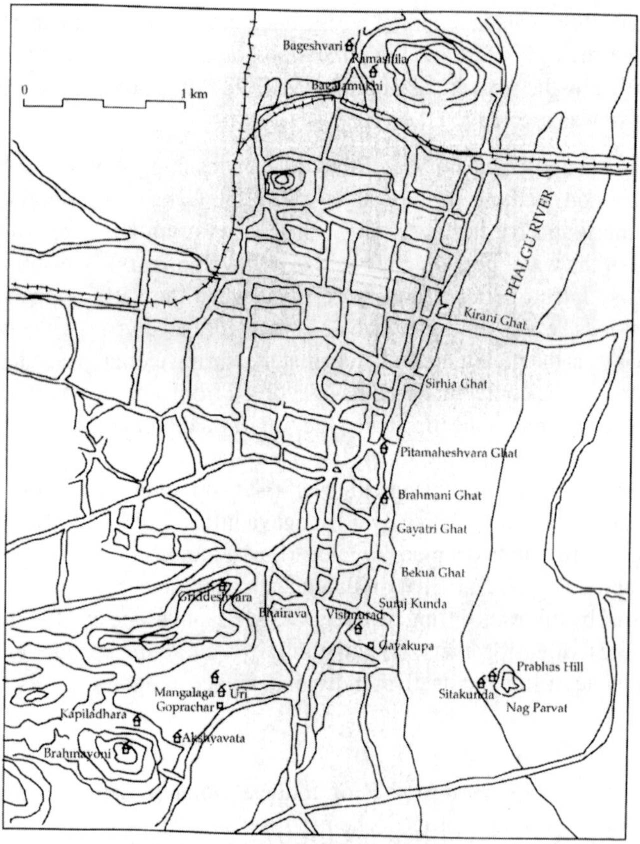

1.3: Gaya Puri is a pilgrim site where Kumbha Mela (Festival of the Pot) is held. It is also a place for obligatory death rituals performed for bringing release to one's forefathers (redrawn after Marshall, Singh, and Malville 1999).

On the Indian subcontinent, numerous terra-cotta figurines of a nude female have been excavated at many Indus Valley sites dating back to 2500 BCE, including caves. Their goddess status is indicated by elaborate headdresses and jewelry. The nude, squatting goddess with a prominent vulva has been found in western and southern India over a long period of time from the first to the eighth century CE. There are at least two examples of her in cave relief carvings—one at Siddan Kotte in northern Karnataka and another at Ellora in Maharashtra, dated eighth century CE.[31]

1.4: Chaitya Cave at Bedsa, Maharashtra, is an example of natural archetype that attracted goddess worship earlier and meditation and contemplation in later times (courtesy American Institute of Indian Studies).

The cave as a natural archetype also finds a strong expression in Buddhist and Hindu sacred architecture as rock-cut caves excavated over a long period (from the third century BCE through the tenth century CE) and as structural edifices. It was common for ascetics to withdraw to caves for meditation and for traveling Buddhist monks to find shelter there during the monsoons. Richard Lannoy in *The Speaking Tree* has poetically described the enhanced modes of consciousness that cave art helped to awaken the monks.[32] The echoing chants, suddenly looming painted figures, profusion of foliage on walls and ceilings, and vibrating forms and colors changing in filtered sunlight led to synesthesia in a dreamlike state of awareness. The surroundings facilitated a retreat to the depths of the unconscious, a psychic death of consciousness and return to beginnings when the ego was undeveloped and psychic duality non-existent. The journey back from the primordial state of being was a spiritual rebirth, an integration of unconscious content into the light of consciousness. In Hinduism this entailed a finding of self as the *atman* (individual soul) becoming one with the *brahman* (universal soul). The metaphor of cave in the heart, an inner space where divinity dwells, is a common one in the *Upanishads,* illustrating the evolution of the cave from a primeval womb/tomb symbol of fertility into a transcendental one. No better example of this can be found than in the Hindu temple, where the inner sanctum of the deity is called *garbha-griha.* Its unadorned walls, dark interior (except when lamps are lit to show the deity to worshippers), and small size recall the interior of a natural cave. As a built structure in Hindu temples, the cave is a cube and above it soars high the temple tower called *shikhara* (mountain crest).

Stella Kramrisch's cogent analysis of the Hindu temple as *purusha* rests upon nature/cosmos conceptualised in the form of the human body.[33] The temple is not only a microcosm but also mnemonic of cosmogony because it encodes the memory of cosmic birth in its physical form. It is a built center where the site's sacred energies are concentrated and given form and shape. The dynamic impulse toward manifestation can be discerned in the temple's plan (or *vaastu purusha mandala*) and in the terminology attributed to its superstructure. The metaphor of cave in the heart is applied to the inner sanctum of the temple where the deity resides. As a womb, it is a place of gestation and generates the creation impulse, resulting in manifestation of the *brahman* into icon. The inner space of cave/heart and outer space of *akasha*/sky are metaphorically equated and metaphysically equivalent.[34] This correspondence points to a realisation of transcendence within and is buttressed by the visual language of temple art and architecture.

The metaphor of temple/mountain recalls the older cosmogonic myth of Indra's pillar separating the skies from earth, thereby engendering the first fundamental duality of the physical environment to which human perception is attuned. The conflation of pillar into mountain is demonstrated in another cosmogonic myth of *devas* (gods) and *asuras* (demons) getting together to churn the primordial ocean for obtaining *amrta,* the elixir of immortality. They churn the ocean with mountain Mandara using serpent

Vasuki as a rope. The process results in a separation of dualities (poison and *amrta*) and the emergence of matter, sun, and moon from the ocean. McKim Malville believes that the myth's coded language describes the state of non-equilibrium in the primordial chaos that preceded creation and differentiation of space.[35] Mythic Mount Mandara appears as Mount Meru, the supporter of heavens and center of cosmos in Puranic cosmology.

The axial pillar is manifested as linga, an aniconic symbol of Shiva representing life and energy, in the cave. A magnificent example is the rock-cut temple of Kailashanatha at Ellora where the mountain is excavated and sculpted to reveal the temple containing the cave/heart/womb. The airborne figures on the temple exterior enable one to perceive the temple sheath as firmament. In the more than one hundred-foot-tall Kandariya Mahadeva temple at Khajuraho, the linga resides in a tiny *garbha griha* of nine and three-quarters feet.[36] The temple tower rising above the *garbha griha* is crowned by *amalaka* (fruit) and a *kumbha* (water pot)—with a finial in north Indian temples—reinforcing its archaic vegetal associations. Thus, in the Hindu temple, the symbol of a tree on the primordial mound achieves its most complete architectonic form.

A Hindu temple is a built abstracted version of natural archetypes. The cosmic tree is the pillar/mountain/temple tower; the natural cave is the *garbha griha*; water goddesses grace the doorways to the sanctum, symbolizing the emergence of life giving waters. In addition sacred trees grow within the temple complex and *kunds* (water tanks) are placed inside for devotees to bathe and purify themselves. The temple's circumambulatory passages, entry axis, and enclosures and gateways (especially in southern Indian style) mark the division of space into four quarters.

CONCLUSION

The widespread presence of archetypes in sacred landscapes reflect deep, perhaps even unconsciously held, beliefs. The archaic symbolism of tree, cave, and water is retained in cosmogonic myths, repeated in rituals, and given an elaborate visual language in the cultural landscape. A natural archetype and its built form are *tirtha*— "ford" or "crossing place"—in a sacred region—*kshetra*. *Tirthas* are conceived at various levels; a sacred landscape may have many *tirthas* and will itself be a *tirtha* in a larger context. The subcontinent is cognised as a network of such nodes. According to Surinder Bhardwaj, "The liberal distribution of sacred places throughout India has created an essentially continuous religious space in which the otherwise great regional cultural diversity becomes less significant for the movement of pilgrims over long distances."[37] How many of these were prehistoric cult sites? Only further research can tell. It is likely that many were. As the concept of natural archetypes suggests, human propensity to attribute sanctity to nature lasts through socioeconomic, technological, and cultural changes.

The restless, spiraling energies of demonic-godly earth spirits were centered first in the great round and then in pillars/temples marking the center of four quarters. Increasing evidence suggests that present predominant pilgrim centers of Hinduism and Buddhism were host to earlier autochthonous gods and goddesses, and it is probable that they in turn were manifestations of the earth spirit residing in waters, hills, and tree groves. Indic religions have incorporated archaic ways of knowing into later strata of thought. Natural archetypes have a significant role to play in this continuity.

It would be tautological to take recourse in mythology in order to prove sanctity of pilgrim complexes, although undoubtedly a site's sacredness increased manifold as myths found a home there, attracted by its genius loci. A place's *numen* may be explained in terms of opportunities for prospect-refuge, coincidence of terrestrial features and solar events, geomagnetic anomalies affecting the body's electrochemical processes, unusual topographic formations suggesting the appearance of land in the midst of a large expanse of waters, and features that have sustained human evolution; yet they shall remain secondary explanations of a phenomenon whose primary rationale lies in man's intrinsic search for spiritual transcendence.

NOTES

1. In D.W. Meinig (ed.), *The Interpretation of Ordinary Landscapes: Geographical Essays by John B. Jackson* (New York: Oxford University Press, 1979), 34.
2. *Ibid.*, 236.
3. Anne Whiston Spirn, *The Language of Landscape* (New Haven: Yale University Press, 1998), 15.
4. Although I have distilled this from many sources, particularly important are J. B. Jackson's writings, especially his *A Sense of Place, A Sense of Time* (New Haven: Yale University Press, 1944).
5. On the nature of nature, see Anne Whiston Spirn, "The Authority of Nature," in *Nature and Ideology: Natural Garden Design in the Twentieth Century,* ed. Joachim WoschkeBulmahn (Washington, DC: Dumbarton Oaks, 1977).
6. Amita Sinha, "Introduction: Varieties of Nature Viewing," in *Landscape Perception,* ed. Amita Sinha (London: Academic Press, 1995), 1–10.
7. Stephen Kellert, "The Biological Basis for Human Values of Nature," in *The Biophilia Hypothesis,* ed. Stephen Kellert and Edward Wilson (Washington, DC: Island Press, 1993), 42–69, suggests that the biophilia tendency can be

described in terms of nine clusters of learning rules that aid human existence and development: utilitarian, naturalistic, ecologistic-scientific, aesthetic, symbolic, humanistic, moralistic, dominionistic, and negativistic. Although Kellert and I share some values (utilitarian, ecologistic-scientific, and aesthetic), the conspicuous absence of any terminology suggesting nature's transcendental dimension makes his scale incomplete in my opinion.

8. Jay Appleton, *The Experience of Landscape* (London: John Wiley, 1975).
9. Rachel Kaplan and Steve Kaplan, *The Experience of Nature: A Psychological Perspective* (Cambridge, UK: Cambridge University Press, 1989).
10. Mike Brill, "Archetypes as a 'Natural Language' for Place Making," in *Ordering Space: Types in Architecture and Design*, ed. Karen Franck and Lynda Schneekloth (New York: Van Nostrand Reinhold, 1994), 61–78.
11. Eric Neumann, *The Great Mother*, second edition (Princeton, NJ: Princeton University Press, 1972).
12. John Mitchell, *The Earth Spirit: Its Ways, Shrines and Mysteries* (New York: Thames and Hudson, 1975).
13. Mimi Lobell, "The Buried Treasure: Women's Ancient Architectural Heritage," in *Architecture: A Place for Women*, ed. Ellen Perry Berkeley and Matilda McQuaid (Washington, DC: Smithsonian Institution Press, 1989), 139–157.
14. Pupul Jayakar, *The Earth Mother* (San Francisco: Harper and Row, 1990).
15. The goddess Bolhai is worshipped in a temple on a megalithic site where a significant number of microliths are found. An earlier traditional site, Bolhai's "kitchen" at the junction of several prehistoric tracks, has oval stones with cup-shaped depressions. On the south bank of the Mula river along a prehistoric route are found several dozen tumuli piled with large basalt rocks in the form of dolmen with capstones and boulders containing cup marks and engraved ovals on two or three faces. One of these mounds with a neem tree in Theur village is the site of the goddess Satavai, represented by red spots on the stones and worshipped by women. See D. D. Koshambi, *Myth and Reality* (Bombay: Popular Prakashan, 1962).
16. Jithendra Das, *The Buddhist Architecture in Andhra* (New Delhi: Books and Books, 1993).
17. Neumann, *The Great Mother*.
18. Mircea Eliade, *The Sacred and the Profane* (New York: Harvest Books, 1959).
19. See Robert Ellwood, *The Politics of Myth: A Study of C. G. Jung, Mircea Eliade, and Joseph Campbell* (Albany: State University of New York Press, 1999).
20. Rudolph Otto, *The Idea of the Holy* (New York: Oxford University Press, 1970).
21. Mimi Lobell, "Spatial Archetypes," *Re-Vision: A Journal of Consciousness and Change* 6:2 (Fall 1983), 69–82.
22. *Omphalos* marks the spot where energy currents of earth spirits are fixed and concentrated on one spot. In Greece, the omphalos stone in the temple of Apollo at Delphi is placed where the sun-god drove a stake through the serpent-dragon Python, thus usurping the site's oracular function, and in Ireland the archangel St. Michael did the same in hilltop shrines. See Mitchell, *The Earth Spirit*.

23. John Irwin, "The Ancient Pillar-cult at Prayaga (Allahabad): Its Pre-Asokan Origins," *Journal of the Royal Asiatic Society* 2 (1983), 253–280.
24. Debjani Paul, "Antiquity of the Visnupada at Gaya: Tradition and Archaeology," *East and West* 35:1–3 (September 1985), 103–141.
25. Irwin, "The Ancient Pillar-cult at Prayaga."
26. Debjani Paul speculates that the Meharauli pillar near the Qutub Minar at Delhi was originally installed at Gaya. Its inscription mentions it was set up on Vishnupada hill by Vaishnava ruler Chandra who may be Chandragupta II of the imperial Gupta dynasty in Magadha. See Paul, "Antiquity of the Visnupada at Gaya."
27. A. Marshall, R.P.B. Singh, and M. Malville, "Pilgrimage, Death, and the Sun at Gaya," in *Proceedings of the Conference on Pilgrimage and Complexity* (New Delhi: Indira Gandhi Centre for the Arts, 1999).
28. Tanks and *ghats* of Phalgu, because of their reputed connection with the underworld, are places for ancestor-related ceremonies. Sita performed the ceremony for her father-in-law, King Dashrath, in a tank known as Sitakund (containing a stone sculpture of the king's arm receiving the offering) and the modern pilgrim visits four other ancient tanks for performing rites. Besides water, hills are sites where contact can be established with the spirit world. For example, Pretashila with its shrine of Pretabhairavi (goddess of ghosts) is believed to be a pre-existing site of folk worship; the old name of Ramashila was Pretaparvata (mountain of ghosts). Both hills now have brahmanical associations with the building of Vishnu and Rama temples but they continue to be places where rituals for propitiating ancestors are performed. The myth of the demon Gaya asur, who is synonymous with the Gaya region and was subdued by the gods, is an apocryphal tale of the earth spirit being vanquished by Vedic gods. See Marshall, Singh, and Malville, "Pilgrimage, Death, and the Sun at Gaya."
29. Peg Streep, *Sanctuaries of the Goddess: The Sacred Landscape and Objects* (New York: Little, Brown, and Company, 1994).
30. Female statuettes celebrating fertility were found in cave sanctuaries—such as the Willendorf goddess in Austria (dating from 30,000 to 25,000 BCE) with her exaggerated breasts and belly and the Lespugue goddess (23,000 BCE) with her egg-shaped breasts and buttocks—and in relief carvings of the goddess with ponderous breasts and pregnant belly in the caves at Laussel overlooking the Beune river and surmounted by a spring (25,000 BCE). The lobe-shaped rock-cut tombs at Xemxiga, Malta, imitate natural caves (and the feminine body—hence gynaecomorphic) and are a prototype of megalithic temples, dating back to 4000 BCE, such as the one in Mgarr with three rounded chambers. See Streep, *Sanctuaries of the Goddess.*
31. J. N. Tiwari, *Goddess Cults in Ancient India* (Delhi: Sundeep Prakashan, 1985).
32. Richard Lannoy, *The Speaking Tree: A Study of Indian Culture and Society* (New York: Oxford University Press, 1971).
33. Stella Kramrisch, *The Hindu Temple* (Calcutta: University of Calcutta, 1946); Kramrisch, "The Temple as Purusa," in *Studies in Indian Temple Architecture,* ed. Pramod Chandra (New Delhi: American Institute of Indian Studies, 1975);

"Space in Indian Cosmogony and in Architecture," in *Concepts of Space: Ancient and Modern,* ed. Kapila Vatsyayan (New Delhi: Indira Gandhi National Center for the Arts, Abhinav Publications, 1991), 101–104.

34. Bettina Baumer, "From Guha to Akasa: The Mystical Cave in the Vedic and Saiva Traditions," in *Concepts of Space,* 105–122.
35. McKim Malville, "Astrophysics, Cosmology, and the Interior Space of Indian Myths and Temples," in *Concepts of Space,* 123–144.
36. Robert Forman, "The Hindu Temple: The Metaphysical Architecture of the Kandariya Mahadeva," in *Man in India* 65:2 (June 1985), 154–176.
37. Surinder Bhardwaj, *Hindu Places of Pilgrimage in India* (Berkeley: University of California Press, 1973).

Chapter Two

Nature: A Transcendentalist View

> "The Indian myths begin with the unmanifest or water principle, the aniconical stone, column or tree, and gradually develop into multiple forms called *avataras*, as in the case of principal deities, or personifications of other natural elements."
>
> —**Kapila Vatsyayan,**
>
> Introduction to the Exhibition "In the Image of Man: The Indian Perception of the Universe Through 2000 years of Painting and Sculpture"[1]

Nature pervades the arts, myths, and legends of Hinduism. In this chapter-I explore the religious and aesthetic sensibilities that have given rise to nature's munificence in different art forms. Nature, regarded primarily as sacred, contains the essence of divinity, manifesting it in varied forms ranging from material to abstract. Attitudes toward nature have not remained constant, and various aspects of sacred, from fearsome to benignly protective, have dominated with time. The terrain, flora, and fauna of the sub-continent are included in myths and legends of the vast pantheon of Hindu gods and goddesses. Natural settings, whether caves or forest groves, have proved ideal venues for hermitages, where philosophical treatises sustaining the great tradition of Hinduism were written.

COSMIC IDEAL

As Diana Eck states:

> One of the most striking aspects of the multitude of Hindu cosmogonic myths is the organic, biological vision that they express. The completed universe is imagined as a living organism, a vast ecosystem, in which each part is inextricably related to the life of the whole. And the whole is indeed alive: it is in constant process and movement, growing and decaying. There is no such thing as objectified "nature" or lifeless "elements," for everything belongs to the living pattern of the whole.[2]

Hindu cosmogony and cosmology throw light on the concept of periodic evolution and dissolution of the universe, on the union of creative forces (nature and divine essence as *prakriti* and *Purusha,* respectively) that bring the cosmos into being, and the homology between human body and nature. These themes in the sacred texts of Vedas, Puranas, and *Brahma sutras* were formulated by the middle of the second millennium BCE.[3]

Creation in Hindu mythology is always re-creation, an endless cycle of birth and destruction that has no beginning or end. This cycle is inferred from the rhythms of nature itself. The trinity of gods—Brahma, Vishnu, and Shiva—are responsible for the creation, sustenance, and destruction of the universe, respectively. The temporal metaphor for the cycle of creation and destruction, based on Brahma's day and night, is derived from the daily and yearly rhythms of the sun. The material world is brought into being by the interaction of nature and the universal spirit—*prakriti* with *Purusha*. The mandala is a visual abstraction of the cosmic energy that is produced by the union of *prakriti* and *Purusha.*[4]

Sleeping on the cosmic waters, Vishnu, as the embodiment of that universal essence, is awakened to give birth to Brahma, who in turns creates the phenomenal world.[5] It is Shiva who in his cosmic dance brings about the destruction of the world and its dissolution back into the cosmic sea. The gods, as manifest forms of divinity, are not only agents of creative emanation and dissolution, but also contain the potential material world within their bodies.

Cosmos and the gods are imagined in the human form. A close affinity between the human body and the cosmos underlies the belief that the body is a miniature universe. The early Vedic hymns describe the emanation of the four *varnas* (from which the castes in contemporary Hindu society are derived) from the dismemberment of the primeval man (*purusha*) in a sacrifice. The human form representing the cosmos (containing plant, animal, and human life; minerals; the sun, moon, and the planets) is visualised within the mandala, implying that the organic and the geometric are synmorphous. *Vaastu purusha mandala,* symbolic of the primal body of the *purusha,* is the basic plan of a temple (*vaastu*—site, *purusha*—human form, *mandala*— geometric form) and represents the creation of order.

The Puranas describe a geography replete with ideal forms—quadpartite and concentric. The imagined world is divided into four continents located in the four cardinal directions and centered on Mount Meru. Later Puranas describe the world as seven ring-shaped concentric continents and seven circumambient oceans. Mount Meru forms the core of the innermost continent—Jambu-dvipa. Each continent is named after a tree; five of them are divided into seven countries, each with seven mountains and seven rivers. Puranic authors constructed this geography based on archetypal forms and numbers rather than the physical reality of the world around them.[6]

MOUNTAINS

Mountains are venerated as residences of gods, and their elevating, commanding presence suggests their conception as cosmic axes linking the earth and heavens. The notion of mountains as abodes of gods is derived from Hindu cosmography in which the center of the cosmos is Mount Meru—the *axis mundi* linking earth with heavens. With panoramic views over the vast plains of the Indian subcontinent, mountains are favored sites for temple building. Structural temples duplicate Mount Meru in their towers over the sanctum and gateways. The Hindu temples have corbelled towers (known as *shikhara*) painted white to signify Meru's snow-covered peak.

The holy Himalayas and Vindhyas contain many pilgrim spots. Shiva lives at Mount Kailash in the Himalayas with his consort Parvati, daughter of Himalaya, king of mountains. Veneration of Mount Kailash suggests a coincidence of physical geography and mythic place. Surrounded by mountains and two lakes and the source of four rivers, it is located at the crossing of trade routes between India and China, which allowed Buddhist monks and travelers beginning in the first century CE to discover its extraordinary geography.[7] The breath takingly beautiful site became the focus of pilgrimages in succeeding centuries because it was congruent with the conceptual image of mythical Mount Meru, similar to Judeo-Christian and Islamic ideas of the world mountain from which the four rivers of life emerge. In the Vindhyan mountain range where the mountains meet the southern bank of river Ganga is the home of the goddess Vindhyavasini. The area has several prehistoric sites and evidence of long-standing *naga* (serpent) worship in the water pool called Naga-kupa.[8] Vindhyavasini is believed to be a local pre-Aryan deity who over time was incorporated into Sanskritic Hinduism as the transcendent Great Goddess.

WATER

Rivers, mountains, seashores, and forest groves nurture the rich mythology of gods and goddesses. The association of pilgrimage centers with water can be clearly seen in the number of sacred spots that lie on riverbanks, at confluences, or on the coast. The devotees bathing in rivers on particularly auspicious days gather spiritual merit (*punya*) and are absolved of their sins. Along with mountains, water is one of the most important natural elements in Hindu mythology, and most sacred sites contain one or both of these elements. Many temples are along riverbanks; others have water in the form of lakes, ponds, or built tanks. Tanks are essential at any worship complex where formless waters need to be forced into a geometric shape for ritual purposes. A place's sanctity increases with its proximity to a river, and river confluences have added ritual importance. The reasons for water's religious significance are many: water precedes creation and reabsorbs it and thus is associated with both evolution and dissolution. Bathing in water is believed to bring about regeneration since immersion implies a temporary regression into the undifferentiated mode of existence while emersion is symbolic of the creation of form. Purification rites at sacred sites involve bathing in a river or built tank within the temple complex.

2.1: The pilgrim city of Hardwar marks the entry of Ganga into the plains of northern India. Its name means the "doorway to Har" (another name of Shiva). Ganga is one of Shiva's wives and the two are frequently worshipped together.

Ganga, the most sacred river in India, is worshipped as both a goddess (the consort of Vishnu and Shiva) and river whose descent from the Himalayas into the parched plains has brought life and nourishment to millions. She is a moving, flowing *axis mundi*—bathing in her waters washes away pollution of sins and being cremated at her banks brings *moksha.* Such is her power that all rivers are contained in her and she in them, an example of spatial transposition in Hindu sacred geography.[9] As Kaveri or Dakshina Ganga, she sustained the political dynasties of southern India, who acknowledged her as a source of divine power and at the same time utilised her waters as a source of irrigation. Kaveri rises from Brahmagiri hill in Western Ghats and, like the confluence of Ganga, Yamuna, and mythical Saraswati at Prayaga, she too is joined by Kanaka and the underground Sujyoti at Bhagamandala where pilgrims bathe to wash away their sins. Temples are sited on her sacred islands—Shrirangapattana, Shivasundram, and Shrirangam—and they form the nuclei of historic cities—Tiruchirappalli, Tanjavur, and Kumbhakonam on her banks.[10]

Apart from ritual bathing in sacred waters, personifications of their life-giving powers abound in mythology and religious iconography. Their maternal, procreative aspect is signified by rivers Ganga and Yamuna and as goddesses adorning temple doorways and guarding the sanctuary. The worshipper is thus purified, metaphorically speaking, upon entering the sanctuary. An essential object of worship in the daily ritual of a Hindu is a pitcher brimming with water. The presence of water in birth, death, and purification rituals is common to many religions, and its elaborate use in Hinduism makes it a very significant element in worship.

VEGETATION

The development from sensual and material to an abstract relationship with nature can be observed in examining the symbolism of vegetation. Ancient tree worship evolved into using trees as a setting for significant events in the lives of gods and sages. The Indus Valley seals show the spirit of the tree in communion with a tiger. The hymns of *Atharvaveda* are about the power of trees to protect and destroy in magical rites of alchemy. The earliest temples were tree shrines. The word *chaitya* in Buddhist literature refers to a sacred tree or a tree with an altar. The cult of the tree was taken over from preexisting animistic practice. The Bodhi tree (*ficus religiosa*) under which the Buddha gained enlightenment at Bodhgaya was probably an existing sacred tree to which offerings were made. In the sculptures of the Bharhut, Sanchi, Mathura, and Amravati stupas (erected between ca. 175 BCE and 225 CE), the Bodhi tree is surrounded by a two or three-storied gallery for worship.[11] Even today banyan and *pipal* trees are venerated in Hinduism and every temple contains these trees within its complex.

The worship of the tree as a sacred power evolved into identifying different types of vegetation with particular Hindu deities. For example, *tulsi* (basil), the most sacred plant in India, is dear to Vishnu and its leaves are believed to possess medicinal power. Similarly, Shiva and Krishna are associated with the *bel* tree and the *kadamba* forest, respectively. In south Indian villages, trees are regarded as embodiments of the village deity.

The fecundity of vegetation finds expression in numerous rituals and folk art. In Indian iconography, voluptuous tree spirits called *gandharvas* and *apsaras* stand holding a branch or with a leg entwined around a stem in various erotic postures, visually connecting the fertility of tree and woman.[12] Kamadeva, the Hindu god of love, uses flowers as his arrows to arouse the emotion of love. Trees represent life and continuity in the material world. The tree represents the universe, and the cosmic tree—*kalpa vriksha*—symbolises the experience of life itself. One metaphor in the *Bhagwad Gita* for renouncing the world is to "cut the tree at its roots."

Paradoxically, the tree motif symbolizing life and fertility is also evocative of withdrawal and detachment from the world. Asceticism is best practiced in forests (or hilly caves), and sages over the centuries have meditated at the foot of a tree, seeking the secrets of the universe and self-knowledge through introspection. The Buddha spent two-thirds of his life giving discourses in forests on the outskirts of the major cities in northern India. The congregation order (*sangha*) and the religious creed *(dharma)* of Buddhism were formulated in the forest. The retreat to nature for meditation is prevalent in Hindu culture, and the forest has always been regarded as a setting conducive to contemplation and metaphysical speculation in the *ashramas,* which became the vanguard of expansion and spread of Hindu faith into peninsular India.

The cult of Soma was brought to the subcontinent by Indo-Europeans and celebrated in the Vedas. The plant *Amanita muscaria* was worshipped as the god of vegetation, and its intoxicating juice as the very elixir of life. The ancient custom of using plants to attain intoxication of the spirit continues today. The various forms of cannabis—*bhang*, *hashish*, and *ganja*—are imbibed extensively by ascetics. This long-standing tradition of use is accepted widely as an aid to meditation and visionary experiences, not surprising for a culture that places such a high value on spiritual transcendence. There is another more Dionysian aspect to its use in ordinary life best known during Holi, the festival of colour. Holi is a celebration of spring's arrival and is marked by bacchanalian revelry during which the normal order of society is suspended. *Bhang* is mixed with sweetmeats and drinks to add to the joyous mood and feeling of gay abandon.

The coconut (*Cocos mucifera*), thought to have originated in the Andaman Islands, has been cultivated on the subcontinent for at least 3,000 years. Its sweet-tasting kernel and milk make it a choice fruit, whether eaten raw or cooked in dozens of different dishes. What has aided its widespread use is its essential role in religious and social rituals. Perhaps because it resembles the human head it was an apt substitute for human sacrifice.

As such, the coconut is ritually split in ceremonies connected with entering a newly built home, using a new machine (such as an automobile), or inaugurating an event. A fresh or dried coconut is also widely used in offerings to the gods, other worship rituals, and gift exchanges on propitious occasions. Coconut, along with banana and mango, symbolises fertility and is used on all auspicious occasions such as birth and marriage. Other utilitarian aspects of the coconut's consumption—oil derived from copra; mats, ropes, and baskets made from coir; leaves in thatching; utensils from its shells—ensure that its cultivation will be of great benefit to the household. The coconut satisfies not just the human desire for sweetness but a complex of psychosocial needs that contribute toward building social capital in this world and gaining religious merit for the next.

Among flowers, the lotus (of the Nymphaeceae family) occupies a very special position and achieved canonical status in South Asian cultures, its fame traveling to Southeast and East Asia with Buddhism. In art and literature, it is often a metaphor for human and natural beauty. The munificence of lotus imagery in art and architectural ornamentation and its widespread use in the narrative tradition ensure its centrality and longevity as a symbol. Like the tulip in Europe, it displays classical perfection in the shape and symmetrical arrangement of its petals. Rising from the waters, its emergence signifies the birth of the cosmos itself. The image of Vishnu slumbering on the primeval waters when the lotus stalk shoots out of his navel, carrying Brahma the Creator, is a common motif. As the seat of gods and goddesses, particularly Vishnu's consort Lakshmi, it is a symbol of stability as well as the dynamic life force, *shakti,* that caused form to emerge out of watery chaos. As such, it girds the square mandala, the all-powerful archetypal symbol of the cosmos, employed in numerous rituals. The lotus-in-the-heart metaphor represents the correspondence of the internal microcosm with the external universe. The *Bhagwad Gita* exhorts us to remain detached from life, and not be affected by travails and successes, just as the lotus remains untouched by water. Thus, an ephemeral flower becomes an icon of transcendence. But there are other associations as well; flowers are universally associated with erotic love and beauty. The beauty of the human (and godly) body is endlessly compared with the lotus in classical Sanskrit literature with the perfect face, eyes, hands, and feet described as lotus-like in their charms. Men and women carry the flowers in their hands, wear its stalks as garlands around their necks, and adorn their tresses with its petals. A symbol of transcendence is paradoxically synonymous with desire. This double meaning is symptomatic not of unresolved duality but most likely of Hinduism's attempts to find a transcendental aspect in every human emotion.

EARTH

Earth, too, has been personified in iconography and vernacular art as a goddess— bhudevi (from *bhu*—earth). The earth energy (*shakti*) is represented through diagrams (yantras), hieroglyphs, and icons.[13] Worship of the earth goddess can be traced back to the onset of human habitation on the subcontinent. Originally a composite of human, plant, and animal features, she transforms after coming into contact with the great tradition of Sanskritic Hinduism. She assumes a secondary position as a consort to the male gods. Hindu goddesses such as Lakshmi, Saraswati, and Parvati rarely stand alone, and the original vegetal and animal aspects become differentiated into the lotus (held in the hand) and the animal vehicle. Earth goddesses abound and are still worshipped in rural India as part of the tradition of autochthonous origins. Her aniconic form as a roughly shaped piece of earth is placed under the trees and she becomes the village deity (*grama devata*) in southern India. As temporary clay images made for certain festivals and then submerged in water, returning to a primal state of formlessness, her icons represent the fundamental energy of the earth. The cult of the mother goddess in her awe-inspiring, destructive aspect harkens back to archaic forms of nature worship. But this aspect of the great goddess was sublimated into a creative, protective, albeit secondary, role as the Hindu civilisation gained a greater understanding and thereby sense of control over nature and began to perceive it through a framework of patriarchal values.[14]

The cult of yakshas—tree spirits and earth genii—can be traced back to pre-Aryan times and the archaic tendency for personification of natural elements. Shiva was probably a yaksha. His autochthonous origins are revealed in his destructive aspect, where as Rudra he performs the cosmic dance of death and burns the world by opening his third eye. His aniconic form, *lingam* (phallus), is worshipped along with yoni (vulva) as symbols of *Purusha* and *prakriti*. Yakshas, which symbolize mineral treasure, precious metals, and earth, are massive figures, charged with sexual energy and power in Buddhist iconography. Lacking spirituality, they are derived from aboriginal traditions. Over time they acquired protective roles and became attendants, guardians, and gatekeepers in mythology and iconography. Their benign, subservient roles in the Hindu pantheon symbolise the dominance of gods transcending nature. Their presence in a group of local divinities marks the incorporation of aboriginal gods in the all-inclusive stream of Hinduism.[15]

2.2: Yaksha attendant in the Great Railing of Bharhut stupa (second century CE). Yakshas and *nagas* are depicted in subservient roles in Buddhist art (courtesy American Institute of Indian Studies).

ANIMALS

Does sanctity extend to the animal world too? All Hindu gods and goddesses have animals for their vehicles. This means that these animals are associated generally with divinity and specifically symbolise the chief virtues (or vices) for which their gods are renowned. Examples, include the owl, which is Lakshmi's vehicle and is associated with the wisdom that Lakshmi embodies; the tiger, a symbol of the great power of the earth goddess in her archaic form; the celestial elephant, Airavata, which is the vehicle of Indra and is associated with the rain-bearing monsoon clouds; and the rat, who as the vehicle of the elephant god, Ganesha, signifies his ability to overcome all obstacles. In addition to symbolising royalty and fertility, elephants support the four directions. Monkeys have played an important role in the saga of god Rama, who with their help defeats the demons. In the sacred hierarchy, the cow occupies the place of honor because she represents the wealth of the early Indo-Aryan settlers. As Kamadhenu, the celestial cow, she is the giver of all desired benefits.

Said to inhabit both this and the nether world, serpents (*nagas*) occupy the most interesting place in the world of mythology and folklore. Associated with man's downfall in Christian theology, the snake has no such negative association in Hinduism. The concept of snakes as symbols of the earth spirit goes back to the archaic period. They are mostly associated with water and inhabit pools, springs, lakes, rivers, and oceans, but their domicile in trees and mountains is not overlooked. They have the power to bring rains and, when angry, can cause storms and floods. Supporting Vishnu on the formless, primeval waters, Shesh-naga is a creature of the aquatic world, keeper of its life energy. In Kashmir valley, springs are called *nagas* and are venues of temples and local pilgrimages. *Nagas* are also supporters of the terrestrial world, as illustrated by the practice of driving a stake to symbolically fix the snake's head. On a spot selected by an astrologer to symbolically represent the center of the world, the foundation stone of the temple or house is laid. In Himachal Pradesh, *nagas* are worshipped as local deities in temples in sacred groves, caves, or lakes near villages.[16] In Kerala, snake shrines are found in groves contained within large compounds of houses. And the snake festival (*nagapanchami*) is celebrated throughout India.

The snake is also a prevalent theme in Indian art. The multiheaded snake icon appears frequently in both religious iconography and vernacular art. The composite images of *nagas,* half serpent, half human, are found in Buddhist sculptural panels of the second century BCE and also adorn later temples and sanctify holy shrines. Like other natural elements, snakes are depicted in a protective attitude, spreading their hoods over the gods. The entwined snake motif on stone slabs (known as *nagakals*) found under trees is a fertility symbol worshipped by women desiring offspring.

As embodiments of divine elements, animals are exalted, worshipped, and loved in India. What then distinguishes the animal world from that of humans and gods and goddesses? In the theory of rebirth, life as an animal is a form of existence inferior to human life and is the result of bad *karma*. But like all living creatures, animals can transcend their given nature.

NATURE AND AESTHETICS

Integral to music, dance, and poetry is an aesthetic principle (*rasa*), or essence, behind various emotions, which is shared by nature. Nature in art and literature serves to intensify feelings and establish the mood. Natural settings convey the prevailing ambience by means of a sympathetic correspondence with the principal characters' emotional states. Whether love, longing, sorrow, or serenity, these feelings are projected into the world of nature. Sanskrit drama and poetry, especially the works of the poet Kalidasa, are based on the similitude between the subjective state of the characters and that of rivers, trees, moon, lotus, and clouds. The close identity between the human body and nature is extolled in describing natural elements in terms of feminine beauty and vice versa.[17]

Nature, if it is attributed gender, is predominantly feminine, although masculine images (such as the sun and mountains as symbols of majestic power) also abound. This kind of poetic imagery does not mark a break between the sacred and secular realms, rather it places erotic love within a religious context. Indeed, the source of nature personification can be traced back to Vedic hymns addressed to the powers of the sun, fire, wind, and storms. In Sanskrit poetry and drama, gods and goddesses play at being human and nature forms a perfect vehicle for illustrating their beauty and emotions.

Much of the action seems to take place in picturesque natural settings, such as royal and public gardens in the ancient cities of Pataliputra, Rajagriha, Sravasti, Vaisali, Indraprastha, and Lanka. These pleasure gardens contain flowering trees, lotus ponds, bathing tanks, exotic birds, and animals, and are located both within and on the outskirts of cities.[18] It is difficult to conjecture their layout from the verbal descriptions; however, there does not seem to be an emphasis on axes, terminal vistas, focal points— elements of classic garden design in the non-picturesque tradition in which the visual image is one of man-made geometric order. These pleasure gardens also are resting places for Buddhist monks. The Sanskrit word for garden, *arama,* came to denote a monastery, once again blurring the distinction between the sacred and the secular.

Since landscapes assume a backdrop to human (and divine) characters in Hindu paintings, it may appear that aesthetic appreciation of nature as a visual composition is lacking. Natural elements, however, are always depicted for their symbolic role in enhancing the emotional state of the human subjects.[19] As in the narrative tradition, miniature paintings show natural settings that succeed in conveying what the heroine is going through in her love trysts. The emphasis is not on realistic rendition of the entire landscape but on individual elements, which consequently assume greater significance than the whole. The word-imagery used in literature is often rendered in pictorial form in paintings, emphasizing allegorical conception rather than objective perception. The lack of perspective tradition to convey distance as one sees it in nature causes elements farther away to appear at the top of the sculptural panel or painting, and those closer, at the bottom. This tradition of non-relational organisation heightens the perception that these are isolated elements evoked for their symbolic meaning, whether sacred or secular.[20] The distinction between spiritual longings and human love becomes diffuse, as in the case of Vrindavan's pastoral scenes showing Krishna frolicking with the cowherdesses. Aesthetic sense is not divorced from the spiritual, and nature inspires both.

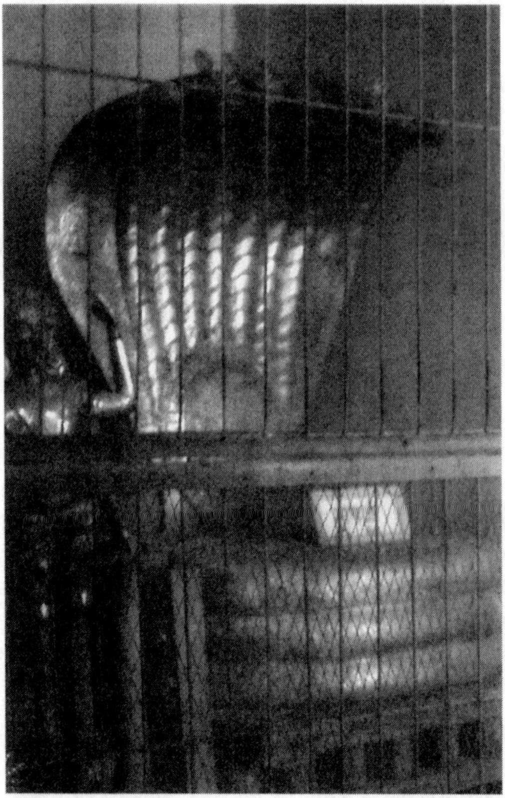

2.3: A metallic sculpture of Shesh-naga, who was incarnated as Krishna's brother Balarama, in Rangji temple in Vrindavan.

VIEWS OF NATURE

It would be misleading to discuss attitudes toward nature as consistent and unified through the diverse cultural strains that make up Hinduism. Great and little traditions have been identified by anthropologists in every aspect of Hindu culture, and beliefs associated with nature do not escape that dichotomy.[21] Added to these diverse traditions are regional differences. Earth goddess, vegetation, and serpent worship play a secondary role in Sanskrit rituals. Deification occurs at the rural level, sometimes in a crude manner with rites performed mostly by female worshippers. In contrast, the power of India's great rivers and mountains has been invoked in the architectural masterpieces of temples and in the location of sacred sites. Nature in the great tradition must be imbued with the divine spirit to bring the cosmos into being. This view is a little different from Christian theology, which regards nature as handiwork of God, and is also different from animistic beliefs in which nature alone is the source of all creation. Just as mythology and philosophy coexist in Hinduism, nature worship is found alongside the metaphysical duality of *prakriti* and *Purusha* without creating unresolved conflicts in devotees' minds.

By attributing an element of divinity to the natural world and invoking its blessings and protective power, Hindus recognize the consciousness common to all elements of the cosmos. The easy transmutations that occur between human beings, animals, and plants highlight this notion. Religious valorisation cannot be regarded as simple animistic worship. In Hindu tradition there is little evidence of propitiation of nature solely because it is feared. Rather nature is a vehicle or conduit for divine manifestation and in that light is regarded as sacred. Consequently, it is venerated rather than controlled, deified and invoked instead of objectified, manipulated, exploited, and bent to human will. Nature is integrated with culture by anthropomorphizing natural elements and establishing them as cultural icons. Nature inspires the arts and folk traditions of India to an enormous extent, demonstrating that the mental constructs of nature and culture are not so dichotomous after all.

Nature is seen essentially in a protective role, and that attitude is reflected in the gentle, benign faces of nature deities and in the many rituals invoking their blessings. It is possible that this protective role was a later development in the religions of India, stretching back to the Indus Valley civilisation in the third millennium BCE. Fecundity is a theme constant through the ages, but nature's fearsome aspect appears to have been subdued over the ages with growth of civilisation. Relics that view nature as awesome and mysterious continue to exist in propitiation rituals of folk practice, in *tantric* rites, and in the cults of Kali and Bhadrakali worship in Bengal and Kerala. Their survival poses an enigma; however, the corpus of beliefs in Hinduism has never been characterised by a single strain and the archaic still lingers in the collective unconscious of its people.

2.4: The sacred banyan tree is often home to icons of gods and goddesses and can become an impromptu shrine, even in the midst of teeming traffic.

Sanskritic Hinduism, with its emphasis on the union of *prakriti* and *Purusha* bringing forth the recurring cycles of the universe, introduced bipolarity, which replaced the earlier unipolar view of nature as the sole creative entity. *Prakriti* and *purusha* are signifiers of feminine and masculine principles, respectively. Their ascendance over the worship of *prakriti* as *shakti,* which goes back to Indus Valley civilisation and aboriginal cults, could be regarded as the victory of masculine over feminine principles until one remembers that *prakriti* and *purusha,* although distinct for conceptual clarity, are complementary and cannot be considered separately. They are frequently represented as a triangle (*trikona*) with the apex of the *purusha* at the top and the point of their union representing creation and existence. *Prakriti,* including the human body and composed of the gross elements of earth, water, fire, air, and ether, cannot be manifested without the power of the divine spirit.

Characterised by veneration, interdependency with the human world, and aesthetic delight, the relationship with nature is definitely not antagonistic in Hindu culture; indeed, harmonious may be the most accurate descriptor. Emerging from an earlier ambivalent view, life-enhancing and protective powers of nature are recognised and invoked in worship within the main body of Hindu traditions. Monotheistic religions have the concept of God as the creator of the universe in which man and nature are separate entities and folk beliefs of tribal communities regard the power of nature as supreme. Hinduism departs from both these views; human beings, God, and nature are not separate entities, nor is nature the supreme God. Rather all of these entities are manifestations of the universal consciousness (*brahman*). Nature, because of its incessant cycle of creation and dissolution, is also *maya* (illusion), and liberation consists of not being subject to its power.

CONCLUSION

To what extent has the transcendentalist view of nature shaped the landscape of India? Hindu mythology is nurtured in landscapes that are interwoven in the religious texts and folklore to form a powerful source of religious imagery. As such, places become icons, reflected and multiplied until sacredness permeates the land. The transcendentalist view recognizes the capability of divinity to be manifested in great numbers and multiplied endlessly. The resulting landscape of pilgrim places and networks is characterised by polycentricity. Diana Eck calls it the imagined landscape of India, not as nation-state but as a shared, living cultural entity.[22] Mountains and rivers—most frequently the Himalayas and river Ganga—are duplicated and transposed. The system of seven rivers and four *dhams* (dwellings) is duplicated at local and regional levels. The metaphor of the body-cosmos suggests the organic unity of the land, especially through the systems of *pithas* created by the dismemberment of goddess Sati.

At the dawn of the twenty-first century, Indian society remains profoundly religious. No better indication of this can be found than in the growing popularity of pilgrimages, the building of new shrines, and the ubiquity of holy people and their *ashramas*. The landscape inscribes these patterns of belief and practice. In addition to providing transcendental experiences and affording a sense of religious community, sacred landscapes perform a didactic purpose. Because Hindu mythology is interwoven with natural features of the land, visits to sacred sites teach new myths or bring back memories of old ones.[23]

Pilgrim centers are distributed throughout the subcontinent and, as sacred sites replete with temples and shrines, they attract devotees from near and far. Many of these sites are landscapes of natural grandeur where temples were built to tap their inherent sacredness. Usually a myth built around a Hindu god and goddess is responsible for worship at that spot.

Pilgrim centers are called *tirthas* (fords or crossings) and signify the place where the final release from life (*moksha*) can be obtained. They are nodes within a *kshetra* (a field of energy) and a place of divine power. This sacred geography has served to unify India's diverse cultural traditions through pilgrim circulation.[24] And this close association of pilgrimage sites with areas of natural grandeur draws the Hindu culture closer into the bosom of nature, thereby transcending the duality between nature and culture.

Even in the industrialised, urban landscape of Indian cities, sacredness in the form of wayside icons and local temples can be found. The gods find a dwelling place under trees at crossroads or any wayside in the midst of the hustle and bustle of urban life. Nodes of sanctity have a tendency to erupt anywhere and everywhere. These auspicious spots often become anchor points for local communities. Benign forces of nature are given an architectonic form in temples dedicated to gods and goddesses. Architectural features concretize natural energies by becoming symbols and icons of natural elements. The spatial configuration of buildings is based upon order perceived in nature, and the shared vocabulary between sacred and secular architecture establishes continuity between temple and house, holy and secular city. The current popularity of *vaastu* (derived from medieval sacred texts on art and architecture) design in housing reflects the strength of belief in tradition.

NOTES

1. (London: Weidenfeld & Nicholson, 1982).
2. Diana Eck, "The Goddess Ganges in Hindu Sacred Geography," in *Devi: Goddesses of India,* ed. John Hawley and Donna Wulff (Berkeley: University of California Press, 1996), 140.
3. Cornelia Dimmitt and J.A.B. van Buitenen (eds.), *Classical Mythology in the Sanskritic Puranas* (Philadelphia: Temple University Press, 1978).
4. Stella Kramrisch, *The Hindu Temple,* 2 vols. (Calcutta: Calcutta University Press, 1946).
5. *Ibid.*
6. See Jai Pal Singh and Mumtaz Khan, "Saptadvipa Vasumati: The Mythical Geography of the Hindus," in *Mythical Space, Cosmology, and Landscape: Towards a Cultural Geography of India* (New Delhi: Manak Publications, 2002), 9–29.
7. Frits Staal, "The Centre of Space: Construction and Discovery," in *Concepts of Space: Ancient and Modern,* ed. Kapila Vatsyayan (New Delhi: Indira Gandhi National Centre for the Arts, Abhinav Publications, 1991), 83–100.
8. Rana P.B. Singh, "Sacredscape, Cosmic Territory, and Faithscape: Goddess Territory of Vindhyachal, India" (paper presented at Pilgrimage and Complexity Conference, Indira Gandhi National Centre for the Arts, New Delhi, 1999).

9. Eck, "The Goddess Ganges in Hindu Sacred Geography."
10. George Michell (ed.), *Eternal Kaveri: Historical Sites Along South India's Greatest River,* Vol. 51, No. 1 (Mumbai: Marg Publications, September 1999).
11. Ananda K. Coomaraswamy, *Elements of Buddhist Iconography* (Cambridge, MA: Harvard University Press, 1935).
12. Sankar Sen Gupta (ed.), *Tree Symbol Worship in India—A New Study of a Pattern of Folk Religion* (Calcutta: India Publications, 1975).
13. Like the mandalas, yantras are mystical diagrams and the two terms are often used interchangeably in Sanskrit literature. For comprehensive definitions of the two, see Gudrun Buhnemann, "Mandala, Yantra, and Cakra: Some Observations," in *Mandalas and Yantras in the Hindu Traditions,* ed. Gudrun Buhnemann (Leiden, the Netherlands: Brill, 2003), 13–56.

    Although mandalas are drawn to accommodate a number of deities, yantras almost always represent the goddess. They can be carried around, in which case they are made of durable materials such as copper, or they may be installed below a deity in the temple. Like the mandalas they may be inscribed in the landscape.
14. Pupul Jayakar, *The Earth Mother* (San Francisco: Harper & Row, 1990).
15. Ananda Coomaraswamy, *Yakshas,* Smithsonian Miscellaneous Collections, Vol. 80, No. 6 (Washington, DC: Smithsonian Institution, 1928).
16. J. Ph. Vogel, *Indian Serpent Lore* (Varanasi: Prithvi Prakashan, 1972).
17. J. Tilaksari, *Kalidasa's Imagery and the Theory of Poetics* (New Delhi: Nawrang, 1988).
18. Ram Bachan Singh, "Cities and Parks in Ancient India," *Geographical Review of India* 36:1 (March 1974), 62–75.
19. Vatsyayan, *Concepts of Space.*
20. O. C. Gangoly, *Landscape in Indian Literature and Art* (Calcutta: University of Lucknow, 1963).
21. McKim Marriott (ed.), *Village India: Studies in the Little Community* (Chicago: University of Chicago Press, 1955); Milton Singer (ed.), *Traditional India: Structure and Change* (Philadelphia: American Folklore Society, 1959).
22. Diana Eck, "The Imagined Landscape: Patterns in the Construction of Hindu Sacred Geography," in *Contributions to Indian Sociology* 32:2 (1998), 165–188.
23. Kelly Alley, "Idioms of Degeneracy: Assessing Ganga's Purity and Pollution," in *Purifying the Earthly Body of God: Religion and Ecology in Hindu India,* ed. Lance Nelson (Albany: State University of New York Press, 1998), 297–331, reports that the number of pilgrims visiting Banaras has steadily increased over the past few decades. Charles Brooks gives the figure of 2.325 million pilgrims per month visiting Vrindavan, birthplace of Krishna, in 1982– 1983, approximately triple the number that visited a decade earlier (*The Hare Krishnas in India* [Princeton: Princeton University Press, 1989]).
24. Surinder Bharadwaj, *Hindu Places of Pilgrimage in India* (Berkeley: University of California Press, 1973).

PART TWO

NATURAL ARCHETYPES

> "Narrative in its essence was a device to regain and reshape memory, to overcome the amnesia that time piles up on a people's psyche. While poetry can appropriate the accretions of lost time, it deals with essences which makes it accessible to connoisseurs— *rasikas*—whereas narrative in its collective aspect uses substances of day-to-day life to materialise memory and scatters it in and around the territories of art taking in its fold the lay and the learned alike. To re-live an experience by reshaping memory ensures the continuance of life through ritual regeneration. Every enactment, recital or visualisation carries elements of the characters being reincarnated into the present. The device of continuous narration served as the ideal means for evoking and recycling the archetypes most effectively."
>
> —**Gulam Mohammed Sheikh,**
> "Story of the Tongue and the Text:
> The Narrative Tradition"[1]

How are the natural archetypes discussed in the previous section woven into the grand narratives of Hinduism and Buddhism? Epics and legends, stories with plots enacted by gods and humans unfolding in space and time, are pertinent to our understanding of how landscapes become sacred. From the vast corpus of mythology and place legends, I select a few as case studies to demonstrate the interweaving of narrative and place around natural archetypes. The landscape patterns decoded in the following chapters can be discerned with some variations in hundreds of sacred sites across the length and breadth of the subcontinent. Chapter 3 decodes the symbolic meanings of nature and landscapes in the Sanskrit epic *Ramayana*. Chapter 4 examines the sacred landscapes of Ayodhya, Chitrakuta, and Kishkindha—sites imprinted over time with the *Ramayana*'s characters and events. Chapter 5 narrates the story of Krishna in Braj, showing how animistic associations of trees, hills, and water were sublimated in a metaphysical conception of sacredness manifested in the landscape. Chapter 6 explores shifting meanings of ancient India's tree of life during the Buddhist period by examining key episodes in Gautama Buddha's life. Chapter 7 traces the evolution of Pavagadh hill as the landscape of the mother goddess.

Landscapes of Braj, those associated with the epic *Ramayana,* where Gautama Buddha spent his life, and Pavagadh hill are believed to be of hoary antiquity. These cultural landscapes are shaped by interpretations of nature found in the grand narratives of Indian culture. For the devout Hindu and Buddhist they are pilgrim destinations, hallowed by the onetime and—to the believer—eternal presence of Krishna, Rama, Devi, and the Buddha. They may be compared to symbolic texts and read by the modern pilgrim for clues to a historic past, an encounter with signs of divine grace, and a reaffirmation of cultural identity. There are other benefits to the visit as well, such as acquiring spiritual merit, fulfilling vows, and shedding sins.

Each pilgrim center is different, although their landscapes share many natural features, especially with regard to the hill-river dyad. At all sites we see archaic animistic myths, which had initially taken root in the landscape but with time were supplanted by the narratives of the current pantheon of gods and goddesses. Each landscape offers a different experience to the pilgrim. The configuration of hills in Chitrakuta are perceived as triangular yantras, the circumambulatory routes of Ayodhya and Braj reveal very different landscapes, the multitude of hills in Kishkindha are crowned by temples that resemble natural outcrops from a distance, and Pavagadh hill is Kalika's yantra and Sati's toe.

The evolving landscapes result from a cyclical process oscillating between natural archetypes and providing a foundation for cultural narratives, and texts (linguistic, visual, and enacted) in turn influence the emerging shape of landscape. Venerated over millennia, these sites have witnessed natural decay, bouts of destruction, and rebuilding over time. Embedded in their narrative structures are psychological archetypes of self, internalised by millions in India and, in the case of the Buddha, worldwide. Rama's story exemplifies the hero archetype, Krishna's legend revolves around the lovable child prankster, Gautama Buddha's life illustrates the archetypal guru, and Kalika Mata is the terrible yet compassionate mother. These universal archetypes resonate with those buried in our individual psyches, endowing these narratives with the power to move us.

As each narrative unfolds in place and time, natural settings play an integral role in a narrative's development and are more than backdrops to events. The poet Valmiki's descriptions of nature in the Sanskrit epic *Ramayana* encompass a dualistic view of her sacred and profane aspects and become an allegory of good and evil. Krishna mythology rests upon pastoralism. The stunning Pavagadh hill symbolises *shakti* (power) and *prakriti* (nature) in all their grandeur. Gardens and tree groves inspire momentous events in Gautama Buddha's life. We learn of nature's many facets—demonic wilderness, benign pastoralism, picturesque gardens, sacred groves, animated spirits, generative and destructive powers, and libidinal potential. A facet comes to light with each occurrence of an event and guides its shape, or plays a formative role in character development.

In reading landscape as text, natural archetypes function as roots of words. Tree, water, hill, cave, and their built versions combine to become sites of events, mythical or actual. Trees at crossroads, hills and water in proximity, river confluences, and unusual configurations of hilly ranges invariably invite legends. The landscape is idealised in linguistic and visual texts. This visionary imagery in turn guides the landscape regeneration if a sacred site is abandoned or destroyed and helps in sacralising new sites. The landscape functions much like the fluid oral tradition of storytelling in which the demands of social relevance continuing through time do not destroy the essential character of the myth. It plays a mnemonic role in providing tangible evidence and is a locale in which collective memories find a home.

NOTE

1. Gulam Mohammed Sheikh, "Story of the Tongue and the Text," in *Narrative: A Seminar*, ed. Amiya Dev (New Delhi: Sahitya Akademi, 1994), 266–267.

Chapter Three

Nature in Ramayana

> "As long as the mountains and rivers shall endure upon the earth, so long will the story of the Ramayana be told among men."[1]
>
> —***Balakanda,*** 2.35

> "Imagine a story that is the *Odyssey*, Aesop's fables, *Romeo and Juliet,* the Bible, and *Star Wars* all at the same time. Imagine a story that combines adventure and aphorism, romance and religion, fantasy and philosophy. Imagine a story that makes young children marvel, burly men weep, and old women dream. Such a story exists in India, and it is called the *Ramayana*."
>
> —**Jonah Blank,**
> *The Arrow of the Blue-Skinned God: Retracing the* Ramayana *Through India*[2]

The age of the Sanskrit epic *Ramayana,* composed by sage Valmiki, is uncertain; it is believed to be set in the pre-Buddhist period around the sixth century BCE in the Koshala kingdom in north-central India.[3] In keeping with India's oral traditions, the epic has been sung by bards through the ages and has inspired classics in different languages.[4] Ramalila, the folk theater, enacts *Ramayana*'s story every year throughout India.[5] In Hindu households, the *Ramayana* is read by individuals daily and sung on important family occasions.

Its popularity shows no signs of waning in the twenty-first century; if anything, it has gathered force. *Ramayana*'s narrative and its characters are archetypal and have had a strong impact on the Hindu collective psyche. Rama, the principal protagonist, is considered to be an *avatara* (incarnation) of God who descended upon the earth to restore righteousness and to punish evildoers. *Ramayana* is a tragic tale of family intrigue, exile, and renunciation. It exemplifies *dharma* (religiously ordained code of conduct) and *karma* (the law of actions and their consequences upon the lives of gods and humans) and, in medieval texts, *bhakti* (devotion). According to Sheldon Pollock, "A great culture's exploration of such central issues as the nature and function of political power and of a hierarchical social order is preserved for us in this poem."[6] I believe that, in addition, the poem preserves for posterity a great culture's concept of nature and landscapes. In this chapter, I decode the symbolic meaning of landscapes and natural features in Valmiki's *Ramayana.* My analysis is based upon the English translation of the Sanskrit text by Robert Goldman and others in the critical edition *The Ramayana of Valmiki: An Epic of Ancient India.*[7]

The *Ramayana* is divided into seven books. *Balakanda,* the first book, is about Rama's birth in Ayodhya to King Dasharatha and his queen Kaushalya, his childhood and adolescence, his protection of sage Vishvamitra from the *rakshas* while the sage performs sacrifices, and his marriage to Sita, princess of the Mithila kingdom, upon his breaking of god Shiva's bow. *Ayodhyakanda*, the second book of *Ramayana,* covers the circumstances surrounding Rama's exile. After King Dasharatha makes his decision to appoint Rama as his successor, Queen Kaikeyi— his stepmother— intervenes and reminds Dasharatha of two boons that he promised her when she saved his life on the battlefront. She asks for Rama's exile and for the throne of Ayodhya to be given to her son, Bharata. Thereupon, in spite of Dasharatha's lamentations, Rama prepares to leave. Sita begs to be taken along and Lakshmana, his half-brother, also pleads to be allowed to accompany him. The three leave the city of Ayodhya for the forest. After wandering for some time, they settle in Chitrakuta, a forested, hilly area. Meanwhile, Bharata, who has been away in his maternal uncle's kingdom, is called back when Dasharatha dies of grief. He blames his mother, Kaikeyi, for the turn of events and refuses coronation. Instead he arrives at Chitrakuta and begs Rama to return. Upon Rama's refusal, Bharata takes Rama's sandals to Ayodhya, symbolically placing them on the throne and ruling on Rama's behalf from the village of Nandigrama on the outskirts of the city where he lives as an ascetic.

Book three, *Aranyakanda,* focuses on Rama, Sita, and Lakshmana's sojourn in the forest, their visits to different ashrams, and their settlement in Panchvati in Godavari river valley. Here Rama kills the *rakshasas*— Khara, Dushana, and Trishiras—when they attack upon their sister Shuprankha's instigation. Their cousin Ravana, demon-king of Lanka, hatches a plot with *rakshasas* Maricha to kidnap Sita. Rama departs to hunt Maricha in the guise of a golden deer with Lakshmana following suit. Sita, left alone, is kidnapped by Ravana and brought to Lanka. Rama is grief stricken and vows to find her. He and Lakshmana are led to the monkey-prince, Sugriva, who had been driven out of his kingdom Kishkindha by his brother, Vali.

In book four, *Kishkindha,* Sugriva and Rama join forces. Rama kills Vali and, in exchange for getting the kingdom of Kishkindha, Sugriva agrees to help Rama and Lakshmana find Sita. He sends out teams of monkeys in all four directions. In book five, *Sundarakanda,* one team that includes the monkey Hanuman, son of wind-god Varuna, manages to reach the shore of the Indian Ocean. Hanuman flies to the island of Lanka and tracks Sita, who is being held captive in a palace garden. Book six, *Yuddhakanda,* describes Rama and Lakshmana's attack of Lanka with Sugriva's army of monkeys and bears after building a causeway across the ocean. Ravana is killed, and Sita is rescued and accepted by Rama only after a purificatory ordeal in fire. Vibhishana, brother of Ravana, who had defected to Rama's camp, is coronated king of Lanka. Rama, Sita, and Lakshmana return victorious to Ayodhya. With the crowning of Rama as king, Rama-rajya commences, a utopian state where morality, prosperity, and good health prevail in the country. The seventh and final book, *Uttarakanda,* serves as an anticlimactic end to the story. Rama banishes Sita on hearing that the citizens of Ayodhya are heaping opprobrium on him for having accepted her after she had spent a year in Lanka in Ravana's captivity. Pregnant Sita seeks refuge in Valmiki's ashram and delivers a pair of twins— Lava and Kusha. Valmiki teaches the twins to sing his composition—*Ramayana.* Rama hears them in his court and asks Sita once again to prove her innocence. She demonstrates her purity by requesting the earth to take her back, and the earth obliges.

Interwoven with the main narrative are numerous secondary stories of births and rebirths of a host of minor entities whose lives intersect with those of the main protagonists. These stories prove the efficacy of the inexorable law of *karma*—one always reaps the consequences of one's actions. Rama himself is a model of *kshatriya dharma,* his life exemplifying that of an ideal son and brother and a just ruler. His life stresses the importance of inculcating various positive values such as chastity, affection, self-reliance, fortitude, truth, righteousness, sacrifice, self-control, altruism, and fulfillment of kinship obligations and duties toward one's guru.

Within this drama of human relationships tinged with idealism and played out in real and imaginary settings, nature imagery is integral to the plot's development. Nature is not merely a stylistic embellishment but intervenes powerfully in a number of ways. Landscape settings and natural elements and processes serve as allegories communicating human emotions, experiences, and actions. Rama's adventure has romantic elements involving the hero's quest to rid the world of *adharma* by defeating evil forces, and this is exemplified by the *rakshasas'* killing of sages and finally Ravana's abduction of Sita. It also has mythic proportions when Rama is considered as God (an *avatara* of Vishnu) in the first and final books.

Northrop Frye puts myth and romance in the general category of mythopoeic literature.[8] Place archetypes, found in different cultures' myths and romances, appear in *Ramayana* as well. The dawning of divine self-knowledge in Rama is the culminating event in a journey that progresses within the realms of cities, forests, and gardens and in the crossing of rivers and ocean. Much of this journey takes place within the uncharted territory of wilderness whose profanity is in striking contrast to the sacred *tapovana,* where ascetics dwell in forest clearings. As in romantic tales the world over, natural forces both hinder and help in the hero's quest. Certain universal place archetypes—trackless wilderness, forest clearings, gardens, mountains, and trees as *axis mundi;* island fortresses and oceans as great barriers— appear in *Ramayana.* The ordered landscapes of palace and city gardens share many characteristics with natural settings. Nature is animated and personified and indeed is often tinged with the transcendent dimension. Neutral in its primeval existence, it serves as a vehicle for the projection of good and evil within the human psyche. *Ramayana* as an *adikavya* (first work of poetry) is the earliest example of the aesthetic theory of *rasa*—affect created with sublimated sentiment and elaborated with nature tropes. The cycles of nature not only mark the passage of time but also resonate with and communicate the characters' shifting moods of grief, despair, and hope.

WILDERNESS VERSUS *TAPOVANA*

Nature is the main thread in the tapestry of settings, particularly evident in books three, four, and five. The landscapes emerging in these books are painted in bold strokes and rest upon a multifaceted view of nature. The natural world is conceived as hostile wilderness, benign pastoral environment, and lush palace garden. The society of the *Ramayana* re-creates the essential configuration of idyllic settings in the forest within the ordered world of palace and city gardens.

Rama, Sita, and Lakshmana's journey to the largely uninhabited south can be understood in this light. Rama and Lakshmana's first encounter with the wilderness is in their youth. Sage Vishvamitra asks King Dasharatha for the two brothers to act as his protectors while he performs sacrifices and meditates in the forest. The brothers accompany Vishvamitra to Tarakavana, named after the yakshi Taraka. Taraka is portrayed as a dangerous and violent creature, attacking the *rishis* practicing austerities in the forest. She personifies the evil inherent in wilderness—disorder, chaos, and mindless violence.[9] The harsh cries of other dangerous denizens— birds, beasts, and reptiles—fills Tarakavana. It is indeed a terrifying place. Rama kills

Taraka, bringing solace to Vishvamitra and other sages. The forest is rid of its dangers; wilderness has lost its violent edge.

Although Rama and Lakshmana return to civilisation, their respite from forays into wilderness is short-lived. When Rama hears news of his exile and Sita insists on accompanying him, he tries to dissuade her. He describes the roar of lions in mountain caves, the intensity of the darkness and wind, the presence of snakes and scorpions, and the tangle of thorn trees. He tells her of the hardships she will have to endure in sleeping upon the ground on a bed of leaves, in being hungry, and in having to fast to the limits of one's endurance.

In the fourteen-years forest sojourn of Rama, Sita, and Lakshmana, the dangers of wilderness continue to assail them. The demons or *rakshasas* are wilderness embodied. They contribute to its disorder by their harmful actions. This aspect of nature is the very antithesis of the order of human society with its code of *dharma*.[10] Scattered in the seemingly impenetrable forests are islands of sanctity—*ashramas,* the vanguard of Indo-Aryan civilisation. The ashramas, established by *rishis,* are instrumental in bringing the order of civilised society with its *dharmic* values into the primeval chaos of wilderness. Retiring to the forest, away from the pleasures and distractions of the vile city, to practice austerities and meditation in order to gain insights and to achieve peace and salvation has been the ideal in Hindu society since time immemorial.

Ascetics lead an austere life in ashramas in the forest's depths. Ashramas in forest clearings are also places to learn the *shastras* (sacred books) by the young twice-born. Enlightened sages often acquire supernatural powers, including insights and knowledge of past and future events, through yogic exercises and meditation. Their highly developed powers of concentration and moral strength imbue their surroundings with their auras and positive energies. Hence, the forest they inhabit is called *tapovana* (forest of asceticism).

Tapovana, although in the midst of wilderness, forms a striking contrast. Here psychological and physical dangers are banished. The inherent fears of evils in the wilderness are conquered by the moral force of sages. Wild beasts and birds are gentle. Trees bear flowers and fruits in profusion. The ashram gives shelter to all. Its pleasant surroundings remove one's tiredness and provide a peaceful environment with freedom from worldly distractions. Fragrant breezes and cool waters nearby make the ashram an attractive sylvan setting. Nature is benevolent. More than benign, it is a paradise-like setting with celestial musicians and dancers adding to the charm and occasionally leading a renouncer astray. In the wilderness of Dandaka, a circle of ashramas where ascetics dwell, is described:

> Kusa grass and bark garments were strewn about it, and, flooded with brahmanical splendor, it was as luminous and blinding to the eye as the sun's circle in heaven (1.2).
>
> It resembled the abode of Brahma; the sounds of *brahma,* the sacred *Vedas,* echoed through it, and illustrious Brahmins who knew the meaning of *brahma* deepened its beauty still further (1.8).[11]

The ashram is a place of spiritual force. Rama, Sita, and Lakshmana in their forest exile visit and live in many such ashramas. Ashramas are nodes in their itinerant path, resting places as the weary threesome make their way into the dense forest. In the ashramas they meet famous sages and imbibe their spiritual teachings. It is in Bharadvaja's ashram near the confluence of the Yamuna and Gangas rivers that they come to know of Chitrakuta hill where they settle down in the early period of their exile. After Bharata's visit to Chitrakuta, they leave for Dandaka forest, visiting Atri's ashram on the way. The *rishis* living there ask for protection from the *rakshasas.*

Rama, Sita, and Lakshmana stay in various ashramas for a total of ten years. The ashramas of sages Sharbhanga and Sutikshana are serene places surrounded by fruit-bearing trees and waterfalls. Agastya's *ashram* is located near a lotus-filled lake surrounded by trees where monkeys and birds live. All creatures are peaceful and forgiving and live in amity. Agastya tells Rama about the Panchvati region where the three could spend the very last year of their exile. After Sita is abducted in Panchvati by Ravana, Rama and Lakshmana travel southwest to search for her. They visit Matanga muni's *ashram* after crossing a dense forest. Shabari's *ashram* is another resting place in their frantic search.

FOREST AND GARDEN

In *tapovana,* near existing *ashramas,* Rama, Sita, and Lakshmana build cottages to live in. *Ramayana* describes two places—Chitrakuta hill close to Mandakini river and Panchvati by the river Godavari farther south in the depths of the Dandaka forest. Both Chitrakuta and Panchvati, as described by Valmiki, possess the attributes of *tapovana.* Wilderness is held at bay in these Edenic settings. Chitrakuta and Panchvati are natural gardens of great beauty. Here Mother Nature is bountiful; there is an abundance of fruits and edible roots and vegetables. Springs, lakes, and rivers are close by. The landscape is described in idyllic terms. The hilly refuge with its wide prospect of rivers makes for aesthetically pleasing and ecologically diverse niches. The leaf hut of Rama and Sita stands between the mountain and the Mandakini river. The lyrical beauty of Chitrakuta brings great happiness to them. The pearl-like waters of Mandakini with its flower-strewn banks, swaying trees on the hill, and garlands of flowers enchant Rama, making his exile feel like an elixir. He addresses Sita:

> Just think of the wild animals as the townsmen all the while, my beloved, of the mountains as Ayodhya, and this river as the Sarayu (89.15).
>
> Being here with you, bathing at the time of the three oblations, and eating sweet fruit and roots, I no longer yearn either for Ayodhya or the kingship (89.17).[12]

Indeed, Rama, Sita, and Lakshmana's stay in Chitrakuta is very pleasant. The hill, rich with minerals, has large shady trees, beehives rich with honey, and sweet, delicious springs, allowing a blissful existence, free from the travails of labour.

Panchvati (where Rama, Sita, and Lakshmana spent the last year of their exile) is not far from sage Agastya's *ashram*. It too is on a hilly area on the banks of river Godavari. This fertile river valley has many fruit-bearing trees growing on its hilly crests, slopes, banks, and where "the woodlands are all in flower" (*Aranyakanda*, 14.2). The fauna is rich as well, the river in particular attracting many birds. Lakshmana describes the beauties of the landscape in the winter season to Rama:

> How beautiful the floor of the forest appears, with the early morning sunlight playing upon it and the meadows slightly dampened by a fall of hoarfrost.
>
> The expanses of forest seem fast asleep, wrapped up in the darkness of hoarfrost, blanketed by the darkness of snow, with not a blossom open.
>
> The sand on the riverbanks is wet with snow, the water thickly covered with mist, and only their cry reveals the presence of cranes (15.20–22).[13]

Another fertile river valley, that of river Tungabhadra, is Rama and Lakshmana's last sojourn as they prepare for launching an attack on Lanka where Sita is held captive. This valley was the kingdom of monkey-king Sugriva, who had promised to help Rama in his battle with Ravana. Yet, Sugriva had been driven out by his brother Vali, who suspected him of usurping his kingdom. Sugriva took refuge in a cave in Rishyamukha mountain near Pampa Lake. The poet paints the landscape in scenic terms. Lotus-covered Pampa Lake has "level landing places and a bed of soft sand. Its silvery, crystal clear waters are deliciously cool, safe and healthful, and charged with the scent of lotuses." Rishyamukha mountain, east of the lake, is a noble mountain yielding treasures to those who dream of them on its peak (*Aranyakanda,* 69.5–32).

Rama and Lakshmana spend the four months of monsoon on Mount Prasravana. Waiting for Sugriva, they pass their time in a cave, sheltered from the rain. The lush natural beauties of a hospitable landscape are a continual source of wonder and amazement. The hills and the river Tungabhadra provide a combination of refuge and prospect, a safe haven from which the rain-drenched landscape can be viewed in all its munificence. Cataclysmic forces of nature and wild beasts of prey have no place in this arcadia. These gardenesque valleys are oases amidst hostile wilderness.

The urban culture of ancient India sought to incorporate features of this natural landscape into its royal gardens and public parks in the cities. Nature, as in other civilisations, was the archetypal model for garden-making. *Ramayana* describes Ayodhya and Lanka as garden cities. Book five, *Sundarakanda,* extensively describes a garden in Lanka called Ashokavanam, which is in Ravana's palace where Sita is held captive. Hanuman, Rama's emissary, finds his way to the garden named after the columnar Ashoka tree. It has a dense vegetation cover; there are even artificial trees designed by the divine architect Viswakarma. There is little evidence of a geometric order apart from the mention of trees being planted in rows as in orchards. Flowers are a significant attraction of the garden, as is evident from its comparison to a young woman adorned with flowers. It is also compared to a sky full of constellations and an ocean glittering with jewels.

Trees provide more than flowers, fruits, and shade. They are path markers and shelter spots. The traditional Hindu concept of the tree as an *axis mundi* finds expression in gardens too. Silver and golden platforms (vedika) surround the trees; it is not clear if the trees are being worshipped for themselves or if they house gods and goddesses. Sita, who appears when Janaka, king of Mithila, is plowing the field and whose name means "furrow," sits under the Ashoka tree in the middle of the garden grove, spending months of captivity remembering Rama and his unmatched prowess. For Sita, the earth goddess, the Ashoka tree is a protecting abode in her state of anguish. The garden serves both secular and sacred purposes. It is primarily a place for recreation where nature can be enjoyed. The primeval sacred grove, however, is not expelled from this garden. Gods find a home in the grove in the garden. In Ashokavanam, Hanuman sees a tall, circular temple with a thousand columns. Certain features of valley landscapes are abstracted in Ravana's palace garden. A stream descends from a cloud like mountain and makes its way to lotus ponds filled with birds. Surrounding an elongated artificial tank with steps made of gemstones and pearls in place of sand is a lovely grove of trees bursting into fruit and flower (*Sundarakanda,* 12.1–37; 13.1–17).

Ayodhya, Rama, and Sita's palace too had an Ashoka vatika. Skilled gardeners had planted many varieties of trees. The garden includes lotus-filled tanks with jeweled steps and marble floors. Cranes and swans grace the water tanks. Sweet warbling of *papiha, koyil,* and parrots can be heard. Arbors with seating punctuate garden spaces. Both Rama's and Ravana's palaces are compared to celestial gardens—Rama's to that of Nandanvana of Indra, king of *devatas,* and Ravana's to that of Chaitraratha of Kubera, king of *yak sas.* Chaitraratha was designed by Brahma himself, creator of the universe and the archetypal designer. To elevate these earthly gardens to a celestial ambiance calls attention to their perfection. Happiness is possible in the earthly paradise.

The gardens of Lanka and Ayodhya are designed in what we call today naturalistic style. They are picturesque settings with temples scattered over the landscape.[14] They are not extensions of buildings or examples of architectonic order. There is little evidence of bending nature to human will. Water is found in canals and built tanks; it does not defy gravity in fountains. There is no mention of topiary or parterres. The grounds are not terraced or stepped. The eye does not travel to a distant vista. The words describe multisensorial experiences and not just visual order. It can be concluded that gardens in the period of *Ramayana* sought to imitate nature, not to improve upon her to the extent that the highly stylised Mughal gardens of India and French and Italian gardens were to do in later ages.

FORM AND AESTHETICS

The lyrical descriptions of *tapovana,* natural landscape, and gardens rest on detailed observations of nature. They convey sensuality in colors and shapes and sympathetic correspondence between the human body and natural elements. When nature is compared to the human form, the distinction between human form and the rest of nature is blurred.

Valmiki seldom mentions trees without creepers. The poet compares the feminine creepers clinging around the masculine trees to lovers in an ardent embrace. When angry Hanuman begins destroying Ashokavatika, Ravana's garden in Lanka, the creepers are fearful like women whose clothes have been torn. When Hanuman is searching for Sita in Ravana's palace, he sees many beautiful damsels sleeping:

> Lying there in slumber, the various sounds of their ornaments stilled, they collectively resembled a vast bed of lotuses whose *hamsas* and bees had fallen silent.
>
> Maruti gazed upon the faces—fragrant as lotuses—of those beautiful women, their eyes closed and their teeth concealed.
>
> Their faces resembled lotuses that had awakened with the waning of the dark and once more closed their petals at night (7.32–34).[15]

Aquatic imagery is also given a feminine form. Rama, Sita, and Lakshmana must cross the river Ganga in the course of their journey from Ayodhya to Chitrakuta. The text explains the river's divine origins and describes it as a young, beautiful, and fragrant woman adorned with buds and flowers. The metaphor extends to lakes and streams. Pampa Lake, the destination of Rama and Lakshmana after Sita is abducted, is conceived as an ornamented young woman, adorned with trees, her beauty enhanced by a covering of lotuses. Other rivers, such as the Tungabhadra and Narmada, are etched similarly.

Clouds and mountains are given masculine attributes. Mountains and hills form prominent features of the landscapes encountered by Rama, Sita, and Lakshmana in their exile. Like trees, mountains and hills provide shelter. In the earlier period of their exile, the three live on Chitrakuta mountain. When they build a cottage again in Panchvati, it is not too far from a mountain. Lanka, Ravana's capital, is situated on Trikuta mountain on an island in the Indian Ocean, making its defence unimpregnable. The hills and mountains are described as majestic, symbolic of valor and perseverance. Mount Mahendra, from where Hanuman prepares his return from Lanka, is described elaborately. It is the greatest of mountains, covered with trees always laden with fruits and flowers, full of creepers and waterfalls, inhabited by lions and tigers, frequented by rutting elephants, and noisy with its flock of mating birds (*Kishkindhakanda,* 66.34–36).

The poet extols Rama's strength with comparisons to nature. The celestial sage Narada describes Rama "as deep as the ocean and as unyielding as the Himalayas.…[I]n his wrath he resembles the fire at the end of time, yet he rivals the earth in his forbearance" (*Balakanda,* 1.16–17). When Ravana comes to take away Sita by force, she tells him:

> I am faithful to Rama, my husband, the equal of great Indra, unshakable as a great mountain, imperturbable as the great sea.

> I am faithful to Rama, the great-armed, great-chested prince, who moves with the boldness of a lion, a lion like man, a lion among men (45.29–30).[16]

The mountain metaphor is used in several contexts. Rama's body assaulted by weapons in his battle with Ravana was like a mountain bearing thunderbolts unflinchingly. Elsewhere Rama is compared to Himalaya mountain in his patience. Ravana's valor is described in similar terms. Assuming the form of a mountain at will, he would "prevent the glorious powers, the sun and moon, from rising" (*Aranyakanda,* 30.16). When Hanuman came to Lanka in search of Sita, he broke into Ravana's palace at night and saw that the sleeping *rakshas* was like Mount Mandara (celestial mountain) "slumbering with its trees, forests, and thickets." He resembled a "storm cloud laced with streaks of lightning and reddened in the sky at twilight" (*Sundarakanda,* 8.5–9).

NATURE AND *RASA*

Human-nature correspondence in formal attributes of beauty extends to physical actions and the psychological sphere of emotions. Natural surroundings, therefore, play an integral role in the plot's unfolding. Tropes linking natural with human world enhance moods, intensify emotional states, and resonate with psychic conditions. Nature, pulsating with life, is capable of experiencing *rasa* (essence of emotions), including eros—*shringara,* separation—*viraha,* fear—*vibhitsa,* pity—*karuna,* valor—*vira,* wonder—*adbhuta,* terror—*bhayanaka,* comedy—*hasya,* and affection—*vatsalya.* In *Ramayana,* vivid descriptions of nature's emotional states bring into focus the protagonist's feelings by striking a resonant chord between the two. On momentous occasions, events in the natural world signify the unfolding human drama. These natural events react to happenings in the human (and godly) world. They set the stage for victories and battles, mark decisions of far-reaching consequences, and resound with the climax. Of the nine *rasas, Ramayana*'s poetry primarily celebrates four—love, sorrow on separation from the beloved, pity, and valor. Experienced by a host of major and minor characters, these four *rasas* would have been incomplete without including nature imagery.

The grief felt by the royal household and Ayodhya's citizens upon hearing that Rama is exiled is reflected in nature. Sumantra—the minister in Dasharatha's court who could not succeed in persuading Rama, Sita, and Lakshmana to return to Ayodhaya as directed by Dasharatha—speaks of universal grief. Even the horses of the chariot that carry them to the kingdom's boundaries shed tears and are reluctant to go back to Ayodhya.

Sumantra tells Dasharatha after returning from his expedition of driving Rama, Sita, and Lakshmana beyond the kingdom's boundaries:

> Throughout your realm, great king, even the trees are tormented by Rama's calamity; they have wilted, flower, bud and branch.
>
> No creatures are moving about, no beasts stirring forth. The forest is overcome with grief for Rama, and its murmur has been stilled.
>
> In the lotus ponds the lilies have closed their petals, lord of men, and the waters have grown turbid. The lotuses have withered, and the fish and birds have hidden themselves.
>
> Blossoms that grow in water, flowers that grow on land, and fruits have lost their familiar luster, and their fragrance is all but gone (53.4–7).[17]

Upon Rama, Sita, and Lakshmana's departure, Ayodhya is plunged into sorrow. The city becomes a wilderness with chaos prevailing. The citizens feel that the moral order has collapsed.

> Let the wilderness where Raghava goes become our city, and the city we abandon turn into a wilderness.
>
> Let all the animals leave their haunts, the snakes their lairs, the birds and beasts their mountain slopes, and take possession of what we left (30.19–20).[18]

Upon Sita's abduction by Ravana from Janasthana, nature is terror-stricken and filled with pity (*karuna-rasa*) for her. When Ravana arrives at Panchakuti where Sita is alone (Rama and Lakshmana are away to hunt the golden deer Maricha), the natural environs quickly realise the *rakshasa*'s intentions. The "trees stopped rustling and the wind died down. The swift current of the Godavari river began to slacken in fear" (*Aranyakanda,* 44.6–7). When Ravana abducts her, Sita implores the forest Janasthana, Mount Prasravana, Godavari river, spirits inhabiting the trees, flocks of birds, and herds of beasts to tell Rama that "the woman he loves more than life itself is being carried off by Ravana" (*Aranyakanda,* 47.29–34). "It was only a gust of wind, as Ravana flew up, that shook the trees with their flocks of different birds, but it seemed they were waving their arms and crying, 'Do not be afraid!' Later lotus overturned, fish and water creatures frightened, sighs rising from their vaporous waters, the lotus ponds seemed to be grieving for Maithali as for a friend" (*Aranyakanda,* 50.32).

Rama returns to find an abandoned hut. The poet compares it to a wilted lotus pond ravaged by winter. The "rustling trees almost seemed to weep, the flowers had faded, the birds and beasts had fallen still, and the spirits of the forest had departed" (*Aranyakanda,* 58.5–7). Grieving Rama begins searching for Sita, running from one tree to the next, from river to river, up and down the mountains. Drowning in an ocean of sorrow, he asks them:

> Have you seen my beloved, *kadamba* tree? She loved you so much. Tell me if you know what happened to my beloved Sita.
>
> Tell me if you have seen her, *bilva* tree. Her breasts are as large as your fruits, her limbs as smooth as your young shoots, and she wears as silky yellow a dress (58.12–13).
>
> Or you there, deer, do you know anything of fawn-eyed Maithili? My beloved might be among the does: Her flashing glances are so like theirs.
>
> Elephant, I am sure you would know if you had seen her. Her thighs are as smooth as your trunk. Tell me, best of elephants (58.20–21).[19]

Rama and Sita beseech mute nature, the sole witness to the danger that has befallen them. They know nature to be empathetic and poignantly believe that she will come to their rescue. Indeed, the deer, hills, and river are helpful but only after a frustrated Rama threatens them. When Sita is nowhere to be found and they can find no trace of what has happened to her, an angry Rama resolves that no creature—yakshas, *gandharvas, pishachas, rakshasas, kinnaras,* and human beings—will remain in peace until he finds her. He tells Lakshmana:

> I will bring the host of planets to a standstill, darken the moon that brings the night, paralyze both fire and wind, blot out the light of the sun; I will grind the mountain peaks to dust, dry up every body of water, uproot every tree, vine, and shrub, annihilate the ocean (60.42 43).[20]

Rama sees Ravana's broken bow and his chariot destroyed in his struggle with Jatatayus, the bird who had attempted to rescue Sita from Ravana's clutches. Sita's search brings Rama and Lakshmana to Pampa Lake. Its poignant descriptions of the changing seasons are unsurpassed in Sanskrit poetry in evoking *viraha-rasa.* When Rama sees the lake, he is reminded of Sita and begins weeping. He says to Lakshmana:

> With gentle breezes and with blossoms and fruit growing on trees, this fragrant spring month is a time of heightened passion, Saumitri (1.6).
>
> This springtime, resounding with birdsongs of every kind, only inflames my pain, Saumitri, for I am without Sita (1.12).
>
> Overpowered by care and grief, Saumitri, I am tormented by that fawn-eyed woman and by the cruel breeze from the spring forest (1.16).

> See, Lakshmana, how this peahen sick with love dances before her peacock mate on the mountain ridges.
>
> Surely the peacock's beloved was not carried off by a rakshasa in the forest. But for me, living without Sita in this month of flowers is unbearable (1.18–19).
>
> And look, there on the brightly coloured mountainsides the deer are with their does, while I am parted from my fawn-eyed Vaidehi (1.46).[21]

The monsoon season brings no relief to Rama. He is constantly reminded of Sita. Ebullient nature overflows with her bounties. In such sybaritic settings, the world is gripped with a mating frenzy, causing Rama profound anguish. He describes the bacchanalian splendor of monsoons to Lakshmana thusly:

> The heavens, which drank the ocean's water through the sun's rays, are giving birth to the elixir of life, their embryo carried for nine months (27.3).
>
> Sighing with gentle winds, the sky, pale with clouds yet tinged by the sunset, resembles a love-sick man anointed with red sandal-paste (27.6).
>
> And like Sita burning with grief, this heat-stricken earth, newly flooded with water, sheds tears (27.7).
>
> Gently sleep approaches Kesava, swiftly the river approaches the sea, joyfully the she-crane approaches the cloud, eagerly the woman in love approaches her beloved (27.22).[22]

Autumn increases Rama's desire to meet Sita. The four-month rainy season had felt like a hundred years to him in her absence. He laments:

> My young wife, whose voice is like the crying of cranes, used to enjoy the crying of cranes in our hermitage; how can she find enjoyment now?
>
> And how can my young wife enjoy the sight of flowering asana trees bright as gold, when she looks about and does not see me? (29.7–8).
>
> Without that fawn-eyed woman, I find no happiness now in wandering through woods and forests, near lakes, rivers, and ponds.
>
> I hope that lovely woman, so young and far from me, is not deeply tormented by love endlessly renewed by nature's charms (29.12–13).[23]

The elaborate descriptions of seasonal activities mirror and intensify Rama's moods.

More than a mirror to the human world, nature serves as a prototype and catalyst to its patterns of forms and actions. Human traits are projected onto rivers, mountains, and animals. Nature is capable of speech, purposeful action, feelings, and expressions and can even assume human form. Conversely, aesthetic criteria derived from natural forms are applied to human beings whose psychological states and instincts are explained with reference to natural processes. Anger and grief are made vivid by nature metaphors. When Rama, Sita, and Lakshmana depart for the forest, Kaushalya is grief-stricken:

> Here, see, a fire kindled by grief for my son has burst forth and is ravaging me, as the earth is ravaged in summertime by the rays of the blazing, holy sun that brings the day (38.20).[24]

Dasharatha laments to Kaushalya:

> Oh Rama! Oh younger brother of Rama! Oh poor Vaidehi! You did not know I would die helplessly in sorrow. Too wide, my lady, is this ocean of grief, too wide for me to cross alive (54.24).[25]

Sita, imprisoned in the Ashoka grove in Lanka and terrorised by Ravana and *rakshasa* women, is overcome by grief:

> Unable to see my husband and fallen into the clutches of *rakshasa* women, I am collapsing under my grief, like a riverbank undercut by water (23.15).[26]

In the great war between Rama and *rakshasas,* nature metaphors once again dominate the scene. The protagonists are compared to trees, clouds, and mountains, transforming the battleground into an animated landscape in the fight between Rama and Khara:

> Awesome clouds resembling crumbled mountains and pouring down blood-red water filled all the space in space.
>
> A dreadful pall of darkness descended and made them shiver with fear, so dense it obscured every quarter of heaven and all points in between (22.8–9).
>
> A cloud-like barrier-omen appeared beside the shining sun, and suddenly, before its appointed time, a total solar eclipse occurred (22.11).
>
> Meteors dreadful to behold came crashing down, and a tremor passed through the earth, mountains, forests, and groves (22.15).[27]

The dark-skinned *rakshasas* are perceived as evening clouds. Rama and Lakshmana are called the sun and the moon, and Ravana is Rahu, god of eclipse. As Rama kills the *rakshasas,* he shines like the sun, destroying darkness and fleeing from Rahu's mouth. Both Rama and Ravana are likened to huge clouds covering the sky with arrows as they fight. Wounded Ravana's escape from Rama's arrows is compared to a cloud driven away by the wind. During the battle, directions are hidden by darkness, the sky is invisible, and falling stars sound like thunderclap. When Ravana is finally killed, the gods are at peace, the directions are happy, the sky is cleansed, the wind quietens down, and sunlight spreads everywhere.[28] In other words, nature breathes a sigh of relief and returns to her natural order. She had been involved in the epic battle at a cosmic scale. With the defeat of evil, stability and order reign once again.

NATURE PERSONIFICATIONS

The magic realism of *Ramayana* rests upon phantasmagorical nature imagery in which personifications and animations abound, making possible an easy flux between human and nonhuman worlds. Besides the terrifying *rakshasas*, in mountains and forest groves reside a host of benign nature spirits variously called yakshas, *kinnaras,* vidyadhars, and *gandharvas* whose couples are perpetually engaged in merrymaking. Human-nature metamorphosis is possible, as in the Ahalya legend. When young Rama and Lakshmana, accompanied by sage Vishvamitra, come upon a deserted *ashram* in a wood near Mithila, they see the cursed Ahalya. She had been wife of Gautama, the ascetic who turned her to stone when he found out that in his absence she had made love to Indra, king of gods. Touching Rama's feet absolves her of her sin and she is restored to life (*Balakanda,* 47.11–32; 48.1–22).

Nature is never impersonal but it is usually a benign, and sometimes evil, force attributed with motives and feelings. It is enlisted by the upholders of *dharma* in the cosmic battle with *rakshasas.* The denizens of the non-human natural world help Rama, the embodiment of righteousness, in his fight against Ravana, the personification of evil. When Sita implores Jatayus, king of vultures, as she is taken forcefully by Ravana, the bird comes to her help. He shatters Ravana's chariot and kills the charioteer and his team. But Ravana clips off his wings and drags Sita away. Rama comes upon the fallen and dying bird as he is searching for his wife and learns what has happened to her. He says to Lakshmana:

> You see, Saumitri, everywhere, even among the animals, can be found good creatures that follow the ways of righteousness, that are brave and provide a sure place of refuge (64.24).[29]

The armies of almost-human monkeys and bears who assist Rama in his cosmic battle with Ravana defy reality. In the realm of myth they symbolize the continuum between human and non-human worlds. Foremost among them is the monkey Hanuman, who finds Sita in Lanka after crossing the ocean and brings back the good tidings.[30] His journey in itself constitutes a heroic adventure in the course of which he meets with obstacles as well as signs of help. Sagara, god of the ocean, asks the mountain Mainaka to rise from the waters so that Hanuman may rest upon its peak as he flies over the great ocean. First Surasa, goddess of serpents, and then the *rakshasa* woman named Simhika test his valor, the former by swallowing him alive and the latter by catching hold of his shadow. In both cases, Hanuman escapes by changing his form and flying away (*Sundarakanda,* 1.1–190).[31]

CONCLUSION

Four facets make up the cultural construct of nature in *Ramayana*: duality of profane wilderness and sacred *tapovana,* natural Edenic settings in forests reproduced in manmade city gardens, analogies between human and natural worlds visible in their shared aesthetic attributes and psychological states, and nature's living creatures helping or hindering the principal human characters in their actions. The facets are not mutually exclusive—animated nature has sacred and profane dimensions and permits the experience of a transcendent realm in the human world. Certain physical settings such as valley landscapes and the gardens of Lanka and Ayodhya are like celestial gardens. Within them, human emotions shared by all—gods, humans, beasts, and vegetation—are experienced poignantly. Natural settings form a backdrop to the unfolding human (and divine) drama and, at times, act as catalysts for actions or actively intervene in the plot.

Ramayana can be read as an allegory of nature's creative and destructive aspects at war, each seeking to annihilate the other. Here nature refers to both inner (within the human psyche) and outer worlds. For *Ramayana* to have achieved the status of an epic myth and have sustained its popularity over such a long period of time, it must resonate with archetypes in the Hindu collective unconscious. Ramayana's characters and landscape settings are symbols that give them a discernible form and therefore are powerfully charged with meanings. Rama's journey to the south results in the profane wilderness giving way to the spirituality of *tapovana* and to human impact on the animated natural landscape. Clearly, *Ramayana* is a moral tale, and therein rests the spiritual force of the poem, which explains its unabated popularity over the last two and one-half millennia. Besides its central message of victory of righteousness over evil and its portrayal of an idealised code of conduct, it is about a culture's relationship with nature—conceptual categories, values, and meanings. This relationship has persisted through time, creating religious valorisation of sacred landscapes and determining aesthetic preferences.

NOTES

1. "The Universe of Rama: Valmiki's Epic Poem," in *The Legend of Rama: Artistic Visions,* ed. Vidya Deheja and trans. Barbara Stoler Miller (Bombay: Marg Publications, 1994), 15–26.
2. (Boston: Houghton Mifflin, 1992), ix.
3. Robert Goldman, *Introduction and Translation of* The Ramayana of Valmiki—An Epic of Ancient India, Vol. 1—*Balakanda* (Princeton, NJ: Princeton University Press, 1984); Robert Goldman and Sally Sutherland, *Introduction, Translation, and Annotation of* The Ramayana of Valmiki, Vol. 5—*Sundarakanda* (Princeton, NJ: Princeton University Press, 1996).
4. They include Bhavabhuti's *Uttara-rama-charita* in Sanskrit (eighth century CE), Kampan's *Iramavataram* in Tamil (twelfth century CE), Krttivasa's *Ramayana* in Bengal (fifteenth century CE), Tulsidas's *Ramcharitmanas* in Avadhi (sixteenth century CE), and *Ramakien* in Thai (eighteenth century CE). See Paula Richman (ed.), *Many Ramayanas—The Diversity of a Narrative Tradition in South Asia* (Berkeley: University of California, 1991) for the many narrative genres based upon *Ramayana,* in particular A. K. Ramanujan, "Three Hundred Ramayanas: Five Examples and Three Thoughts on Translation," in *Many Ramayanas—The Diversity of a Narrative Tradition in South Asia,* ed. Paula Richman (Berkeley: University of California Press, 1991), 22–49.
5. Stuart Blackburn, "Creating Conversations: The Rama Story as Puppet Play in Kerala," in *Many Ramayanas.* See Philip Lutgendorf, *The Life of a Text: Performing the Ramacharitmanas of Tulsidas* (Berkeley: University of California Press, 1991).
6. Pollock makes a distinction between Viradha and Kabandha of Dandaka forest and the *rakshasas* of Lanka. The former are marginal creatures of the forest, physically and morally deformed, while the latter live in an enchanted city not unlike Ayodhya. What marks them from *rakshasas* is their continual transgression of *dharmic* code violence and their aggressive sexuality. See Sheldon Pollock, *Introduction, Translation, and Annotation of* The Ramayana of Valmiki—An Epic of Ancient India, Vol. 3—*Aranyakanda,* ed. Robert Goldman (Princeton, NJ: Princeton University Press, 1991).
7. Robert Goldman (ed.), *The Ramayana of Valmiki—An Epic of Ancient India,* Vols. 1–5 (Princeton, NJ: Princeton University Press, 1984).
8. Northrop Frye, *Anatomy of Criticism* (Princeton, NJ: Princeton University Press, 1957).
9. According to Goldman, *The Ramayana of Valmiki,* this event can be traced to the archetypal legend of an enchanted forest being guarded by a yaksha who devours those seeking to enter it. It constituted a rite of passage to adulthood in Rama's life, signified by the killing of a sexually charged devouring mother and the granting of magical weapons by the surrogate father, Vishvamitra.

10. Sheldon Pollock, *Introduction, Translation, and Annotation of* The Ramayana of Valmiki— An Epic of Ancient India, Vol. 2—*Ayodhyakanda,* ed. Robert Goldman (Princeton, NJ: Princeton University Press), 136–137.
11. *Aranyakanda,* 87.
12. *Ayodyahakanda,* 217
13. *Aranyakanda,* 121.
14. In Tulsidas's *Ramacharitmanas* (Gorakhpur, India: Gita Press, 1938) Rama and Sita's first meeting occurs in a garden in Mithila, where Sita had come to worship in the temple of goddess Parvati. The sacred and erotic aspects of nature are captured in this episode.
15. *Sundarakanda,* 32.
16. *Aranyakanda,* 84.
17. *Ayodhyakanda,* 197.
18. *Ayodhyakanda,* 147.
19. *Aranyakanda,* 213–214.
20. *Aranyakanda,* 220–221.
21. Rosalind Lefeber, *Introduction, Translation and Annotation of* The Ramayana of Valmiki, Vol. 4—*Kishkindhakanda,* ed. Robert Goldman (Princeton, NJ: Princeton University Press, 1994), 55–57.
22. *Kishkindhakanda,* 118.
23. *Ayodhyakanda,* 164.
24. *Ayodhyakanda,* 198.
25. *Ayodhyakanda.*
26. *Sundarakanda,* 180.
27. *Aranyakanda,* 134.
28. *Srimad Valmiki-Ramayana,* intro. and trans. in Hindi (Gorakhpur: Gita Press, 1969).
29. *Aranyakanda,* 228.
30. According to Northrop Frye in *Anatomy of Criticism* (Princeton, NJ: Princeton University Press, 1957), a romance usually has helping animals in the hero's quest, the horse central among them. In *Ramayana,* monkeys play that role.
31. Joseph Campbell in *The Hero with a Thousand Faces* (New York: MJF Books, 1949) describes the hero's journey into the underworld's magical threshold as a metamorphosis for the hero, a self-annihilation and a rebirth. The symbol of the underworld is a womb image, such as the belly of a whale among the Eskimos of Bering Strait, the elephant among the Zulus, and the sea monster who swallowed the Greek hero Herakles.

Chapter Four

Landscapes and the Ramayana Legend

> "Because of a common conceptual framework or microphysics, self-organizing systems are characterised by self-similarity and fractal geometries, in which similar patterns are repeated with different sizes or time scales without changing their essential meaning. The body, temple, and universe, as well as movement throughout them, may be self-similar. The pilgrim may follow a pathway that represents the universe from centre to periphery or mimics the evolution of the universe from creation to death."
>
> —**J. McKim Malville,**
> "Complexity and Self-organisation in Pilgrimage Systems"[1]

Sacred landscapes sustain and authenticate myths and legends far beyond their oral and textual traditions. The pilgrim experiences the power of place and encounters the living presence of gods. His faith and belief in religious texts are strengthened through encountering the reality of landscape, temples, rituals, and fellow pilgrims. This is undoubtedly true with *Ramayana* legend as well. Ayodhya, Chitrakuta, Panchvati, Kishkindha, Ramesvaram, and numerous other places celebrate events in Rama's life, giving the devotee a firsthand experience of the environs where Vishnu's *avatara* once lived.

The landscapes of Ayodhya, Chitrakuta, and Kishkindha possess characteristics that make them inherently sacred to folk and brahmanical belief systems. Valmiki's *Ramayana* names these places and describes them in a manner much embellished by the poet's vivid imagination and style. The river valleys of Mandakini in Chitrakuta and Tungabhadra in Kishkindha are painted in words as Edenic settings. In comparing the text and actual sites as they exist today, we encounter landscape archetypes that constitute sacred *kshetra* and *tirtha*. The sanctity attributed to them is inherent in their physical configurations and natural attributes that evoke a strong charge in the believer as well as the non-believer. Their religious affiliations change over time depending upon ascendancy and decline of gods, but their symbolic meanings as sites of hierophany and means of crossing over to the godly realm remain.

AYODHYA

Ayodhya, capital of the kingdom of Koshala, is the birthplace of Rama and the city from which he rules as king-avatar. As such, it is the Rama legend's most sacred site. Valmiki's *Ramayana* describes it as a fortified city, situated on the banks of the river Saryu, 12 yojanas (42 km) in length and 3 yojanas (10.5 km) in breadth. It has handsome palaces (with seven courtyards) for members of the royal family, wide streets for chariots, and parks and gardens. According to *Kalika Purana,* it is laid out in the auspicious shape of a bow (as in *karmuka mandala*) along the Saryu.[2]

I have drawn upon Hans Bakker's exhaustive study of Ayodhya and Peter Van der Veer's introductory chapter for the following description.[3] The Saryu encircles the city on three sides. Rama's fort on elevated ground is situated south of the river. About eight kilometers to the west, the river fords and forms the old *tirtha* Gopratara (oxen ford) where Rama, along with Ayodhya's

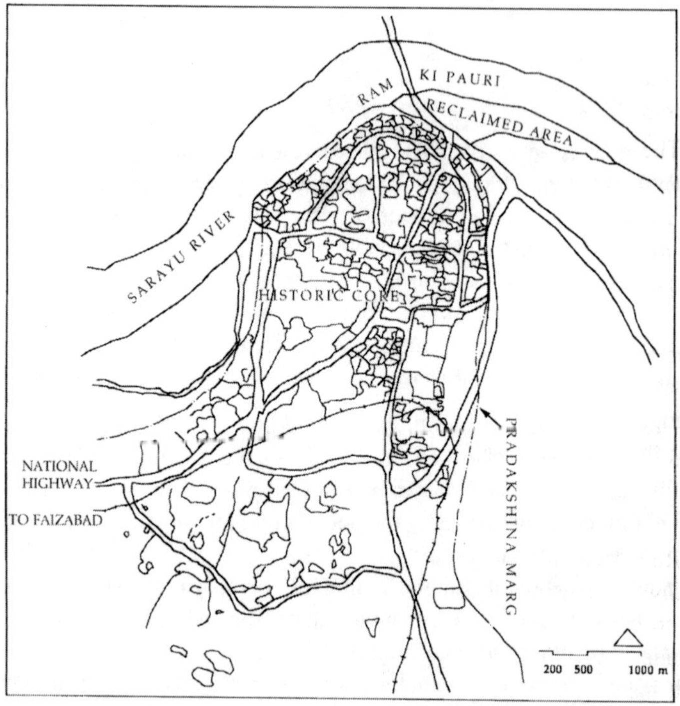

4.1: Ayodhya was built on a hilly peninsula surrounded on three sides by the river Saryu. The historic fort was situated on a promontory (redrawn after Dewan 1990).

citizens, is believed to have ended his earthly life. Svargadhara, which consists of a stretch of *ghats,* is now believed to be the spot where Rama's body was cremated. The *ghats* lie between the Shaivite temple of Nageshvarnath (associated with Rama's son Kush) and Sahasradhara, a *naga* sanctuary on Lakshmana *ghat.* (Lakshmana is said to be an incarnation of Shesh-naga, king of serpents.) The banks are named after Rama and Lakshmana— Ramakunda or Rampauri, and Sahasradhara or Lakshmana *ghat* (where Lakshmana left his mortal body to reunite with the cosmic serpent, Shesh-naga). There are two *ghats*—Rinamochan and Papamochan—where the bathers can be freed from debts to ancestors and gurus and shed their sins.

The excavations carried out in the fort area by B. B. Lal in 1975 and 1976 show that the site's earliest habitation dates back to the seventh century BCE but the rise of Ayodhya as a major pilgrim center occurred some 1,500 years later. This paralleled the rise in the worship of Rama as the principal incarnation of Vishnu. According to Bakker,

> [t]he tendency to reify the realm of saga occasioned a remarkable new development. It contributed to the new conception of the *avatara* of God on earth as a historical event which eventually resulted in the transformation of the site Ayodhya into a holy place.
>
> The deification of Rama runs parallel with the reification of the city of Ayodhya.[4]

Bakker traces the beginning of this process to the reign of Kumaragupta I or Skandagupta in the mid-fifth century CE when the royal court of Pataliputra moved to Ayodhya. Marking the spot of Rama's birth, the Ramjanmabhumi temple was built during the eleventh and twelfth centuries in the Gahadvala period. The Gahadvala kings of Kannauj, Chandradeva, and Jayachandra built Vishnu temples—Chandrahari and Dharmahari on the bathing *ghat* Svargadhara. Over the centuries, a skyline of temple spires along the riverbank began to emerge. In the twelfth century at least five Vishnu temples were in Ayodhya—on Janmabhumi, on the east and west sides of Svargadhara *ghat,* at Chakratirtha *ghat,* and at Gopratara *ghat.*

Reflecting the increasing importance of Rama, the oldest version of *Ayodhyamahatmya* belonging to the Vaishnavakhanda of *Skandapurana* was compiled in the thirteenth century. The *Ramayana* legend was now grounded at specific locales— Dantadhavan-kunda where Rama would brush his teeth, Maniparvata where he created a pleasure grove for Sita, Yajnavedi where he performed sacrifices, Kanakamandapa as the site of Rama and Sita's palace, Ashoka vatika with Sitakund on the northern bank of the river Tilodaki near its confluence with Saryu, and Bharatkunda where Bharata stayed in Nandigrama during Rama's exile.

Rama's legend as Vishnu's incarnation began to grow into a religious cult during the period of Islamic depredations. For five centuries, Islamic rule precluded building officially sanctioned Hindu temples in Ayodhya, the capital of Avadh province now ruled by Muslim governors. The Ramjanmabhumi temple was destroyed on Moghul prince Babur's orders in 1528 CE and a mosque (Babri masjid) was built. (The later destruction of this mosque on December 6, 1992, by Hindu *karsevaks* reveals the deep significance of this site, the very exact location of Rama's arrival on earth.) During Mughal emperor Aurangzeb's reign (1658–1707 CE), the twin temples on the Svargadhara *ghats* were replaced by mosques. This Muslim appropriation of historically significant religious sites, however, did not deter the rediscovery of legendary sites; on the contrary, the process gathered force in the sixteenth century with the rise of the *bhakti* movement.

The temples in Ayodhya date from the liberal rule of Shia Nawabs during the eighteenth century. Their Hindu ministers constructed shrines; Naval Ray, minister to Safdar Jung (who ruled from 1739 to 1754 CE), built temples along Svargadhara *ghat;* and Tikayat Ray, minister to Asaf-ud-daulah (who ruled from 1775 to 1797 CE), constructed Hanumangarhi, temple to Hanuman, on the eastern gate of the ancient fort Ramkot.

Bakker has traced the transformation of the shrine guarding the eastern gateway of Ramkot from yaksha/*bhairava* shrine to Hanuman temple.[5] By the sixteenth century, Hanuman was worshipped at Ramchaura under a tamarind tree on top of the mound Hanumantila. This mound was the remains of the old guarded entry to the fort. The earlier place-deities—yakshas Ajita, Mattajajendra, and Bhairava—had given way to Hanuman, Ramayana's celebrated monkey-warrior. The significance of Ramkot as ancient Ayodhya's royal fortress was by this time well established. The mounds on the southwest and southeast are called Kubertila and Sugrivatila, respectively, with the *tilas* of Nal and Nila (who had built the bridge to Lanka) between them. Kanak Bhavan, a small temple at the site of Rama and Sita's golden palace, was enlarged and embellished by Rani Krishnabhanu Kunwari of Orchcha in 1891 CE. The new Janmasthana temple, founded by Sadhu Ramdas shortly after Babur destroyed the old one, includes Sita *rasoi* (kitchen). Sumitrabhavan (birthplace of Lakshmana and Shatrughana) and Kaikeyibhavan (birthplace of Bharata) are shrines as well. *Ghats* were built by Raja Darshan Singh (who ruled from 1827 to 1851 CE) and new ones were built after 1964 when the river Saryu had to be diverted to build a new bridge.

Ayodhya is now a city of temples—it reputedly contains 5,000—and is believed to draw as many as 400,000 pilgrims for its main festival,

Ramnaomi, commemorating Rama's birthday.[6] The major pilgrimage circuit, *Chaurasi kos parikrama,* lasts for twentyfive days, leading the pilgrim to the major shrines along the Saryu's banks and concluding on Janakinaomi, the birthday of Sita. Shorter circumambulatory routes are *chaudah kos* and *panch kos parikrama.* In the month of Shravan, Rama and Sita idols are brought out of the temples and placed in swings for the celebration of the *jhula* festival. Other festivals are celebrated at their respective sites—Ramnaomi in Rampauri and Ramajanmabhumi, Janakinaomi in Kanak Bhavan and Sitakund, *nagapanchami* and Maha Shivaratri at Nageshvarnath temple, and Saryu jayanti with a dip in the waters of Saryu, celebrating the descent of the river from the heavens.

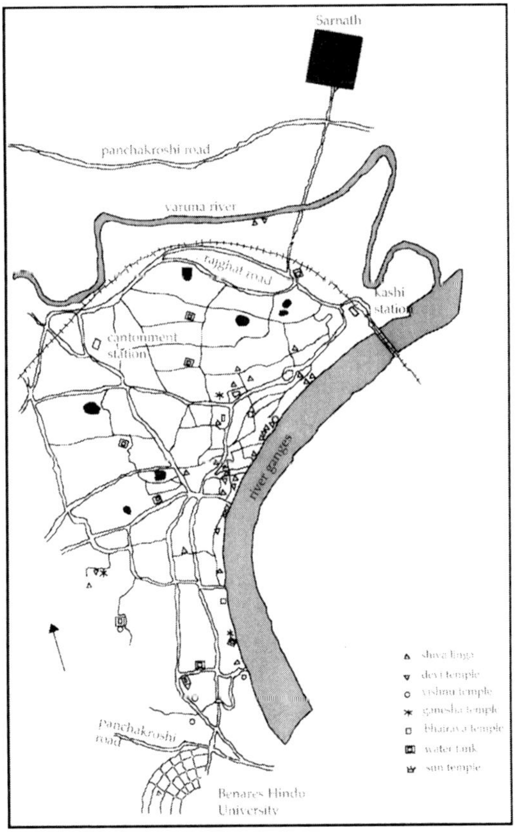

4.2: The layout of Varanasi is shaped by the crescent sweep of the Ganga and appears to be similar to *karmuka mandala.* Its concentric streets are also circumambulatory paths (redrawn after Eck 1982).

Ayodhya shares certain topographic features with Varanasi and Mathura. The three are part of the "seven holy cities" (*saptapuri*), along with Ujjain, Dwarka, Kanchi, and Hardwar, where death brings *moksha*. The gods have made these cities their homes, and their landscapes play no small part in establishing them as sacred *kshetras*. Mathura is said to have been laid out in a crescent shape along the banks of the Yamuna by Rama's brother Shatrughana after he slew the demon Lavana. The two-kilometer stretch of *ghats* along the riverfront attracts large numbers of pilgrims to its numerous fairs, festivals, and *parikramas*. The *ghats* of Vrindavan curve convexly toward the river.[7] *Karmuka mandala* is evident in Varanasi as well; the city rises from the western bank of the river Ganga, stretching northward in a broad crescent sweep.[8] There are seventy bathing *ghats* on the stretch of land bordered by the Ganga between the rivers Asi and Varana. The temples extending along the *ghats* are fifty to seventy feet above the river, creating a magnificent skyline. The oldest part of the city was on the Rajghat plateau at the Varana-Ganga confluence with rivers to the east, west, and north.

These cities all are located in peninsular regions, surrounded by water on three sides.[9] Clare Cooper Marcus, in discussing another peninsular community in Findhorn, Scotland, traces its power of place to negative ions proliferating because of the presence of water.[10] The ancients in India chose these locations for that and other reasons—the presence of water in swift currents of river, lowland basins, and river confluences, which made it possible to consider the site as a ford. Coupled with plateaus or hilly terrains, these sites provide a combination of natural features favoured by gods of epic and Puranic mythology. That these sites also are strategic locations for forts and defensible settlements adds to their attraction. I believe that in Ayodhya, as in Braj *kshetra*, local gods and goddesses were overtaken by the supreme gods of Hinduism. Mount Govardhan and Manasi Ganga in Vrindavan originally began as nature deities of hills and water, and later were incorporated into Krishna *bhakti*. Could Ayodhya's deities—such as those of Nageshvarnath temple and Hanumangarhi, which represent earlier shrines and were ultimately co-opted into the *Ramayana* legend—have suffered the same fate?

CHITRAKUTA

Chitrakuta was Rama, Sita, and Lakshmana's first sojourn in their wanderings through the wilderness during their fourteen-year exile. The *kshetra* is named after Chitrakuta hill, which is part of the Vindhyan spur and the center of the holy region. The rivers Mandakini and Payasvini carve a valley in this hilly landscape, meeting near the town of Sitapur. The two landscape elements considered most sacred in Hindu tradition—

river confluences and hills—are present in the region. Their significance to pilgrims undoubtedly derives from events narrated in *Ramayana,* such as Rama, Sita, and Lakshmana's stay in a thatched cottage on Chitrakuta hill; their meetings with sages Atri and Valmiki at their respective *ashramas;* Bharata's arrival with news of their father's death; and Rama's coronation. But Chitrakuta appears to have attracted ascetics long before Rama's arrival. Lalapur hill, 25 kilometers east of Chitrakuta, is believed to be the site of Valmiki's *ashram,* and Atri's *ashram* is only 8 kilometers south of the hill. Atri's wife Anusuya is believed to have brought the river Ganga, known as Mandakini here, by force of her *tapas*. Bharatkupa, 7.7 kilometers west of Chitrakuta, reputedly contains the waters of all holy rivers brought by Bharata for Rama's consecration. Ramghat marks the place of Rama's bathing, Raghava Prayaga—the confluence of rivers Mandakini and Payasvini—is where Rama performed the rites of his father's death; Sphatikashila is the stone platform on the riverbank where Rama and Sita sat, admiring the landscape; Ramashaiyya is where the couple slept one night; and Sitakund is where the couple sported. Other significant places include Kotitirtha, hallowed by the penance of sages; Siddhashrama, a natural cave with a spring; Gupta Godavari, which has a number of limestone caves, including one with a stream; and Hanumandhara, shrine of Hanuman, which is bathed by a stream and located on a hill

The presence of Sita *rasoi* (kitchen) adds an interesting dimension to the place narrative. Phyllis Herman speculates that the kitchen shrines in Chitrakuta and elsewhere symbolize *shakti* or the power of earth goddess Sita—the one who transforms raw material into edible food and is the source of the bounties in Rama-rajya, the utopian reign of Rama. As she is the ideal wife of Rama and mother of his sons, her fertility and life-sustaining aspect is grounded in the landscape's caves or structural shrines. Like the *shakti pithas* where the goddess is worshipped in the form of crude stones, these sites commemorate her powers in stoves, grinding stones, and rolling pins. At Lalapur hill, the *rasoi* is in a small cave where Sita cooked for her sons during her second exile to Valmiki's *ashram* and at Chitrakuta, where Sita *rasoi* is built at the top of the hill and lends its name to the peak.[11]

Kalidasa describes Chitrakuta in *Raghuvamsa,* but as with other Rama sites, it only attained popularity in the sixteenth century.[12] Tulsidas (1540–1623 CE) extolled its virtues in his *Ramacharitmanas*. With the compilation of *Chitrakuta Mahatmya* in the eighteenth century, more sites were added to the list of sacred places. The temples of Chitrakuta were mostly constructed in the eighteenth and nineteenth centuries. Sites on the edge of *kshetra,* such as Gupta Godavari and Bharatkupa, are sacred to

Shiva. Raja Aman Singh of Panna established a linga at Gupta Godavari in 1754 CE. Before the sixteenth century, Bharatkupa was referred to as Jyesthanstana, sacred to Shiva in *Mahabharata, Padmapurana,* and *Bhushundi Ramayana*. Worship at the shrine of Mattagajendranath, which is Shiva as the *kshetrapala* or "territorial guardian" at Rama *ghat,* initiates the pilgrimage of Chitrakuta.[13] Shiva guards the sacred *kshetra* on its margins at Siddhashrama, Kotitirtha, Bharatkupa, and Gupta Godavari. Thus, he could rightfully be called the ancient deity of Chitrakuta. Yet, there is another and older tradition of worshipping Chitrakuta as Kamnath or Kamatnath, who is not identified with Rama, Shiva, or the goddess. Diana Eck suggests that this older tradition represents an ancient yaksha cult that was incorporated into Vishnu *bhakti* similar to the worship of Mount Govardhan in Braj.[14]

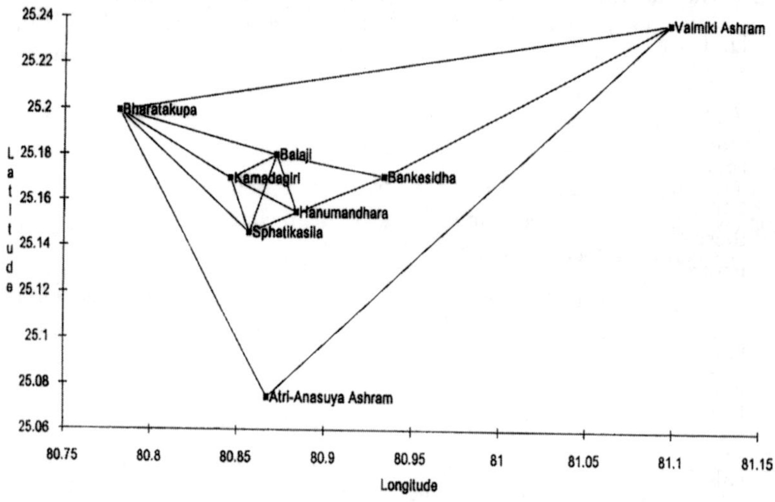

4.3: The sacred sites at Chitrakuta fall into the pattern of three interlocking triangles. The bisectors of the two larger triangles align with sunrise and sunset on summer solstice (courtesy Rana P.B. Singh).

B. Dubey, Rana Singh, and John Malville have studied the spatial alignments in the landscape and consider "the intersection of mythohistoric traditions with the natural landscape to be of great interest and continuing puzzle."[15] The sacred sites of Chitrakuta fall into a pattern of three interlocking isosceles triangles. Their alignments mark the sunrise and sunset on solstice. Singh calls them "cosmic geometries" since they connect different levels of the cosmos—macrocosm of stars, planets, moon, and sun; mesocosm of the natural landscape; and microcosm of city, temple, home, and body. The largest triangle is formed by Valmiki *ashram,* Atri-Anusuya *ashram,* and Bharatkupa. Sphatikashila, and Balaji in turn constitute another triangle containing the innermost triangle formed by Kamadgiri (Chitrakuta mountain), Balaji, and Sphatikashila. The arms of the largest triangle are roughly equal—the distances between Valmiki *ashram* to Atri-Anusuya *ashram* and Bharatkupa are 29.4 kilometers and 32.15 kilometers, respectively. The second isosceles triangle has sides of 9.3 and 9.6 kilometers and the third has sides of 2.4 and 2.7 kilometers. Nine sites lie on the bisector of the largest triangle, which stretches for 30 kilometers between Valmiki *ashram* and Gupta Godavari. It aligns with the direction of sunrise on summer solstice. The bisector of the second triangle, extending from Bharatkupa to Hanumandhara, aligns with the sunset on summer solstice.

Are the triangles, constituted by visual axes, yantras inscribed on the landscape to gather sacred spots into a meaningful pattern? *Chitrakuta Mahatmya* describes the triangles as Rama's bow and arrow. Singh, in another context, that of Vindhyachal's hilly range, shows the yantra embedded in the three goddess shrines of Lakshmi, Kali, and Ashtabhuja (Saraswati).[16] Here the triangle is the goddess's aniconic form, her yantra a mystical diagram used for concentration. It is likely that the discovery of these sacred sites was aided by a preexisting, extraordinary configuration of natural features established by sight lines and equivalent distances.

At Chitrakuta, the pilgrim's belief that he is indeed at the center is strengthened by experiencing the sunrise and sunset on hills. On Kamadgiri hill, center of the *kshetra,* he would see the summer solstice sunrise near Balaji and the winter solstice sunrise near Hanumandhara. On the summit of the hill at Sita *rasoi* near Hanumandhara, he would see the summer solstice sunrise near Valmiki *ashram* hill and sunset above Kamadgiri hill. Indeed the hill summits appear to graze the skies and bring about the sun's birth and death. Kamadgiri—which means "hill that grants desires"—is particularly significant because it derives its power from being the location of Rama, Sita, and Lakshmana's huts and is therefore the *axis mundi.* The stone-paved circumambulatory pathway around the hill (4.5 kilometers long and constructed by the queen of Bundela chief Chhatrasal in 1725 CE) takes the pilgrim to fifty-six temples, including the four mukharvind, which are located in the cardinal directions. As the pilgrim navigates this path, he retraces the steps of Bharata. In five days he completes the pilgrimage circuit by visiting all the sites in Chitrakuta that Bharata had visited before leaving for Ayodhya.[17]

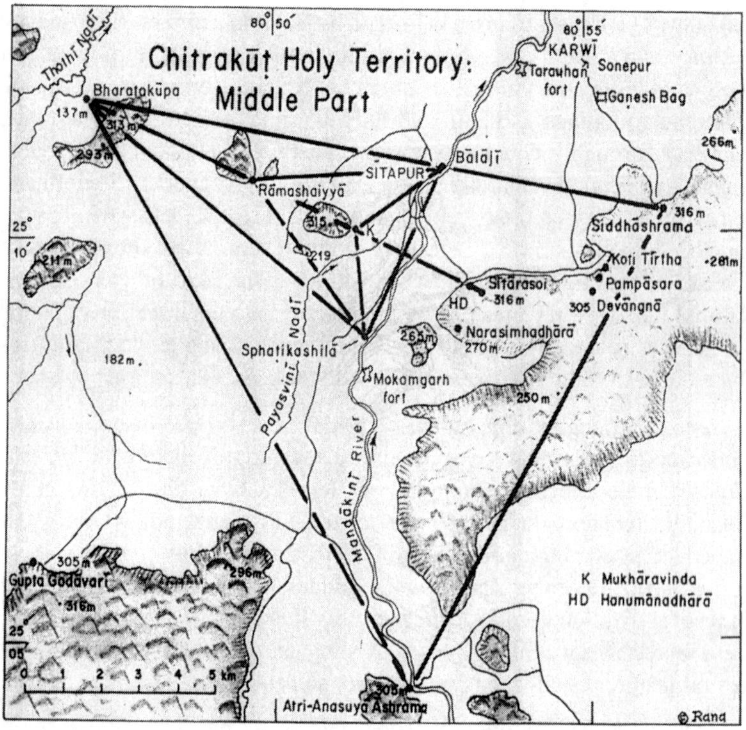

4.4: Chitrakuta mountain is the center of the hilly landscape at the confluence of the Mandakini and Payasvini rivers. This was the site of Rama, Sita, and Lakshmana's sojourn during their forest exile (courtesy Rana P.B. Singh).

KISHKINDHA

The ruins of Vijayanagara in central Karnataka are spread over the landscape of the famed monkey-kingdom, Kishkindha, of *Ramayana* legend. Like Chitrakuta this area is hilly and on a riverbank, in this case the river Tungabhadra, which makes a northward turn at this point. Here Rama and Lakshmana arrive to search for Sita; here they meet Sugriva, Hanuman, and other monkeys; here Rama kills Vali; and here the brothers wait out the monsoons before embarking upon the journey southward with the army of monkeys and bears to rescue Sita. The landscape is read as the site of these events and is an ever-present, physical reminder of the narrative. Yet the many other and older narratives associated with this site are evidence that its particular geography is myth prone. The river valley of Tungabhadra, like that of Godavari and Mandakini, possesses the combination of a meandering river and hillcrests, making it a sacred place archetype in folk and Sanskritic traditions. Here myths of succeeding epochs are validated by the power of place.

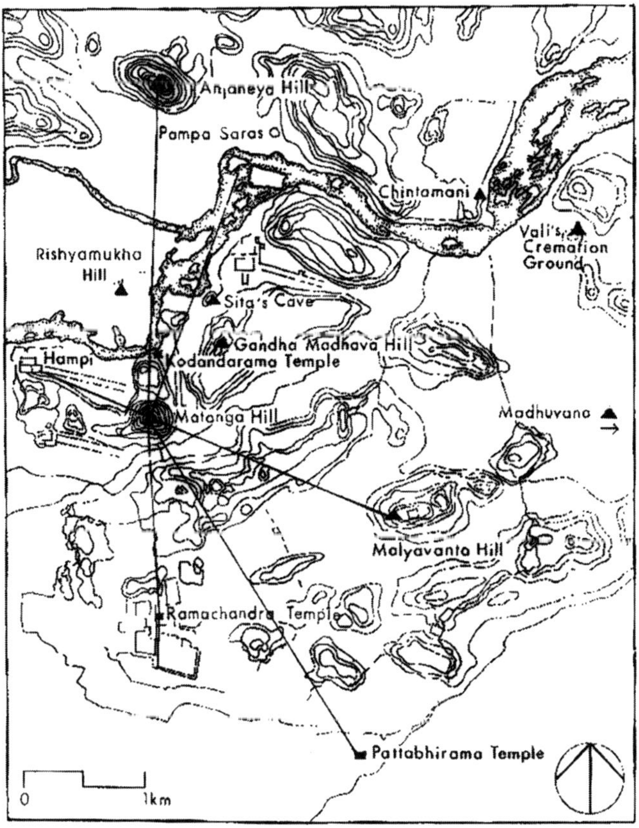

4.5: Sacred sites at Kishkindha are connected into a pattern of visual axes that intersect at Matanga hill. The visual superimposition of temple spires creates a powerful effect (courtesy McKim Malville).

Philip Wagoner points out that the Sanskrit text *Hemakutakhanda* and the Kannada *Pampamahatmya* describe the site as Hemakuta *kshetra* after the sacred hill Hemakuta.[18] The hill is home to Virupaksha (one of Shiva's forms), who married Pampa, the daughter of the sage Matanga. The sage's hermitage is located on another hill, which is named after him, and it is on this Matanga hill "where hares chased hounds" that Sugriva finds protection from his brother Vali in Treta Yuga. According to *Rayavacakamu,* a Telugu historical text dating from the sixteenth century, sage Vidyaranya founds a city on this hill and installs King Harihara on the throne in *Kali yuga.*[19] The city is named Vijayanagara and becomes the capital of a medieval Hindu empire that collapsed in 1565 CE with the sacking of the city by armies of adjoining Muslim kingdoms. The power and authority of its kings were derived from the city's site as much as from its structure of temples and palaces. Shiva's fierce warrior form, Virbhadra, protected the city from his temple on the summit of Matanga hill.

Malville has studied spatial alignments of the site's landscape features using data from the Global Positioning System (GPS).[20] Although there are no triangular yantras formed by visual axes as at Chitrakuta, natural features and their architectural embodiments (such as temples) are consistently aligned with each other, establishing strong visual axes that provide for a spectacular experience. The building activities of Vijayanagara kings sought to accentuate the sacred features of the landscape and reified the *Ramayana* saga as Gahadvala kings did on a smaller scale in Ayodhya. The temples' verticality strengthened the impact of the preexisting hillcrests.

Matanga hill lies at the intersection of at least three visual axes—between Ramachandra temple (the royal shrine of Vijayanagara kings), Kodandrama temple (where Lakshmana crowns Sugriva king of Kishkindha), and Hanuman temple on the summit of Anjenadri hill (where Hanuman was born); between Raghunatha temple on Malyavanta hill and Virupaksha temple on Hemkuta hill; and between Prasanna Virupkasha, Sugriva's cave (where jewels dropped by Sita are hidden), and Pampa *sarovar* (by Shabari's *ashram*). It is also the center of other radial lines extending outward to other natural and built features.

The north-south axis links the royal center, Matanga hill and the lake at its base, Kodandarama temple, Chakratirtha on the northward turn of Tungabhadra river, and Anjenadri hill with a Hanuman shrine at its summit. The *shikhara* of Virbhadra temple on Matanga hill is only 0.8 arc minute from true north when viewed from the gateway's center to the royal enclosure. Matanga hill is framed in the doorway of Ramachandra temple. From the entry avenue of Ramachandra temple, the devotee sees its *shikhara* and that of Anjenadri temple separated by only 7.0 arc minutes. Kodandarama temple also faces Anjenadri hill. The *shikharas* of Virupaksha and Raghunatha temple lie on a straight line, differing by only 1 arc minute from 180 degrees.

The visual superimposition of temple spires has a powerful effect. The natural landscape is enhanced by architecture and its most prominent hill framed in openings, keeping its sacred energies, munificence, and powers of protection forever in view. John Fritz and George Mitchell, who have conducted extensive studies of Vijayanagara's archaeological remains, describe three phases in the sacred site's transformation into a royal capital and the assimilation of local deities into the *Ramayana* tradition.[21] Temples were built in the tenth and eleventh centuries CE in Hemakuta *tirtha,* which is famous for its legend of Virupaksha and Pampa, whose symbols were Hemakuta hill and Pampa lake. The boundaries of the *tirtha* are ritually enacted by taking the god and goddess in a circumambulatory tour *(giri-pradakshina*) twice a year even in present times.[22] The Vijayanagara kings built the huge Virupaksha temple complex and Manmatha tank, down the hill and north of the temple, making it the sacred center of the city. In the final phase around the beginning of the fifteenth century, Rama gained ascendancy and the Vijayanagara kings began to identify themselves with the king-avatar. *Ramayana* themes began to be depicted in sculpture and Ramachandra temple was built in the center of royal enclosure.[23] It was visually aligned with Rishamukha hill (an island in Tungabhadra) on the north and Malyavanta hill in the northeast, points of Rama's arrival into Kishkindha and departure to Lanka, respectively.[24]

As in Chitrakuta and Ayodhya, a process of transformation in site and temple worship can be discerned. The sacred site's local god and goddess were assimilated into Shiva mythology. According to legend, as in Chitrakuta, Shiva was worshipped by Rama at Kishkindha. He continues to preside as *svayambhu* (self-manifested) linga in Virupaksha temple and at Raghunatha temple. The pilgrims worship him by visiting the landscape sanctified by Rama and Lakshmana's stay. When Vijayanagara kings styled themselves in the image of Ayodhya's divine king, the sacred center of the city shifted from the Virupaksha temple complex to their royal chapel, and pilgrimage to Kishkindha sites became popular.

CONCLUSION

Clearly the Rama legend was not solely responsible for sanctifying these three sites. In fact, it appears that temple-building and worship at these sites occurred before Rama's arrival. At the beginning of the second millennium, the dormant *Ramayana* tradition was revived and gathered force with royal patronage and as the *bhakti* movement gained ground. Accordingly landscapes discussed in the epic were rediscovered— their legendary existence now became a physical reality. Some scholars argue, as Singh points out, that Panchvati, Kishkindha, and Lanka were within the Vindhyan range, in close proximity to Chitrakuta.[25] The existence of numerous Sita *kunds,* Sita *rasois,* and Hanumandharas in north and central India is evidence of other claimants to *Ramayana*'s significant sites and lends credence to the notion that landscapes imbibed the *Ramayana* tradition over time. Eck calls the incorporation of a local *tirtha* with a pan-Indian tradition as the geographical equivalent of Sanskritisation.[26]

What do Ayodhya, Chitrakuta, and Kishkindha have in common that over time attracted those who worshipped the goddess, Shiva, and Rama? Do their landscapes possess inherent qualities that invite myths and attract *sadhus,* preachers, devout followers, royal patronage, and pilgrims? For the Rama *bhakta,* of course, this is hallowed ground where once upon a time Rama, Sita, and Lakshmana walked and where Ramarajya—utopia on earth—flourished. The faithful are nourished by interaction with the physical environment as much as by participating in rituals and communing with fellow devotees. This physical environment is the holy mountain meeting the confluence of holy rivers; it is the skyline of temple spires on *ghats*, accentuating hill summits and coinciding with the appearance and disappearance of the sun; it is a network of numerous *kunds,* bathing *ghats,* and circumambulatory paths to locations already made familiar with daily readings of *Ramayana.*

Underlying the complex, self-sustaining institutional systems that the pilgrimage complexes are today are certain topographic features that have lent themselves to sacred meanings over millennia. As landscape archetypes their physical configurations have been associated consistently with encountering the numinous and transcendent in Hindu thought. Diana Eck and Surinder Bharadwaj have drawn attention to natural features that have become for the Hindu symbols of the process of climbing and crossing the mundane world of existence to *moksha* and liberating themselves from the cycle of birth and death.[27] To the believer the river ford is a physical representation of the spiritual journey of the *atman* (individual soul) to the *brahman* (universal spirit). A dip in the flowing waters is a metaphor for moral cleansing and shedding of *papa* (sins). The rivers, believed to have fallen from heaven to the earth, are flowing *axis mundi,* in the same way that mountains, thrusting upward from the earth's bowels into the rarefied realm of the gods, are perceived as centers of the universe and its borders. In Puranic cosmology, Mount Meru is conceived as the center of the universe surrounded by four island-continents. The river Ganga falls from the heavens directly above Mount Meru. In Valmiki's *Ramayana,* mountains rim the known world.

It is not surprising that river confluences are *tirthas* and mountains are the homes of ascetics. The combination of hilly terrain and river (or rivers) in a valley landscape would therefore be even more significant. The mountain-river dyad constitutes a landscape archetype that forms the structure of sacred sites in Indian geography. Are they natural symbols of masculine and feminine principles and therefore representative of a complementary totality, a wholeness found in the natural landscape? Mount Kailash and Lake Mansarovar are the homes of Shiva and Parvati, respectively, and the prototypes of similar configurations revered beyond the Himalayas. Numerous holy sites display this complementarity in the naming and worship of natural features: Mount Govardhan and Manasi Ganga in Braj, Kamadgiri and Mandakini in Chitrakuta, and Mount Hemkuta and Pampa *sarovar* in Kishkindha. Chitrakuta, Panchvati, and Kishkindha have Mandakini, Godavari, and Tungbahadra rivers coursing through hilly terrains. In Ayodhya, Maniparvata, Sitakund, and the fort itself are located on a plateau with the Saryu flowing below it.

India's *tirthas* are grounded in the folk tradition of the genius loci of groves, pools, and hillocks. The yakshas and *nagas* as spirits of the place were, and still are, worshipped for guarding against evil and as benefactors. Epic mythology, with its cosmography and dyads of *prakriti* and *Purusha* and of *atman* and *brahman,* treated the natural world as a vehicle for transcending *samsara.* The ancient sacred sites were perfect locales for practicing the evolving metaphysics in rituals that included the worship of more powerful gods who descended to earth periodically to set the moral order right.

The choice of sites in folk and later Sanskritic traditions is not an accident—their selection is an example of geomancy. It can be compared with fêng shui stemming from East Asia's Taoist tradition, which favors sites with a balance of ch'i. At these sites, mountains and rivers are interdependent and complementary landscape features, expressive of passive and active energies, whose balance is a key to Tao-like harmony. I believe that Hindus also sought harmony in the landscape and found harmonious landscapes conducive to thoughts of liberation from the cycle of birth and death. They duplicated this harmony in architecture of temple *shikharas* and stepped tanks, creating *tirthas* out of built form.

Mythology and landscape's concrete reality together contribute to the "power of the place" experienced by pilgrims. There are perhaps psychological and physiological explanations behind what causes such places to be charged, such as the presence of negative ions, prospect and refuge views, ecologically diverse niches, and the visual coincidence of natural and heavenly phenomena. Science may offer physical explanations but mythology provides us with the symbols upon which the pilgrim's faith rests. And the complexities of the pilgrimage experience can be better understood by exploring the psychological impact of the landscape, in particular its role as an anchor to the religious beliefstructure.

NOTES

1. Keynote address to the International Seminar on Pilgrimage and Complexity (New Delhi: Indira Gandhi National Centre for the Arts, January 1999).
2. Atindra Nath Bose, "Oldest Indo-Aryan Cities," in *Journal of Indian History,* Madras 21 (April 1942), 60–82.
3. Hans Bakker, *Ayodhya* (Groningen: Egbert Forsten, 1986); Peter Van der Veer, *Gods on Earth—The Management of Religious Experience and Identity in a North Indian Pilgrimage Centre,* London School of Economics Monographs on Social Anthropology, no. 59 (London: Athlone Press, 1988), 127–135.
4. Bakker, *Ayodhya,* 11, 16.
5. Hans Bakker, "The History of Hanumat Worship at Ayodhya," in *Pilgrimage Studies: Text and Context,* ed. D. P. Dubey (Allahabad, India: The Society of Pilgrimage Studies, 1990).
6. Jatin Dewan, "Development of Land-Water Interface: Ayodhya" (unpublished B.Arch. thesis, Chandigarh College of Architecture, 1990).
7. Rajat Ray, "Ghats of Mathura and Vrindavan," *Architecture+Design* (November– December 1989), 61–69.
8. Diana Eck, *Banaras: City of Light* (New York: Alfred Knopf, 1982).
9. This configuration extends to nonpilgrim cities as well. Ahmadabad, for example, is located on the eastern bank of the river Sabarmati, on an elevated plain known as Bhadra that has *nalas* (streams) on the north and south and undulating topography to the east. Ahmad Shah Abdali built his palace in 1411 CE on this plain, which supported an earlier Hindu settlement called Ashaval. The *Padmapurana* mentions Pinchumandarka *tirtha* in the area, and several stone images of Surya have been recovered pointing to sun worship dating back to the eighth century. See R. N. Mehta and Rasesh Jamindar, "Urban Context," in *Ahmadabad,* ed. George Michell and Snehal Shah (Bombay: Marg, 1988), 16–29.
10. Clare Cooper Marcus, "Designing for a Commitment to Place: Lessons from the Alternative Community of Findhorn," in *Dwelling, Seeing, and Designing: Towards a Phenomenological Ecology,* ed. David Seamon (Albany: State University of New York, 1993), 299–330.
11. Phyllis Herman, "Sita in the Kitchen: The *Pativrata* and *Ramarajya,*" in *Manushi: A Journal About Women and Society* 120 (September–October 2000), 5–11, and "Siting the Power of the Goddess: Sita *Rasoi* Shrines in Modern India" (paper presented at the International Ramayana Conference, Northern Illinois University, Dekalb, Illinois, September 2001). At Panchvati near Nasik in Maharashtra, Herman found a cave with a kitchen shrine and, across it in a structural complex, dioramas of Sita cooking, Sita giving food to Ravana disguised as an ascetic, her twin sons, and Rama hunting the golden deer Maricha.

12. D. P. Dubey and Rana P.B. Singh, "Chitrakut: The Frame and Network of the Faithscape and Sacred Geometry of a Hindu Tirtha," in *The Spirit and Power of Place: Human Environment and Sacrality,* pub. 41, ed. Rana P.B. Singh (Varanasi: National Geographic Society of India, 1994), 301–332.
13. Diana Eck, "Following Rama, Worshipping Siva," in *Devotion Divine: Bhakti Traditions from the Regions of India,* ed. Diana Eck and Francoise Mallison (Groningen: Egbert Forsten, 1991), 49–71.
14. *Ibid.*
15. See Dubey and Singh, "Chitrakut"; and John Malville and Rana P.B. Singh, "Pilgrimage Cosmologies at Chitrakut and Vijayanagara: Emergent Geometries and Self-Organisation" (paper presented at the Twenty-sixth Annual Conference on South Asia, Madison, Wisconsin, 1997).
16. Rana P.B. Singh, "Varanasi Cosmic Order and Cityscape: Sun Images and Shrines," *Architecture+Design* (November–December 1994): 75–79; Rana P.B. Singh, "Sacredscape, Faithscape and Cosmic Geometry: Goddess Territory of Vindhyachal, India" (paper presented at the Sixth International Conference on Built Form and Culture Research, University of Cincinnati, 1997).
17. Dubey and Singh, "Chitrakut."
18. Philip Wagoner, "Architecture and Mythic Space at the Hemakuta Hill: A Preliminary Report," in *Vijayanagara: Progress of Research, 1985–87* (Mysore, India: Directorate of Archaeology and Museums, 1985), 142–148.
19. Philip Wagoner, *Tidings of the King: A Translation and Ethnohistorical Analysis of the Rayavacakamu* (Honolulu: University of Hawaii Press, 1993).
20. John M. Malville, "Astronomy at Vijayanagara: Sacred Geography Confronts the Cosmos," in *The Spirit and Power of Place: Human Environment and Sacrality,* pub. 41, ed. Rana P.B. Singh (Varanasi: National Geographical Society of India, 1994), 171–188.
21. John Fritz and George Mitchell, "Interpreting the Plan of a Medieval Hindu Capital, Vijayanagara," *World Archaeology* 19:1 (June 1987), 105–129.
22. Wagoner, "Architecture and Mythic Space at the Hemakuta Hill."
23. Anna Dallapiccola, "The City of Vijayanagara: Kiskindha, the Monkey-Kingdom," in *The Legend of Rama: Artistic Visions,* ed. Vidya Daheja (Mumbai: Marg Publications, 1994), 61– 72.
24. John Fritz, "Vijayanagara: Authority and Meaning of a South Indian Imperial Capital," *American Anthropologist* 88:1 (March 1986), 44–55.
25. Rana P.B. Singh, "Rama's Route After Banishment: A Geographic Viewpoint," *Journal of Scientific Research* (Varanasi: Banaras Hindu University, 1991), 323–344.
26. Diana Eck, "India's Tirthas: 'Crossings' in Sacred Geography," *History of Religions* 20:4 (May 1981), 323–344.
27. *Ibid.*; Surinder Bharadwaj, *Hindu Places of Pilgrimage* (Berkeley: University of California Press, 1973).

Chapter Five

Sacred Landscape of Braj

"Budding mango trees tremble from the embrace of rising vines.
Brindaban forest is washed by meandering Yumna river waters.
When spring's mood is rich, Hari roams here
To dance with young women, friend—
A cruel time for deserted lovers." (33)

— *The Gita Govinda of Jayadeva*[1]

Braj, a major pilgrimage center in the state of Uttar Pradesh, offers a glimpse into the special relationship between sacredness and landscape. This relationship evolves with our changing comprehension of nature's meaning within the religious framework. Archetypal associations of nature, such as animism and sexuality, are transcended as we recognize a more metaphysical understanding of sacredness manifested in nature.

Braj is a cultural zone demarcated by language, customs, and topography in northern India. It is located by the river Yamuna and is a point of entry into the region called Doab formed by the Himalayan ranges to the northwest and the Thar desert and Aravalli hill ranges to the southwest. Numerous routes pass through this region leading farther east and south into India. Until recently this area was primarily woodland and pasture interspersed with a few villages. The ancient city of Mathura, located on a curve of the river Yamuna, forms the nucleus of this sacred zone. Other sacred centers include the adjacent villages of Gokul, Vrindavan, Govardhan, Nandgaon, and Barsana.

Founded in the seventh century BCE, Mathura has several legends associated with its origin. The commonly accepted one is that it was founded on the site of the forest Madhuvana in which dwelt a demon called Madhu and his son Lavana. They were killed by Shatrughana, brother of Rama, king of Ayodhya, and god-incarnate of the epic *Ramayana*. Madhuvana reached its height of prosperity between the second century BCE and third century CE and is associated with the three major religions of India—Jainism, Buddhism, and Hinduism. As a religious center it has suffered the depredations of iconoclastic Islamic rulers since the eleventh century. A thriving city today, it has maintained a continuous pattern of settlement with historically significant sites located in a series of three concentric semicircles on the banks of the river Yamuna. The pattern is based on *karmuka mandala* and has symbolic value. Although Mathura is the center, the landscape of Braj contains many other sacred foci. The coexistence of several significant sites is based on a religious tradition that encompasses more than one way of understanding nature and incorporating her into devotional worship.

Krishna, god-incarnate of the epic *Mahabharata,* is born in Mathura and returns to it after growing up. His childhood and adolescence are spent in adjacent areas of Braj and are far more significant in the minds of his devotees. Krishna was born to Devaki and Vasudeva in prison. They are confined there by Devaki's brother, Kansa, king of Mathura, who believes that his death will occur at the hands of his sister's child. After Kansa kills six of Devaki's newborns, Vasudeva transports newborn Krishna across the river Yamuna to Braj in the dead of night. It is believed that the river Yamuna, which is in high spate at the time, miraculously calms down to a shrunken level in order to facilitate Vasudeva's crossing. Having reached the other bank, he places Krishna in the care of Nanda, headman of a nomadic pastoral community, and his wife, Yashodha.

LANDSCAPE OF BRAJ—PASTORAL AND ANIMISTIC ASPECTS

The pastoral character of the landscape is reflected in toponymy and the defining incidents of Krishna's life as he grows up in the community of cowherds.[2] Braj is derived from the Sanskrit root *vraj* (to go) and alludes to the nomadic character of a pastoral community in its meaning as the place where cows wander. Gokul, now the name of a village, originally referred to any enclosure for cattle. Govardhan, the name of another adjacent village, means that which increases cattle. The name Mathura may be derived from the Sanskrit root *math* (to churn) in reference to the churning of milk and curds, a prominent activity in a community whose economy is based on milk products. Such a community is known as that of *ahirs* (from the root *abhi*—circum, and *ir*—wanderers) and *gwalas* (from *go*—cow and *pala*—keeper). The cattle graze in forests of which twelve are frequently mentioned in texts on Krishna's legends. Villages are named after these forests; for example, Khadira village is next to Khadira ban (forest of *acacia arabica*).

Nature veneration, or what Eck calls the locative form of religiousness, was prevalent in this community of cowherds.[3] There is evidence of cattle, snake, tree, and mountain worship in many Braj legends associated with Krishna and in rituals celebrating him. Reverence for nature was incorporated in Krishna (or Vaishnavaite) tradition and thereby in mainstream Hinduism. The manner in which this was done bears scrutiny because it represents a unique attempt to come to terms with earlier animism. Instead of declaring it an act of profanity, nature worship is incorporated into Hinduism by anthropomorphizing its deities and making them members of the Hindu pantheon, albeit secondary ones.

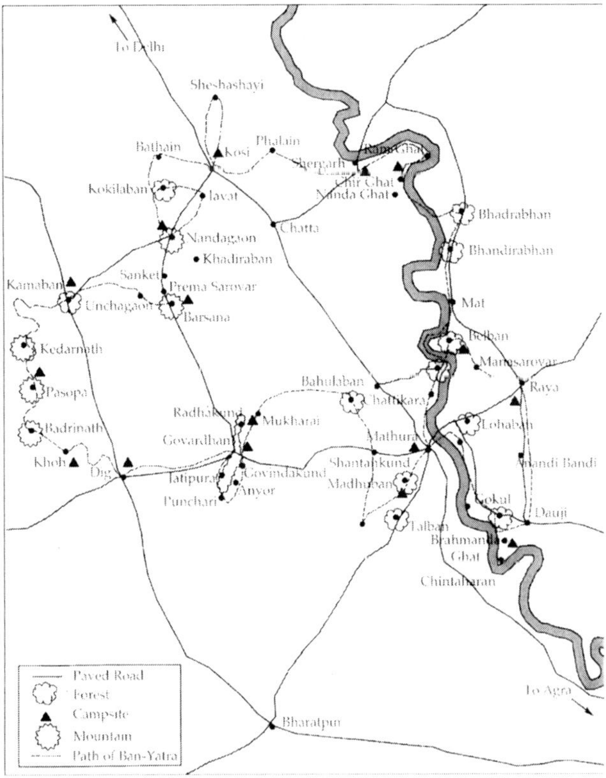

5.1: Twelve forests, Govardhan hill, and river Yamuna are present in the Braj *kshetra*, which has many settlements besides Mathura (redrawn after Haberman 1994).

Krishna, as he is growing up, reveals his divinity by performing miraculous feats and sub-duing demons that lurk in forests and inhabit the watery underworld. As a mischievous child, he does it effortlessly and playfully in the form of *lila*. When he is barely walking, his foster mother Yashoda, tired of his pranks, ties him to a wooden mortar but, as soon as her back is turned, Krishna drags the heavy mortar between two immense trees growing in the courtyard in an effort to free himself. As the trunks are felled in an enormous crash, the tree spirits (yakshas) are freed. Later, Krishna and his brother Balarama, along with other cowherd boys, are grazing cattle in the forests of Braj when they encounter demons disguised as animals that attack cattle. Their killing of the ass-demon, bull-demon, crane-demon, and horse-demon Kesi represents a victory over the dark, chaotic forces lurking in the wilderness.

The legend of Krishna's lifting Mount Govardhan in Braj exemplifies the resuscitation of nature veneration in the pastoral community of cattle worshippers. Govardhan, meaning that which increases cattle, is the name given to the hill deity in its theriomorphic form as a bull. Krishna urges the cowherders to worship the mountain instead of Indra, the Vedic sky god, who retaliates by sending monsoon clouds over Braj. For seven days and nights Krishna protects the community from the torrential downpour by lifting up Mount Govardhan, under which everyone gathers. Indra yields and pays obeisance to Krishna. The incident represents not only the supremacy of Krishna over Indra but also the strengthening of a traditional practice prevalent in the community. To celebrate the victory, cattle are decorated and led around the mountain and Krishna makes himself identical with the mountain deity and accepts the cowherders' offerings. The occasion is still celebrated as the *annakut* (referring to the mountain of food offered to Krishna-Govardhan) festival in which an anthropomorphic form of the mountain, made with cow dung on the courtyard's floor, is worshipped by women. In pictorial representations of Krishna, Mount Govardhan is represented as a conical peak held aloft.

This so-called mountain is really a narrow hilly range about four or five miles long with an average elevation of 100 feet, with the town of Govardhan occupying a break in the range. The most revered spot in the town (and perhaps the whole of Braj) is a tank called Manasi Ganga. According to local tradition, the village of Paitha (entrance), situated at a short distance from the southwest corner of the range, marks the spot where Krishna entered the hill in order to lift it from below. At the range's southern extremity stands the village known as Puchri (tail). Charlotte Vaudeville has suggested that these place-names indicate that the hilly range was conceived of as having the form of a bull with its mouth and tail symbolised by the two holy spots.[4] The range's association with snakes is indicated by the tank, Manasi Ganga, which is named after the snake goddess, Manasa Devi.

The wide prevalence of snakes in traditional nature worship and their incorporation into Hindu mythology as inhabitants of the netherworld are manifested in several other incidents. When the infant Krishna is transported across the river Yamuna on a stormy night, the snake-god Vasuki protects him by spreading his hood. Nanda and Yashodha's son, Balarama, is considered an incarnation of the cosmic serpent Shesh-naga on whom Vishnu slumbers as he floats over the primeval waters. Furthermore, Krishna subdues Kaliya naga, who dwells in the depths of Yamuna, poisoning its waters. Krishna does not kill the snake but humbles him by dancing on his hood and leaving an imprint. These incidents prove the supremacy of Krishna over gods of the sky and the underworld, symbolising his victory over the deified forces of nature. Krishna's ascendance and their defeat, however, do not result in their total banishment from the Hindu pantheon. Vestiges of their archaic worship persist in festivals today.

EROTICISM AND THE LANDSCAPE OF BRAJ

As Krishna reaches adolescence, his *lila* or divine play occurs in the forests of Braj, where nature forms a perfect setting for his amorous dalliances with the cowherdesses. The Dionysian aspect of the Hindu love-god finds expression not in the midst of the village community or the city's structured space but in untrammeled wilderness and its association with sexuality unfettered by social norms. Krishna plays the flute as he grazes the cows, casting a bewitching spell over the flora and fauna of Vrindavan as well as the women of Braj. The wives of the cowherds think little of their families, children, and husbands as they follow the beckoning divine flute. Krishna's favorite among them, Radha, is immortalised in Jayadeva's twelfth-century poem "Gita Govinda." With time and the growth of the Krishna-Radha legend, she came to be recognised as *shakti,* residing in the godhead. Various natural metaphors are used to symbolise the complementary aspects of male-female duality—Krishna and Radha as thunder and lightning, bees and flowers, night and day. Their love play occurs among the bowers and arbors of the Vrindavan forest in Braj where Radha must steal away from her home to follow the intoxicating call of Krishna's flute.

Again toponymy reifies a particular view encapsulated in the legend, enabling its continuity over time. A spot halfway between Nandgaon (Krishna's home) and Barsana (Radha's home), where the couple used to meet, came to be called Sanket, meaning "sign." Ajnokh was so named because it was the place where Krishna applied *anjan* (kohl) to Radha's eyes, Piasya (related to *piasa,* meaning "thirsty") where Radha revived a fainting lovelorn Krishna with a drink of water, Javakban where Krishna decorated Radha's feet with the red Javak dye—all living testimony to the couple's love trysts. Krishna's play with the other cowherdesses is not ignored. Sankari khor (narrow opening between two hills) commemorates Krishna's pranks when he would demand a toll of kisses from the cowherdesses with their milk pail as they attempted to cross. Chirghat is the name given to the bank of Yamuna where Krishna stole their clothes and hid in the branches of the kadamb tree as they bathed in the river.

In traditional Indian lore, the forest is usually the setting for the *ashramas* of sages who have renounced the world and chosen to meditate in the lonely wilderness, away from the distractions of civilisation. Krishna's amorous exploits are an antithesis to this classical tradition, expressing an archetypal connection to nature that was symbolised in the tamer version of nature, the royal garden.

LANDSCAPE OF BRAJ—A TRANSCENDENTAL VIEW

Both erotic and animistic aspects of nature are sublimated in a religious tradition that emphasizes transcendence through love. Accordingly, the mundane landscape is transformed and imbued with sacredness. It becomes a site of hierophany, a manifestation of God, of Krishna who descended into the earthly realm as an incarnation of Vishnu. His activities are *lila* and create bliss in the hearts of his devotees. Not accidentally Krishna chose a pastoral community and a forest setting for expression of his divinity. His delightful childhood—during which he steals milk and butter (and love) from the people of Braj, playfully grazes the cattle while defeating the demons of the forest, dallies with the cowherdesses, and enchants them with the call of his flute from the wilderness—found an appropriate setting in a pastoral landscape with pockets of pristine nature. The physical environment signifies the gratification and sensuality of his childhood and adolescence.

The eroticism of Krishna's life and its extension into the landscape of Vrindavan is celebrated in the Puranic texts and Sanskrit and vernacular poetry. In modern scholarship, J. L. Masson's and Sudhir Kakar's interpretations of Krishna mythology as signifying infantile sexuality and omnipotence are only psychoanalytic reductions.[5] Krishna *bhakti* as a form of love transcends the carnal. In medieval India, *bhakti,* the tradition of selfless devotion, was considered a more effective path to communion with God than the path of action (*karmayoga*) or intellectual knowledge (*jnanayoga*). In Braj, Krishna's roles—naughty child, playful companion, deceiving lover—provide models of devotional sentiments for the worshipper to experience and seek transcendence in an exalted state of adoration. The intensity and constancy of *bhav* (emotion) transform it from a human emotion into a sublime one. The contrast with other advocated methods of salvation in Hinduism—emotional detachment and meditative contemplation—could not be greater.

Of all the different emotional modes of *bhakti bhavs* and their aestheticized forms (*rasas*), those of *vatsalya* (parental or fraternal affection) and *madhurya* (romantic love) are elaborated in devotional poetry and encouraged in the Krishna cult. The landscapes of Braj, including its temple architecture, instill these sentiments in devotees through daily worship and year-round festivities. Cultivation of intense devotion is made possible by living physically in Braj, or imagining oneself there, and dwelling on Krishna's pastimes, thereby evoking the associated moods and feelings.

The transcendence achieved through emotional and aesthetic experience is rooted in the physical landscape. Braj, and particularly Vrindavan, is not just the site of the onetime descent of Krishna, but rather his eternal play. The normal comprehension of time and space is suspended in Braj. Temporal and spatial boundaries dissolve as time stands still and space flows between earthly and heavenly realms, blurring their distinction. Pilgrims narrate visions of child Krishna; walled gardens in Vrindavan are believed to be the site of Krishna and the cowherdesses' daily nocturnal dance. The unmanifest *lila* of Krishna is revealed to the initiated only under auspicious circumstances. In the devotee's imagination, Vrindavan is the mythic garden of Eden with its abundant flora and fauna, overflowing rivers, rich pastures, and picturesque bowers. It is the land of everlasting bliss.

CULTURE OF BRAJ—LITERATURE AND ARCHITECTURE

Literary texts in both Sanskrit and vernacular poetry have celebrated Krishna's legends in Braj for centuries. One of the earliest sources is Bhasa's *Balacharita* (written between 200 and 300 CE), which describes Krishna's childhood. Krishna's life was elaborated in further detail in *Harivamsa,* a text that was meant to be an appendix to the epic *Mahabharata* and composed around 400 CE, and in *Vishnupurana,* composed sometime between the fifth and seven centuries CE. The devotional poetry of the Alvar poets of south India inspired *Bhagavatapurana,* which was written in the ninth and tenth centuries. Jayadeva's *Gita Govinda,* written in the twelfth century, is a celebration of Krishna and Radha's love, which reached its apotheosis in *Brahmavaivartapurana,* compiled in the sixteenth century. Vernacular poetry includes the lyrics of Maithali poet Vidyapati (1350–1450 CE), fourteenth-century Bengali poet Chandidas (1400 CE), the Rajput princess Mirabai (1500–1565 CE), and Gujarati poet Narsi Mehta (1500–1580 CE), in addition to Surdas's *Sursagar,* which was composed in the Braj dialect around 1582 CE.

The continuous outpouring of lyrical poetry and sacred prose was both the cause and manifestation of the growth of Krishna devotion across India.

Along with painting, literature has played an important role in popularizing the sacredness of Braj's landscape. The main impetus to modern pilgrimage, however, was provided by saints Vallabhacharya and Chaitanya, who visited and settled in Braj in the sixteenth century. They founded sects, attracting large numbers of followers, and built temples at various holy spots. In 1552 CE, Narayan Bhatt compiled *Vrajabhaktivilasa,* the most exhaustive listing of Braj's sacred places, thereby affirming Krishna mythology's imprint on the landscape at the places made holy by various episodes in his life.

The power of place is reified in temple architecture. That architecture is conceived as an abstraction of the forces imbued in the natural surroundings is indicated by the terms *kunj* (bower) and *niikunj* (arbor) applied to buildings with a Krishna shrine. Earlier temples did not survive Islamic iconoclasm. The place where Krishna was born is the site of continuous depredations, the temple built there being first sacked by Mahmud of Ghazni in 1017 CE. Its replacement was destroyed by Sikandar Lodhi, and another built in the early seventeenth century was demolished by Aurangzeb and replaced by the mosque that still stands at the site. A few temples built during the tolerant reign of Akbar in the sixteenth century survive but the majority of standing temples were constructed in the past 150 years. Built on the model of vernacular courtyard housing, they are subdued in style when compared with the magnificent edifices of the typical Hindu temple.

PILGRIMAGE TO BRAJ

The culture and landscape of Braj are experienced firsthand in the pilgrim's journey. Braj, particularly Mathura and Vrindavan, draw pilgrims from all over India. It is foremost in a hierarchical ranking of sacred places in India. The best way to directly experience the landscape is through circumambulation of the region. The rite is known as *Chaurasi kos* (84 kos, which is a distance of about 300 km) *parikramu* (circumambulation). The journey begins and ends in Mathura but includes individual villages, groves, and tanks and their individual circumambulatory paths as part of the extended route. The sacred circuit is not exactly circular as it connects nodal points marked by significant incidents in Krishna's childhood and adolescence. The river Yamuna flows through this landscape with holy spots on both its eastern and western banks. There is no strict hierarchy among the sacred foci as such, although certain places, such as Vrindavan and Govardhan, receive more pilgrims than others do. And the order in which places are visited does not seem to follow the chronology of events as they unfold in Krishna's life.

Apart from full circumambulation of Braj, individual circumambulations of places along the circuit can be done. For example, the circumambulation of the city of Mathura is known as *panch kos parikrama* (5 kos, or 16 km, pilgrimage circuit). In every case, the journey is not considered complete until the pilgrim returns to the point of origin. The pilgrimage, once begun, should be completed and, in the event of a disruption such as illness, resumed. The practice of circumambulation, which forms a major feature of pilgrimage, is archaic and can be traced back to the pastoral community's circumambulation of Govardhan hill during Krishna's times as a propitiation rite for the hill deity.

The present landscape has little left of the flora and fauna depicted in paintings and described so eloquently in poetry. Sacred groves and tanks and reputed sites of mythological events dot the agricultural landscape and form part of the pilgrimage itinerary. Settlements, with the exception of Mathura, are small in size, with temples as the most prominent architectural structures. The flat topography of the land makes the eastern and western hill ranges (of which Govardhan is the most revered) dominant elements in the landscape.

Pilgrims arrive in Braj throughout the year but the number surges between July and September during northern India's monsoon season. It is then that Krishna's and Radha's birthdays are celebrated as festivals, which draw many pilgrims. The rainy season transforms the dry, parched earth into a verdant landscape with the river Yamuna surging. The days associated with new and full moons during these months are particularly auspicious for circumambulations and bathing.

Since medieval times oral tradition has included a form of dance-drama known as *ras lila* in Braj. Krishna's circular dance with the gopis is called *rasa* and is re-enacted along with other incidents from his life by performing troupes at the very spots where they originally took place. (The performing area for this dance is called *ras mandala* and may be in a temple, a wealthy devotee's home, or a temporary encampment for pilgrims.) This dance-drama is performed every year over a month-long period during monsoons when pilgrimages to Braj are most frequently undertaken. For the witnessing pilgrim visiting all the holy spots in the circumambulatory tour of Braj, the setting thus comes alive. The pilgrim also visits temples, joins in chanting divine names, and listens to sermons extolling devotion to Krishna. The householder becomes a temporary ascetic, renouncing material comforts by going barefoot everywhere and sleeping only on the ground, and lives in a state of ritual purity through regular bathing and eating only certain kinds of food.

Kirtan (communal devotional singing), fasting, and arduous trips (*dandauti parikrama*—circumambulation done with prostrate body) are occasions that induce epiphany. The daily and annual cycles of temple rituals also help in keeping the focus on Krishna's life. For example, what is known (and imagined) about the child Krishna's daily life is commemorated in an eightfold cycle of worship—*mangala* (act of awakening), *shringara* (decoration), *govala* (grazing the cows), *rajbhog* (meal at noon), *uthapan* (awakening from the midday nap), *bhoga* (light meal), *sandhya* (twilight when the cows are brought home), and *shyan* (retirement for the night). Each event is celebrated in the form of *darshan* and *aarti* of the temple deity, providing opportunities for the state of enhanced experience. This vivid reenactment of events in Krishna's life with the consecrated temple idols brings into present the distant reality. *Bhakti* and associated *bhavs* generated by an aspect of Krishna's life are facilitated by aconcrete focus.

The purpose of the journey to Braj is not primarily to acquire material benefits in this life or gain spiritual merit in the after or next-life but to experience transcendence through immersion in Krishna's *lila* in the here and now. It is likely that the believer is transported into the heavenly Vrindavan having crossed the mundane reality. The spatiotemporal boundaries shift and stretch, producing an altered state of consciousness, a total forgetfulness of self, and engrossment of all senses in the reality of Krishna. This state of heightened consciousness has been called *flow* and occurs as a result of the combination of the devotee's personal faith and the powerful charge that the sacred place's environment produces.[6] The experiential state is eased by the mental disposition of the devotee who has come prepared to seek the deity's blessings.

CONCLUSION

The story of Braj reveals certain dimensions of the meaning of sacred landscape in the Indian context. Like other sacred centers, Braj is the site of hierophany, of divine manifestation, a place of *avatar* (from Sanskrit root *tr,* "to cross," and the prefix *ava,* "down, across"; therefore, it means "to cross downward"). As a center or *axis mundi,* where communication with other worlds is possible, crossings take place from godly to human realms and vice versa. Rivers flowing from heaven to earth like the Ganga, mountains and temple towers built in their imitation, and even sacred trees with branches soaring upward and roots reaching into the netherworld are means of crossing, physical symbols that make the ascent possible. This is why pilgrim complexes that contain many of these features in India are called *tirthas*.

Krishna, like other incarnations, descends ostensibly to restore righteousness when there is a preponderance of evil. His *lila* imbues the landscape with a much richer significance than his primary mission on earth. What makes Braj unique is not the descent of Krishna but his continual presence in the eternal Vrindavan, which is manifest to the believer. This belief is fostered by its landscape, toponymy, architecture, rituals, festivals, flow of pilgrims, and faith of resident devotees; in short, the culture of Braj, which makes immersion in the perceived flow of divine love possible. Whereas journeys to other pilgrim complexes (such as Varanasi, Gaya, and Hardwar) are undertaken for performance of ancestral rites, propitiation of sins, and fulfillment of vows, Braj *yatra* is undertaken for a different kind of experience—one in which the divinity's human aspects are the object of devotion.

The sacred is to be found in the profane, the sublime in the sensuous. The archetypal associations of nature expressed in metaphors of animism and eroticism are transformed into metaphors of transcendence. Braj becomes a mandala, symbolizing the entire cosmos. It is experienced in the circumambulation rite, the path being analogous to that of the sun as it journeys around the cosmos. Thus, the sacred zone, a microcosm, is demarcated in ritual practice. This mandala is only conceptually circular; when translated into the physical circumambulatory path, it follows the exigencies of the landscape. Besides the structural correspondence between cosmic and local landscape, there is psychic correspondence between human and natural realms in the projection of human emotions and spirituality into the larger landscape.

NOTES

1. Barbara Stoller Miller (ed. and trans.), *Gita Govinda of Jayadeva: Love Song of the Dark Lord* (Delhi: Motilal Banarasidass, 1984), 75.
2. F. S. Growse, *Mathura: District Memoir,* third edition (Ahmedabad: New Order Book Company, 1978).
3. Diana Eck, "India's Tirthas: 'Crossings' in Sacred Geography," *History of Religions* 20:4 (May 1981), 323–344.
4. Charlotte Vaudeville, "The Govardhan Myth in Northern India," *Indo-Iranian Journal* 22.1 (January 1980), 1–46
5. J. L. Masson, "The Childhood of Krsna: Some Psychoanalytic Observations," *Journal of the American Oriental Society* 94:4 (1974), 454–459; Sudhir Kakar, *The Inner World: A PsychoAnalytic Study of Childhood and Society in India,* second edition (Delhi: Oxford University Press, 1981).
6. Mihaly Csikszentmihalyi, *Flow—The Psychology of Optimal Experience* (New York: Harper & Row, 1990). Other books and articles on Krishna include P. Banerjee, *The Blue God* (Bombay: Lalit Kala Series of Indian Art, 1981); Edward Dimock, "Lila," *History of Religions* 29:2 (1989), 159–173; A. W. Entwistle, *Braj—Centre of Krishna Pilgrimage* (Groningen: Egbert Forsten,

1987); Robert Goldman, "A City of the Heart: Epic Mathura and the Indian Imagination," *Journal of American Oriental Society* 106:3 (1986), 471–483; Enrico Isacco and Anna Dallapiccola (eds.), *Krishna, the Divine Lover—Myth and Legend Through Indian Art* (Bombay: B. I. Publications, 1982); Friedhelm Hardy, "Krnaism," in *Encyclopedia of Religion,* ed. Mircea Eliade (New York: Macmillan, 1987), 384–392; John Stratton Hawley, *Krishna, the Butter Thief* (Princeton, NJ: Princeton University Press, 1983); David Kinsley, *The Sword and the Flute—Kali and Krsna, Dark Visions of the Terrible and the Sublime in Hindu Mythology* (Berkeley: University of California Press, 1975); McKim Marriott, "The Feast of Love," in *Everyday Life in South Asia,* ed. Diane Mines and Sarah Lamb (Bloomington: Indiana University Press, 2002), 249–260; Behaula Shah, "The Making of Krishna's Playground: The Reconstruction of Structure and Meaning of a Sixteenth-Century Landscape Named Braj," unpublished thesis (Radcliffe College, Cambridge, 1997); W. M. Spink, *Krishnamandala: A Devotional Theme in Indian Art* (Ann Arbor: Center for South and Southeast Asian Studies, University of Michigan, 1971); Doris Srinivisan, *Mathura— The Cultural Heritage* (New Delhi: American Institute of Indian Studies, 1989); Charlotte Vaudeville, "Evolution of Love—Symbolism in Bhagavatism," *Journal of the American Oriental Society* 82 (1982), 31–40; Charles White, "Krsna as Divine Child," *History of Religions* 10:2 (November 1970), 156–177.

Chapter Six

The Cosmic Tree in Buddhist Landscapes

> "The Tree of Life, the Earth-Lotus, theWord-Wheel, the Lotus-Throne, and the Fiery-Pillar—these symbols can be traced back beyond their first representation in Buddhist iconography through the aniconic period of the Brahmanical Vedas, even into the Rigvedic period itself; they represent a universal Indian symbolism and set of theological concepts."
>
> —**Ananda Coomaraswamy,**
> *Elements of Buddhist Iconography*[1]

Natural landscapes played a momentous role in Gautama Buddha's life and nurtured the development of Buddhist doctrine. Natural settings are described in the canon and in other writings on Gautama Buddha's life and natural elements are depicted in Buddhist art, but their deeper meanings and their impact on his life and philosophy are often overlooked. Certain archetypal meanings of nature can be drawn on to explain the symbolic significance of momentous events in Buddha's life. In his birth, death, and attainment of nirvana and in the practice of meditation and the development and dissemination of his philosophical doctrine, the natural landscape was crucial. He was born and died in a grove of trees. He attained enlightenment under a tree and subsequently spent all his life as an itinerant monk, stopping in parks and forests on city outskirts only during rainy seasons.

A new symbolic meaning of nature emerges in the narrative of the Buddha's life— that of transcendent wisdom, clearly an evolution from prevailing animistic tree worship. The tree of life was transformed into the tree of wisdom, symbolizing the transition from folk practice of religion to a higher transcendental religious creed followed by people in those regions of India where Buddhism began to flourish. Serene natural settings formed the locale of *sangharama* (congregation of monks) in natural settings outside the city where institutionalisation of the Buddhist creed took place. Even the origins of Buddhist architecture, with its *stupas, viharas* (monasteries), and *chaitya grihas* (halls for assembly of congregation), lie in meanings attributed to features of the natural landscape.

ANCIENT INDIAN LANDSCAPE

Around the sixth century BCE, the Gangetic basin on the Indian subcontinent was the cradle of an emerging complex civilisation as pastoralism gave way to agriculture and large human settlements. These settlements ranged in size from villages and market centers to administrative capitals of aristocratic republics and monarchical kingdoms. The landscape consisted of cultivated land and human settlements separated by stretches of virgin forests with trade routes crisscrossing the land. Rivers and trade routes determined the location of major cities. Cities such as Shravasti, capital of the Koshala kingdom, and Rajagriha, capital of the kingdom of Magadha, were fortified with walls. Smaller settlements were surrounded by cultivated fields and pasture; beyond were the great forests.

Commerce in cities took place on bustling streets, lined by mansions of rich traders. Palaces and houses of wealthy noblemen had gardens containing shady trees, lotus ponds, pavilions, and flowers. Within the residences were stepped bathing tanks, occasionally with subterranean chambers. Vegetation consisted of both fruit and flowering trees with swings. Vines and fragrant creepers of jasmine formed arbors. The royal family also possessed orchards and parks called *arama* on the outskirts of the city, to which they retired frequently. For the king and his entourage, there were hunting preserves, such as the deer park at Isipitana (Sarnath) on the outskirts of Banaras.

In the forests close to human settlements were sacred groves where trees were venerated. Hermits of different schools of thought found a home here or in caves in the hills surrounding Rajagriha and elsewhere, where they performed meditation, sacrificial rites, and the yogic practice of subduing desires of the body and senses. The forest also sheltered the wandering philosophers, called *paribhajakas*, during monsoons when travel was impossible. They were held in high regard by the urban dwellers who came frequently to listen to their discourses.[2]

GAUTAMA BUDDHA'S LIFE

The Gangetic valley had achieved a high level of urban development and material wealth by the sixth century BCE. Its central position is indicated by the term *Madhya Desha* ("middle country"), which was used in both Sanskrit and Buddhist literature to refer to this area. Two kingdoms—Koshala and Magadha—in the eastern part of this region and a host of smaller aristocratic republics—Sakyas, Koliyan, Moriyans, and Mallas—occupied a belt of territory from the northwest to southeast between the Himalayas and the river Ganga. It was in the Sakyan republic with its capital at

Kapilvastu at the foothills of the Himalayas that Gautama Buddha was born in 563 BCE. The strong oral tradition (although writing was not unknown) was perhaps responsible for no full-length biography being written until six hundred years later, about the same time that his images began to be made. Based upon the *vinaya,* which is one of the three divisions of the Buddhist canon in Pali, works composed in Sanskrit include *Mahavastu, Lalitavistara,* and *Buddhacharita* and include details about Buddha's life.

Siddhartha Gautama's father, Suddhodana, was the elected head of a small territory. Kapilavastu was not as large as Shravasti or Rajagriha, but its location on the northwest-to-southeast trade route made it an important and thriving town. Siddhartha's birth occurred in a sacred grove at Lumbini, halfway between Kapilavastu and Devadaha. His mother, Mahamaya, was en route to Devadaha, her birthplace, when she was seized with labour pains and delivered the child standing under a *sala* tree, holding its branches for support. Since Mahamaya died soon after, Siddhartha Gautama was brought up by his aunt and stepmother, Mahaprajapati. He was surrounded by luxury, living in three different houses with pleasure gardens, during the summer, winter, and monsoon seasons. As a *kshatriya* prince, he was well versed in martial skills. He married Yashodara, the daughter of a chieftain, and had a son, Rahula. He became increasingly dissatisfied with his life of luxury and indolence, however, and often pondered the causes of human misery and unhappiness. Despite his sheltered life, he happened to see an old man, a sick man, a dead man, and finally a beggar on his chariot rides into the town. These sights triggered thoughts on the evanescence of happiness and the futility of satisfying desires in the face of inevitable decline and death. The palace's distractions and comforts did not decrease his anxiety. Having no peace of mind, he left home in search of truth at the age of twenty-nine.[3]

His journey can only be understood with reference to the prevailing religious climate of the times. The Brahmin priestly class was consolidating its hold on society through prescribed rituals that had degenerated to exploitative practices and castebased discriminations; hence, their views were continually challenged by others. Various schools of thought existed, including those of *vedanta* and *sankhya,* among whom some debated the existence of the soul and others its relationship to the creator.[4] A group of materialists challenged the concept of a creator and moral laws and believed that the way to true happiness lay in whatever gave pleasure. It was in this environment of vigorous philosophical debates that Siddhartha Gautama, on his way to the east, first sought guidance from Brahmin teachers who expounded the doctrines of *Upanishads.* He rejected them because their essence was vitiated with brahmanic emphasis on rituals. He then met two teachers, Alara Kalama and Udraka, ascetics who meditated in the caves in the five hills surrounding the city. He learned from them the practice of rigorous meditation giving rise to a state of non-existence of ego. He wished, however, for a state of unbroken concentration in which anxiety and desires never reared their ugly heads. Not finding their teachings satisfactory because his anxieties returned when he ceased to meditate, he traveled south toward Gaya.

There he practiced austerities for six years with five disciples in a forest on the banks of the river Nairanjana close to the village Uruvela (modern Bodhgaya). He fasted for lengthy periods and periodically was exposed to inclement weather yet failed to obtain release from anxiety or gain insights that could redress human distress. Realizing that austerities had failed to produce results, he then started begging for food to gain physical strength, at which point his disciples abandoned him. At that time, he remembered how once he had sat under a rose apple tree when his father had taken him to a plough festival, and he had entered into a peaceful, contemplative state that he now perceived as the way to enlightenment.[5]

After recovering his physical strength, he resolved to meditate under a *pipal* tree on the banks of the river, about three kilometers south of Pragbodhi hill, vowing not to rise until he was enlightened.[6] It was here on that fateful night that he was assailed by terrible fears, temptations, and doubts. They took the form of Mara, god of death, who came to be equated with desire and sensual pleasure in Buddhist thought. Mara tempted him with his young, nubile daughters who were well versed in the art of seduction. He then wreaked nature's fury upon Gautama in the form of tempests. The Bodhisattva was not perturbed in his meditation. He did not give in to his fears, firm in his belief that they have to be faced before one can overcome them. In resisting them, he was sustained by his moral discipline. He then touched the earth with the tip of his fingers as if summoning the earth-mother as a witness to his conquest of the demons of desire.

In four stages, during the dark, stormy night at the end of three weeks of meditation, he gained increasingly higher levels of understanding until illumination washed over him. He had transcended ordinary planes of thought, the here and now of the given state of existence, in his sudden knowledge of infinity and eternity.[7] He had conquered the constraints of both time and space by being able to see all creatures of the worlds, his experiences in past lives, and those of others. In a sudden flash of understanding he perceived the chain of causes behind human misery and suffering. He was now completely free from the bonds of *karma* and the cycle of rebirths. He had attained nirvana. As the sun rose in the east, the

Buddha, the enlightened one, still sat blissfully under the tree. For the next seven days, according to the legend, a terrible storm raged as the Buddha was protected by the snake-king Mucalinda, who coiled himself around Buddha's body and spread his hood over him. A great event in the history of mankind had occurred.

The event may be explained in terms of individuation, which Jung believed was the realisation of the transcendental archetype of the self in one's life. It could only happen when the contents of the unconscious are confronted with the form of numinous images in consciousness. Mara's figure was the shadow image, representing shadow forces in the psyche that Gautama faced that fateful night. The struggle culminated in his experience of "self as an immeasurable spatial expanse, a universe of images within as the universe without."[8] The "eternal" self emerged, the inner core of reality, hard as the adamantine platform *(vajrasana)* upon which he sat under the tree and which became the symbol of his enlightenment, together with the tree.

Forty-five years elapsed before the Buddha's death in 483 BCE. In this period the Buddha, in the tradition of *paribhajakas,* led a peripatetic existence, preaching the way to enlightenment to others, including kings and commoners living in the cities of the Gangetic plain. Immediately after obtaining nirvana, he left for the deer park at Isipitana in the vicinity of Banaras, a great center of learning and a holy city. There he gave his first sermon, an event known as Turning of the Wheel, to the five disciples who had abandoned him at Uruvela. He advocated the middle path, neither extreme austerities, which could harm the body, nor the life of sensual pleasures with an ever-increasing appetite for desires, fueled by indulgence. He pointed out that life is suffering, the cause of suffering is clinging to desires, and an end to suffering can be brought about by extinction of desires. The path leading to their extinction lay in the practice of eight principles of conduct—right view, aspiration, speech, conduct, livelihood, effort, mindfulness, and meditation. This sermon inaugurated a new phase in his life totally devoted to helping others benefit from his insights on the causes of human sorrows. For his doctrine to be disseminated to the wider community, he established *sangha* (a congregation of celibate monks and nuns). This *sangha* was based on the premise that the law of causation—cause and effect of actions—is not limited to the individual but operates at the collective level, since an individual is anchored in a community whose improvement in turn benefits him.

Most of his discourses were given in major urban centers—Shravasti, Rajagriha, Vaishali (capital of the Licchavi republic), Koshambi (capital of the Vamsas republic), and Kapilavastu. In the rainy season, he and his followers were forced to remain at one place as their travel routes were flooded. *Aramas,* pleasure grounds on city outskirts that had been donated by the royalty and nobility to Buddha and his followers, were their headquarters during this period. The Buddha entered the city only to beg for alms or partake of a meal by invitation. The *arama*'s natural surroundings were conducive to meditation and the daily round of activities, which included contemplation, philosophical discourse among the monk community, and communication of tenets to gatherings of laypersons.

Many of the *aramas* were bequeathed to the Buddha and his followers. Bimbisara, king of Magadha, presented a bamboo grove named Veluvana in Rajagriha. A rich physician, Jivaka, donated a park. A wealthy merchant of Shravasti, Anathapindaka, bought a grove called Jetavana from Prince Jeta for the Buddha. In Saketa, the banker Kalaka donated Kalakarama; in Nalanda, the merchant Pavarika presented Pavarika Ambavana; and in Vaishali, the royal courtesan Ambapali gifted a mango grove called Ambavana. In Kapilavastu, the Buddha stayed in the banyan grove Nigrodharama in the woods near the city, and in Koshambi at Ghostiarama and Kukkutarama.

His last journey is described in the canonical text *Mahaparinirvana sutra.* He was returning to Kapilavastu from Rajagriha where he had spent many rainy seasons when he died en route at Kushinagara, a small town on the banks of the river Hirayanavati. At Beluva village, he gave his last sermon, announcing his coming end. Later in his journey, he halted at the mango grove of the blacksmith Cunda in the village Pava and at Cunda's house ate a meal, which severely sickened him. Nevertheless he continued his journey with his two disciples, Ananda and Aniruddha, and finally in the *sala* grove of the tribe of Mallas at Kushinagara, he lay down on his right side between two trees with his head pointing to the north, attaining parinirvana, the final release. His body was cremated and the relics divided among claimants, including the king of Magadha, the citizens of Vaishali and Kapilavastu, the Malla tribe, and the Brahmin Vethadipaka. The recipients built stupas to contain the relics at the centers of crossroads in their respective cities, as befitting the remains of a great person.

SIGNIFICANCE OF NATURE

This rather brief summary of the major events in the Buddha's life points to archetypal meanings of nature, particularly of vegetation, that can be drawn on in explaining nature's significance in his life and in the emerging religion. Mircea Eliade in his exhaustive study of vegetation symbolism has described the tree as a symbol of life and inexhaustible fertility, as signifying periodic regeneration, as center of the world and supporter of the universe; and he has described the tree altar as constituting an effective microcosm.[9] The belief in the tree of life underlies the prevalent practice of tree worship in ancient India. We see a shift occurring in its meaning; the tree becomes a symbol for the Buddha's enlightenment, its branches a metaphor for psychic growth, and its elevation a breaking free from and rising above the mundane plane of sorrows and desires. In Buddhist iconography and architecture, the tree signifies the center and axis of the world and a place of transcendence.

Tree and serpent worship venerating powers of life and fertility in nature was the primitive religious faith of the oldest inhabitants of the Indian sub-continent and was incorporated by the Indo-Aryans in their religious practices. To this day, it is part of folk-worship. The trees were worshipped not for themselves but as *chaityas* or dwelling sites of spirits, such as yakshas and *nagas*.[10] The yakshas represented nature's fertility powers and were venerated as such, particularly by women desiring offspring. They also acted as protective benefactors or guardian deities of a place. Their human images were charged with superhuman energies and the female spirits, *yakshinis,* assumed the form of beautiful damsels. Their cult was popular in the Buddha's time and in later centuries. Buddhist iconography, especially the relief carvings on the stupas of Bharhut and Sanchi, shows them in large numbers and they often appear in *Jataka* stories preserved in the Buddhist canon.

The guardian deities of springs, lakes, and pools were often *nagas* who dispensed nature's gifts when propitiated or withheld her bounties when ignored. These folk deities were incorporated in Buddhist legends as helpers, protectors, and worshippers of the Buddha and his relics, thus, channeling their energies toward benevolent purposes in service of a higher authority.[11] The snake-king Muchalinda, who protected the Buddha during a storm, was the *naga* of a tank south of the bodhi tree in Uruvela. The symbolic role of folk deities is significant in the interpretation of other momentous events in the Buddha's life. Siddhartha Gautama's birth in a grove and its depiction in Buddhist art with his mother, Mahamaya, holding a branch of the tree in the manner of a *yakshini* acknowledges nature as a life-giving force. Located at the crossing of two routes, the grove was sacred to Rummin-dei, a local village goddess. An Ashokan pillar marks the spot, and Mahamaya, identified with the local goddess, is worshipped by the villagers in a small, nearby shrine.[12] The Buddha's death under the *sala* tree in a grove in Kushinagara marks the end of life as the inevitable cycle of birth and death in nature. Of nature one is born and to her one must return.

6.1: The snake-king Muchalinda coils around the Buddha and spreads his hood to protect him from the raging storm, second century CE, Pauni, Maharashtra (National Museum, Delhi).

The Buddha visited Nalanda's mango grove on many occasions to give discourses. The site derived its name from its guardian deity, a mythical *naga* called Naga Nanda who lived in a water tank. Other tanks and shrines in the area were dedicated to sun worship. Tree worship was also practiced. The adjacent village of Bargaon was named after the sacred *bar* tree, now enclosed in a *bhairava* shrine and worshipped by local inhabitants.[13]

Although the cult of tree worship played no part in early Buddhist creed and it is doubtful that the Buddha or his followers ever perceived trees as spirited, the presence of yakshas and *rukkha-chaityas* (sacred trees) continued to be felt among the people. Buddhist literature mentions *chaityas* as halting places for the Buddha during his itinerant travels. According to legends, the Bodhisattva was mistaken for a yaksha by Sujata, daughter of the village headman, when he was meditating under the tree in Uruvela. She propitiated him by offering food when her son was born.

In his selection of the spot under the *pipal* tree, Gautama Buddha was influenced by the Hindu practice of concluding ceremonies for their dead ancestors at the *Shaiva* shrine under the banyan tree (*akshaya vata*) in Gaya.[14] Like the pilgrims who seek *moksha* for their deceased relatives, the Buddha too sought escape from the fetters of desire and the cycle of birth and death under the *pipal* tree, twelve kilometers to the south of the eternal banyan. *Akshaya vata* was popular since the times of the epic *Mahabharata* (ca. 800 BCE) and housed the *shiva-linga* known as Lord of the Banyan, which is attested to by an inscription dating back to the eleventh century. It is likely that the Bodhi and *akshaya vata,* trees of identical genus (*Ficus*) and *axis mundi* for Buddhists and Hindus, respectively, were originally worshipped as trees of life.

The tree of life transformed into tree of wisdom became the world axis in Buddhist iconography and architecture. The numerous depictions of the Bodhi tree made it the most important aniconic symbol of the Buddha before his image became popular.[15] Ashoka, who became the ruler of Magadha in 270 BCE, upon conversion to Buddhism, initiated the worship of the Bodhi tree in Bodhgaya by constructing a shrine around it. This two-storied shrine, with a stone seat at the base of the tree, is depicted in a Bharhut relief sculpture. It became a structural temple with towers during the Kushana period in the second or third century CE.[16] Ananda Coomaraswamy's analysis of Buddhist carvings show the earliest tree shrines to consist of platforms enclosed by railings for people to venerate trees by circumambulating and giving offerings.[17] In the representations of the Bodhi tree dated between 175 BCE and 225 CE at Bharhut, Sanchi, Mathura, and Amravati, it is surrounded by two or three-storied structures, known as *bodhi-gharas,* perhaps the earliest temples in the region.

Even during the Buddha's lifetime, the cult of the Bodhi tree was spreading. What facilitated the cult was the ease with which the original Bodhi tree could be propagated. A seed of the tree at Uruvela was planted in front of the Jetavana monastery at Shravasti by the Buddha's disciples.[18] The Ananda bodhi, as the Jetavana tree was known, was worshipped by people during the Buddha's absence. *Jataka* no. 479 describes the ceremonies as the festival of the Bodhi tree.[19]

SHIFTING MEANINGS

The Bodhi tree marks the center of the world. Sacredness is no longer diffused over the landscape in the guise of nature spirits but has acquired a historical and place specific dimension. It has now consolidated itself in places and events associated with the Buddha's life. In *Buddhacharita* by Asvaghosha, the tree under which Bodhisattva obtained enlightenment is described: "For this is the navel of the earth's surface, entirely possessed of the highest power; for there is no other spot on earth which can bear the force of his concentrated thought."[20]

The transition in symbolic meaning from the tree of life to the tree of wisdom signifies a higher form of thought in which well-being is achieved not through propitiation of gods and sacrifices but through the eightfold path of right conduct. Earthly and heavenly pleasures are not the goals in life; rather transcendence is sought through the extinction of desires and finally liberation from the never-ending cycle of birth and rebirth and its miseries. In India the natural surroundings had always been a refuge for seekers of truth who sought through introspection and meditation the answers to metaphysical questions. The Buddha told his disciples at the end of a philosophical dialogue to withdraw to a shady grove: "Here are trees; think this matter out."[21] The tree was a perfect metaphor for enlightenment, its form representing growth in psyche and its individuation, as the twentieth-century psychologist Carl Jung would explain.[22] The tree, symbol of growth into wholeness, represents a profile view of the self whose cross-section may be seen in a mandala. Jung's patients' drawings showed the tree turning into a cross, as a quaternity symbolic of the self. Emperor Ashoka's pillar at Sarnath with its capital of four lions manifests the archetype of a totality image divided into four.

In the following centuries, vegetation continued to represent traditional nature worship, albeit with a few changes. Tree spirits were depicted in relief carvings on stupas of Bharhut and Sanchi but they had lost their preeminent position to the Buddha. The Bodhi tree was a symbol not only of his enlightenment (a time and place-specific event) but also of the doctrine named after him. Unlike the capricious tree spirits, well-reasoned Buddhist principles of conduct promised salvation to individuals who practiced them. Viewed in terms of Eliade's categories, the symbolism shifts from that of vegetation's in exhaustible fertility and periodic regeneration to the tree as center and support of the universe.

Sanskritic Hinduism also exhibits similar shifts in nature's sacred associations. By the second millennium, place deities became subservient to gods of supraregional significance and were incorporated into their legends. Folk deities residing in the trees, rivers, and mountains became kin, helpers, or manifestations of Hinduism's supreme gods—Vishnu and Shiva. Tree motifs are universal in religious art, and mutations in their forms and meanings are inevitable with social and historical change. In his wide-ranging book, Simon Schama traces the survival of pagan animism in Judeo-Christian theology in his discussion of the symbolism of wood, water, and rock.[23] Gothic cathedrals reconstructed the primeval sacred grove. The biblical tree of life in the Garden of Eden became the verdant cross in Christian iconography and landscape paintings.

In ancient India, nature was not only worshipped as a divine symbol and perceived as conducive to meditation but also enjoyed for its aesthetic beauty. In Buddhist thinking, however, pleasures of the senses were the root cause of suffering. It was perhaps Kama, god of desire, who as nature's life-force appeared as Mara, god of death, to tempt the Bodhisattva when he resolved to get nirvana under the *Bodhi* tree. Thus, it was fitting that the royal pleasure gardens, *aramas,* became *sangharamas,* the dwelling places for Buddhist congregations.

CHAITYA *GRIHAS* AND *VIHARAS* IN ARAMAS

A magnificent destiny awaited the *aramas* as the centuries unfolded. A *sangharama* typically consisted of *viharas, chaitya grihas,* and stupas. It grew into a large complex over hundreds of years, functioning as a nucleus of the monastic order and a center of learning. The *viharas* consisted of rows of cells on three sides of a central courtyard. Built individually or in clusters by royal patrons and wealthy devotees on the same site again and again, they show successive layers of construction in many pilgrim centers. They played a key role in making the itinerant monks of the wandering sect settle down in an established order. The walled pleasure garden was transformed into a walled retreat for ascetics.

The *chaitya griha* grew out of the need for a common meeting hall for the congregation. The word *chaitya* is derived from the root *chit,* meaning to think or meditate. Typically the *chaitya griha* was a rectangular structure with a rounded apse and roofed by a barrel vault. It evolved from an elliptical ground plan or a combination of circular and rectangular plans. The excavations at Ambavana in Rajagriha, capital of Magadha, reveal the foundations of two long, parallel, elliptical structures with circular short ends.[24] Their apsidal ends arose from the necessity of circumambulating a ritual object, such as a stupa or a Buddha image placed at the end of the halls.

At Jetavana in Shravasti, the Buddha stayed in wooden buildings, called Gandhakuti and Kosambakuti, built by Anathapindaka for *sakyamuni*'s use. The remains of temples built during the Gupta period mark these spots. King Prasenjit constructed other buildings in the park and much later Emperor Ashoka erected two pillars surmounted by a wheel and a bull at its eastern gateway. The remains of many Buddhist monasteries and stupas can be seen in this place now called Saheth while Maheth, half a kilometer away, contains the ruins of the ancient city.[25] In Kushinagara the remains of ten monasteries lie in the vicinity of the Nirvana temple containing the colossal statue of the Buddha.[26] The *viharas* surrounding the main stupa and Nirvana temple form a walled complex. At Sarnath, a *mahavihara* (consisting of many *viharas*) was built as recently as the twelfth century CE close to the apsidal shrine holding the Ashokan pillar and marking the site of the Buddha's first sermon.[27]

Sukumar Dutt has described in detail the evolution of early monastic architecture in the parks of ancient Indian cities; therefore, it is possible to re-create, even if somewhat imperfectly, the surroundings where the Buddha and his followers spent their lives for the benefit of hundreds of thousands of Buddhist pilgrims who visit these sites in the twenty-first century.[28] To the modern pilgrim, too, is owed the peaceful serenity that must have suffused the environment where once upon a time the Buddha lived and meditated.

PILLARS AND STUPAS

The living tree is reified and becomes a symbol of the cosmic axis in the free standing pillars attributed to Emperor Ashoka. Located at Sarnath, where the Buddha preached his first sermon, the lofty column with its capital of four lions surmounting a plinth with four animals and four wheels proclaims the Law of the Turning of Wheel. The wheel, identified since time immemorial with the sun and its movement, crowns the pillar, the world center where the way to escape the temporal cycle of suffering was shown.[29] John Irwin has argued convincingly that some of the so-called Ashokan pillars are in fact pre-Buddhist.[30] They were built at crossroads and their sites line up on Uttarapatha, a northwest-southeast route in the Indo-Gangetic plain. In their vicinity sacred trees and remains of ancient tumuli are found, pointing to pre-existing site worship. Among the artifacts discovered when mounds at the Lauriya-Nandangarh pillar site were excavated early in the century was a gold image of a nude female deity, an earth goddess. Out of forty pillars, only four (Rummindei, Nigali Sagar, Rampurva, and Sarnath) could have definitely been erected by Ashoka. He inscribed edicts on existing pillars and left at least three uninscribed. Evidence that these pillars were worshipped, possibly since pre-Mauryan times, comes from Sanchi and Bharhut reliefs in which they are shown adjacent to tree shrines and stupas. An Archaeological Survey of India report in 1931 mentions that those at Lauriya-Nandangarh and Vaishali were regularly worshipped by people. This phenomenon represents a folk tradition stretching back to prehistory when wood and later stone pillars reified the sacred tree.

6.2: The pillar is depicted in relief in the Sanchi stupa gateway. Pillars have marked sacred sites since pre-Buddhist times and were objects of folk worship (courtesy American Institute of Indian Studies).

The Buddhist stupa retains this universal axis in the form of a wooden mast in the center of the top of the hemispherical dome bearing the umbrella (*chattravali*), the ancient emblem of royalty. Here Irwin calls attention to the stupa's Bodhi tree associations.[31] A stone *harmika,* akin to altars under tree shrines and surrounded by the threshold railing (vedika), crowns the dome where the pole (*yashti*) protrudes from the dome. This association is strikingly portrayed on a stupa relief on the drum slab of Amravati, which depicts the wooden pole as a tree crowned with lush foliage.

6.3: A stupa in Sanchi in Madhya Pradesh with the railing, vedika, around the hemispherical mound defining the circumambulatory passage. Gateways known as *toranas* mark the cardinal directions. Another vedika at the top of the mound surrounds the *harmika* and *yashti* crowned by a *chattri* (courtesy American Institute of Indian Studies).

In the origin and evolution of the stupa lies further evidence of archaic cult-of-place worship. The earlier stupas were low mounds lacking *yashtis* and included those commemorating events and containing relics. In some stupas relics were inserted to reinforce sanctity of an already sacred edifice.[32] The term *stupa* referred not only to a pile of earth but also to the upper part of the head and its top. As a memorial rather than a sepulchral monument, it celebrated place, event, and person rather than death. As such its symbolism is of cosmic regeneration, manifesting in periodic enlarging through superimposition. The existence of wooden and stone pillars (*yupa*) in many stupas reinforces the concept of center and *axis mundi*.

Irwin speculates that both Buddhist *yashti* and Vedic *yupa* were derived from an older, non-Sanskritic tradition.[33] In Vedic sacrifices the *yupa* first appeared as a wooden pillar carved out of a tree in the sacred grove where Vanaspati, Lord of Forest, resides and later was replicated in stone. Linga, functioning as an axis in Hindu temples and in the grave mounds of holy men, is also a version of the cosmic pillar. The ancient symbols—primordial mound and tree of life—were adopted by Brahmins and Buddhists, to serve their respective mythology and doctrine.

BEYOND THE BUDDHA'S LIFE

Sacred landscapes of Buddhism allowed the doctrine to spread and flourish. *Viharas, chaitya-grihas,* pillars, and stupas constituted its primary structures. If we examine their settings carefully, a landscape pattern

6.4: Fragment of the Great Railing from the Bharhut stupa (courtesy American Institute of Indian Studies).

emerges. Stupas, as markers of the Buddha's physical presence and as relic chambers of the Buddha's remains, were monumental nodes in the vast network of Buddhist centers spread through the Indian subcontinent. Gregory Schopen explains that their power originated in the belief that the Buddha actually resided in them.[34] This belief attracted larger numbers of relic deposits of Buddhist monks and followers in votive stupas, which crowded around the main stupa in a haphazard fashion through the ages. The Buddha's relic was equivalent to his person, his personal attributes, and his right to personal property. In medieval Buddhist *viharas,* the Buddha continued to reside as an image in a chamber, frequently called Gandhakuti after the original one in Shravasti.[35] Images were now equivalent to the living person and were ceremoniously buried in stupas. A site's sacredness stemmed from the belief that the Buddha was a living presence there in the midst of the monastic community. But where were the stupas and *viharas* located? Kurt Behrendt separates Buddhist pilgrimages into three categories: sites in the center retracing Buddha's path to enlightenment, places at the threshold where he performed miracles, and sites at the periphery where his relics were enshrined in stupas.[36] Landscapes supporting this hierarchy in the Buddhist pilgrimage universe are very similar, as are their architectural elements. The sacred geography of Buddhism, although revolving around the person of the Buddha, relates to that of Hinduism, both in turn drawing upon ancient and folk cults of nature worship. Bodhgaya near Gaya and Sarnath near Banaras are the best known examples of sacred sites shared by Hindus and Buddhists.

Of the peripheral sites that the Buddha never visited but which nevertheless became important through enshrinement of his relics or images, many are located along merchant routes. The widely accepted explanation for their location is that they served to propagate Buddhist doctrine and were supported by merchant patronage. What has yet to be thoroughly studied is the preexisting sacred character of these sites, which was inherent in their landscapes and embraced by succeeding religions. Koshambi speculates that the trade routes linking Buddhist cave monasteries originally were movement tracks of pre-agricultural people.[37] They crossed at their mother-goddess cult sites, scenes of ceremonial festivities and blood sacrifices. Mother-goddess worship, banished when the caves were occupied by Buddhist monks, returned when the monks abandoned the caves.[38] In Andhra Pradesh, megalithic mounds containing mother-goddess figurines have been found along the Krishna river valley.[39] The mounds are attributed to local tribes called yakshas and *nagas,* named after nature spirits, who accepted Buddhism under the tutelage of the Satavahanas and Ikshvakus kingdoms, builders of the great stupa complexes in Amravati and Nagarjunakonda.[40]

River confluences, combinations of hills and water, unusual formations of hilly ranges, and curvilinear flows of rivers were landscape types that attracted Buddhist, Jain, and Hindu religious complexes. Buddhist, Jain, Hindu and even Sufi shrines in the ancient city of Rajagriha (Rajgir), which is surrounded by five hills and contains hot springs, found a home in the nearby caves. The Buddha used to meditate in Pipala cave in one of the hills (Gridhakuta?) after his midday meal, according to Fa Xian's account. The guardian deity of the city was Maniyar Naga whose sculpture was excavated in a Jain shrine.[41] These sites and their guardian deities—yakshas and *nagas*—had been venerated since prehistoric times. The lesser-known mother-goddess worship also flourished in sacred groves, caves, and hilltops. It is likely that natural protuberances and built mounds signified her womb and the landscape itself was equated with her anthropomorphic form. Buddhist sites, those blessed with the physical presence of the Buddha and those where his presence continued in relics and images, may in fact have been deliberately selected for their genius loci.

NOTES

1. (Cambridge, MA: Harvard University Press, 1935).
2. I have based these descriptions of ancient Indian urban landscapes on the following sources: T. W. Rhys Davids, *Buddhist India* (Delhi: Motilal Banarsidas, 1971), T. Ling, *The Buddha* (London: Temple Smith, 1973); Ram Bachan Singh, "Cities and Parks in Ancient India," *Geographical Review of India* 36:1 (March 1974): 62–75.
3. I have consulted the following sources for details of Buddha's life: Hermann Oldenburg, *Buddha: His Life, His Doctrine, His Order,* trans. W. Hoey (Delhi: Indological Book House, 1971); Edward Thomas, *The Life of Buddha as Legend and History* (New York: Alfred Knopf, 1927); Alfred Foucher, *The Life of the Buddha According to the Ancient Texts and Monuments of India,* trans. Simone B. Boas (Westport, CT: Greenwood Press, 1963); Ananda Coomaraswamy, *Buddha and the Gospel of Buddhism* (New York: Harper and Row, 1964 [reprint]).
4. *Vedanta* is aimed at nonduality—the merging of the soul with the Supreme One (Universal Soul), from whom it had emanated, through *karmayoga,* or yoga of action, which is doing one's duties effectively with equanimity and unattachment and leaving the results to God; *jnanayoga,* or yoga of knowledge, which is seeing God as the soul in everyone and considering the basis of actions as contact of senses with sense objects; *bhaktiyoga,* or yoga of devotion, which is the fixation of mind on God with devotion and gratitude for His glories and instances of His help through motivation and circumstances; the goal of *sankhya* was to free the soul from the shackles of body and senses through the practice of meditation on God.
5. H. Nakamura, *Gotama Buddha* (Los Angeles: Buddhist Books International, 1977).

6. J. Leoshko, "The Case of Two Witnesses to the Buddha's Enlightenment," *Marg* 39:4 (1988): 39–52.
7. Neuroethology, the study of the neurobiology of religion and spirituality, has some interesting observations on the neural circuitry of the brain that gets activated in transcendental experiences. Andrew Newberg and Eugene d'Aquili, in their book *Why God Won't Go Away* (New York: Ballantine Books, 2002), report brain-imaging data they collected from meditating Tibetan Buddhists and praying Franciscan nuns, whose feelings of infinite space and sense of unity with the world were accompanied by quietness in the superior parietal lobe on the top and back of the brain. If this part of the brain, called the "orientation association" area, receives no sensory input, it cannot determine the boundary between the body and the world. Michael Thalbourne, a psychologist at the University of Adelaide, makes the observation that people are likely to have spiritual experiences if their unconscious thoughts tend to break through into consciousness more readily. See Sharon Begley, "Religion and the Brain," *Newsweek* (May 7, 2001), 52–57.
8. Herbert Read, Michael Fordham, and Gerhard Adler (eds.), *The Collected Works of C. G. Jung* (London: Routledge, 1953–1978); quotation from Anthony Stevens, *Jung,* Vol. 4 (New York: Oxford University Press, 1994), para. 331.
9. Mircea Eliade, *Patterns in Comparative Religion* (New York: World Publishing, 1963).
10. Ananda Coomaraswamy, *Yaksas* 80:6 (Washington, DC: Smithsonian Miscellaneous Collections, 1928).
11. L. Bloss, "The Buddha and the Naga: A Study in Buddhist Folk Religioisity," *History of Religions* 13:1 (August 1973), 36–53.
12. D. D. Koshambi, "At the Crossroads: Mother Goddess Cult Sites in Ancient India," *Journal of the Royal Asiatic Society of Great Britain and Ireland* (Cambridge: Cambridge University Press, 1960), 17–31, 135–144.
13. T. Bloch, "The Modern Name of Nalanda," in *Journal of the Royal Asiatic Society* (1909).
14. Frederick Asher, "Gaya: Monuments of the Pilgrimage Town," *Marg* 40.1 (1989), 45–60.
15. Ananda Coomaraswamy, *Elements of Buddhist Iconography* (Cambridge, MA: Harvard University Press, 1935).
16. G. Malandra, "The Mahabodhi Temple," *Marg* 40:1 (1989), 9–28.
17. Ananda Coomaraswamy, "Early Indian Architecture," *Eastern Art* 2 (1930), 209–235.
18. T. O. Ling, "Bodhi-Tree," in *A Dictionary of Comparative Religion,* ed. S.G.F. Brandon (New York: Scribner, 1970).
19. Coomaraswamy, "Early Indian Architecture."
20. E. H. Johnston, *Asvaghosha's Buddhacharita or Acts of the Buddha* (Delhi: Motilal Banarsidas, 1984), 201.
21. Rhys Davids, *Buddhist India.*

22. Carl Jung, "The Philosophical Tree," in *The Collected Works of C. G. Jung*, Vol. 13, ed. H. Reed, M. Foreman, and G. Adler and trans. R.F.C. Hull (Princeton, NJ: Princeton University Press, 1967).
23. Simon Schama, *Landscape and Memory* (New York: Alfred Knopf, 1995).
24. Debjani Mitra, *Buddhist Monuments* (Calcutta: Sahitya Samsad, 1971).
25. M. Venkaramayya, *Sravasti* (New Delhi: Archaeological Survey of India, 1981).
26. D. R. Patil, *Kusinagara* (New Delhi: Archaeological Survey of India, 1981)
27. John Huntington, "Sowing the Seeds of the Lotus—A Journey to the Great Pilgrimage Sites of Buddhism," Part 1, in *Orientations* (November 1985), 46–61; Part 2, in *Orientations* (February 1986), 28–43.
28. Sukumar Dutt, *Buddhist Monks and Monasteries of India* (London: George Allen & Unwin), 1962.
29. Coomaraswamy, *Elements of Buddhist Iconography.*
30. John Irwin, "Ashokan Pillars: A Reassessment of Evidence," *The Burlington Magazine* 115:848 (November 1973), 706–720.
31. John Irwin, "The Stupa and the Cosmic Axis: The Archaeological Evidence," in *South Asian Archaeology,* Vol. 2, ed. M. Taddeir (Naples: Instituto Universitario Orientale, 1979), 799– 837.
32. Irwin, "Ashokan Pillars."
33. John Irwin, "The Axial Symbolism of the Early Stupa: An Exegesis," in *The Stupa—Its Religious, Historical and Architectural Significance,* ed. A. Dallapiccola (Wiesbaden: Franz Steiner Verlag, 1980).
34. Gregory Schopen, "Burial 'Ad Sanctos' and the Physical Presence of the Buddha in Early Indian Buddhism—A Study in the Archaeology of Religions," *Religion* 17 (1987), 193– 225.
35. Gregory Schopen, "The Buddha as an Owner of Property and Permanent Resident in Medieval Indian Monasteries," *Journal of Indian Philosophy* 18 (1990), 181–217.
36. Kurt Behrendt, "Lay and Monastic Pilgrimage in Ancient India" (unpublished paper delivered at Pilgrimage and Complexity conference, Indira Gandhi National Centre for the Arts, New Delhi, January 1999).
37. Koshambi, "At the Crossroads."
38. A relief image of goddess Yamai is worshipped in Bedsa vihara cave. At Karle, the relief image of the goddess Ambabai is carved at the *chaitya* entrance and she is identified with the stupa and worshipped by Koli fishermen. At a Junnar cave on Manamodi hill, the goddess Manamodi is worshipped as Ambika.
39. At Nagarjunikonda in Andhra Pradesh is found a headless stone figure of a nude seated female with spread knees, donated by a queen of the Ikshvaku dynasty in the third century CE, cited in Jatin Das, *The Buddhist Architecture of Andhra* (New Delhi: Books and Books, 1993).
40. Ashoka added the Buddha's relics to the pre-Mauryan stupa at Amravati, enlarging it in the process. The site derives its name from the Amareshvara (a form of Shiva) temple, which is visited by large numbers of pilgrims. In the

neighboring village of Dharanikota (ancient city of Dhanyakataka, capital of Satavahana empire) are found fragments of a stone pillar inscribed with a few lines of Ashokan edict. Das, *The Buddhist Architecture of Andhra.*

41. Upendranath Thakur, *Buddhist Cities in Early India—Buddha Gaya, Rajagriha, and Nalanda* (New Delhi: Sundeep Prakashan, 1995).

Chapter Seven

Kalika at Pavagadh: Landscape of the Mother Goddess

> "O Goddess, by you everything is supported; by you is the world created;
> By you is it all protected, and you always consume it at the end of time.
> At the world's emanation you have the form of creation; in its protection you have the form of steadiness;
> Likewise at the end of the world you have the form of destruction, O you who consist of the World!"
>
> —*Devi Mahatmya* (1:57)[1]

With the slow absorption of prehistoric earth-goddess cults into the cultural geography of Hinduism and Buddhism, the great mother archetype resurged in the guise of Devi, the Great Goddess, and her various manifestations. Her presence could be anywhere but more often than not she chose natural archetypes—mountainous caves or hill-water dyads—as her sites. Her locative aspect is often overlooked in the voluminous literature on goddess worship in India.[2] Yet, a careful look at the topography of goddess sites, together with her iconography, yields rich insight into aspects of her divinity. Mythology anchors and grounds her manifestations in the lay of the land, so that her sites become centers in the vast network of Hindu belief systems.

Who is Devi? As the primordial great goddess, she is the transcendent reality that creates the cosmos as well as sustaining and destroying it. The *shakti* and *tantric* modes of worship elevate her above all male gods and she is equivalent to *brahman*, the ultimate reality. She is not accorded this position in the Vedas, but with the passage of time we see her mounting significance in the Puranic lore.[3] Her elevation from that of tribal goddess to the all-pervading supreme entity is evidence, although far from complete, of incorporation of non-Aryan deities into the Hindu fold.

In Pavagadh, Gujarat, she resides as Kalika Mata, a dark, terrible goddess but also a compassionate one. Pavagadh hill, formed through volcanic eruptions, is a striking feature in the otherwise flat landscape of eastern Gujarat. Home to the *Bhils* and other tribes, it was inhabited in the eighth century by the feudal vassal of the Solanki Chalukyan ruler of Patan-Ahilwada.[4] By the eleventh century, it had been claimed by the Rajputs (Hindu warrior clans) and the hill became their sanctuary from the invading Muslims. Like the goddess worshipping *Bhils,* the Rajputs also worshipped the great goddess in the form of Kalika Mata who was their *kuldevi,* or the tutelary goddess of their clan. The Rajput rule survived until 1484 CE when the Islamic rulers of Gujarat brought about its downfall. With the subsequent destruction and defacement of temples, goddess worship declined and was revived only in the nineteenth century with the rebuilding of her temple. The twentieth century saw a massive resurgence in her worship, with over 2.4 million pilgrims climbing to the hilltop each year to receive her *darshan.*

7.1: Champaner city at the foot of Pavagadh hill was the last of fortified settlements built to take advantage of the opportunities afforded by the topography. The earlier forts on the hill were built by Rajputs who worshipped Kalika Mata as their *kuldevi* (Department of Landscape Architecture, University of Illinois at Urbana-Champaign collection).

The strong association of the goddess with mountains, forests, and rivers begs the question: how might we better understand her divine attributes through natural symbolism? The location of 108 *shakti pithas* on the Indian sub-continent is a testimony to the role of natural archetypes in the making of sites sacred to the goddess.[5] Many are well-known—Vaishno Devi in

Jammu, Kamakhya in Assam, Vindhyavasini in Uttar Pradesh, Kalighat in West Bengal.[6] The *pithas* draw pilgrims from near and far and are associated with the fallen parts of the goddess Sati's body. The *shakti pithas*, however, house aniconic and iconic forms of other goddesses from the Indian pantheon (such as Kali, Lakshmi, and Saraswati), suggesting a plurality of mythic traditions and the presence of local deities.

TOPOGRAPHIC SYMBOLISM

The prehistoric and continuing historical sacrality of Pavagadh hill and its evolution into the cultural landscape of pilgrimage suggest that we might examine its physical environment for a deeper understanding of how divinity is inscribed on the landscape. The multifaceted and paradoxical nature of Devi is manifest in the character of the hill's primeval landscape and its subsequent fashioning at human hands. The Devi at Pavagadh is worshipped as Dakshina-Kali, a dark, fierce, and wrathful four-armed goddess. She wears a garland of human heads and a girdle of decapitated arms and hands, and her arms hold a trishul (a kind of weapon), scimitar, conch, and the head of the demon Mahishasur. With her tongue lolling out, the goddess stands over the supine body of Shiva.[7] This image contrasts with the peacefully benign visage of other beautifully attired goddesses who are consorts of male gods. From a Jungian perspective, Kali is the personification of the terrible mother archetype, one to be revered for her fearsomeness. She, however, is also the giver of boons to her worshippers and rushes to their aid in times of trouble. How can we reconcile her wrathful and compassionate aspects? Only by understanding that her anger and blood-thirstiness are directed against evildoers and demonic characters, not against her believers who follow the path of *dharma*.

The pilgrim is made aware of Dakshina-Kali's paradox and her simultaneous transcendence and immanence through the landscape. The 830-meter-high Pavagadh hill has steep and formidable slopes in the southern and western directions but gently cascades and connects with a number of plateaus in the northeast. Its steep escarpments and crags, striking silhouette, and reddish tinge of rhyolite rock make it seem like a primal force of nature—a result of tremendous upheaval of the earth. One could describe Kali in those very terms, an embodiment of *shakti* (power) and *prakriti* (nature), an overwhelming, overpowering presence that is majestic, fascinating, and mysterious.

Indeed the hill is perceived by the believer to be the metonymic form of Devi. Its crest, jetting from its uppermost plateau, is Sati's toe in the mythic imagination. Extending the analogy, the rest of the hill could stand for Sati's body, parts of which fell elsewhere. Another popular reading of the hilly crest is that it resembles the conch that Kali carries in one of her four hands. Seen from above, the hilly range appears like a yantra of intersecting triangles with the Kali temple at its center.[8]

The yantra is a powerful aniconic form of Devi that is worshipped below her eyes (*gavashka*) in the *garbha-griha* of the temple. The symbolic meanings can be read at multiple levels. The *garbha-griha* (womb house) represents the cave in the mountain. As the Devi's abode or womb, it contains and emanates her powers over life and death. Situated at its center is the yantra, symbolizing the mountain and Devi. Thus, totality (of landscape and existence itself) emanates from the center, the *bindu* (point) within the yantra. The whole (macrocosm) is contained in the part (microcosm), its energies concentrated at the center, which is its miniature replica.

7.2: The yantra, a symbol of Kalika Mata, is an object of worship at the goddess temple at the top of Pavagadh hill. Metallic engravings of yantras are sold in shops along the pilgrim path (Department of Landscape Architecture, University of Illinois at Urbana-Champaign collection).

The temple's location at the top of the hill signifies Devi's transcendence. The arduous climb to reach the pinnacle culminates in euphoria when arriving at what feels like the top of the world. The sense of exhilaration and danger is enhanced by the glimpse of abrupt cliff edges plunging into deep valleys. One false step and one could hurtle into oblivion to the depths below. The wind at the top speaks of Devi's might and lends its name to the hill—Pavagadh, "castle of the winds."[9] The culmination of this landscape experience is the *darshan* of Kali, to see and be seen by her to receive her blessings and partake of her grace.

The fearsome (*raudra*) exterior Dakshina-Kali is believed to hide a peaceful, beneficent (*saumya*) interior for her worshippers. She is also known as Kalika Mata, the nurturing mother, giver of life. Her nurturing aspect manifests itself in the landscape as well. In the many plateaus of the hill are *talaos* and *kunds* (bodies of water) made by damming and diverting water's natural flow. These bodies of water, originally constructed by historic "water-intelligent" communities, represent an ingenious system of rainfall collection. Their utilitarian aspects have a religious significance drawn from the life-sustaining, munificent aspects of the nurturing mother goddess, as evident in the *talaos'* names. The highest part of the hill appears to have risen from Dudhiya (milk) *talao*. The pilgrim is enjoined to bathe in its waters and be purified before the *darshan* of Devi. (A small temple known as Ghat Mandir lies directly on the axis to Kalika mandir, which is used for ritual tonsure of children.) Chassiya (curd) *talao*, located on the second highest plateau, has the oldest temple of Lakulisa (Shiva) on its banks. Below on Machi plateau are the Teliya (like oil) and Annapurna (goddess whose name means "full of food") *talaos* Water, the sustainer of life, is thus equated with the maternal, care-giving Devi. Thus, the topography of Pavagadh combines both the fearsome and benign aspects of Kalika Mata.

MYTHOLOGY OF PAVAGADH

Although Devi is visualised in and through the landscape, it is mythology that anchors her narratives to specific sites. Myths and oral traditions act as mnemonic tools that bring alive for the pilgrim Kalika Mata's eternal presence at various sites and her involvement in site history. One group of myths reaffirms her presence by linking Pavagadh topography to Shaiva and *Ramayana* mythology. Pavagadh is seen as the son or a part of the Himalayas and the local river, Vishvamitri, is viewed as a branch of the Ganga.[10] Another group of myths concerns the vicissitudes of Rajput history. These myths reveal the full dimension of Kali's personality, including her wrathful side. Kalika was the patron goddess of the Rajputs and the stability and prosperity under their rule derived from her benevolence. She could withdraw favors as easily as she had given them if the rules of *dharma* were transgressed. Although this view is refuted by many believers, folklore suggests that Rajput ruler Patai Rawal was defeated because of his moral transgressions.[11] The first group of myths imbues the topography with significance, relating them to places that are central to the grand narratives of Hinduism. Pavagadh's Devi is thus no longer a local goddess but one drawn by her association with the hill into the mythic web that covers the subcontinent. The second group of myths draws upon the Devi's main purpose: to vanquish demons who are threatening the moral order. They rationalize the defeat of the Rajputs by Muslim rulers, who as alien aggressors may have been imagined as possessing demonic qualities. Devi refused to give the Rajput ruler Patai Rawal her protection because he broke the rules of *dharma.* For the believer, myths constitute the living history of Pavagadh and provide a fuller understanding of Kali's divine nature.

LANDSCAPE OF PILGRIMAGE

The remnants of Rajput and Islamic forts on Pavagadh hill are in ruins now, as is the fifteenth-century city of Champaner that was built at the foot of the hill. The Kalika temple was rebuilt in the nineteenth century by the Marathas, likely to commemorate their victory over Islamic armies elsewhere. More recently, the historic pilgrim path has been restored. Temples, both Jain and Hindu, dot the present-day landscape and are visited by pilgrims. Each temple is a node in the mesh of the hill's sacred landscape, a point of concentrated holiness. Shrines, mostly found on the pilgrim path, are smaller replicas of temples and they add to the holy aura that envelops the entire hill.[12]

Besides the Kalika Mata temple at the top, the hill is dotted with numerous Devi temples—a Kali temple is inside historic Champaner and at the base of the hill, and Khudiyar (a tribal goddess) Devi's shrine is located where the pilgrim path begins. Ambaji temple is located on the lower Machi plateau; a shrine to Khappar Jogini, Bhatiji, and Bahachur Devi is near the upper reaches of the pilgrim path; and Bhadrakali (elder sister of Kalika Mata) temple is on Bhadrakali plateau. In addition, small shrines to Kali are housed in the many *ashramas* functioning in Pavagadh. Devi temples at the foot of the hill serve those who are unable to climb to the top. Bhadrakali temple is built at the edge of a steep elephant valley in the vicinity of Rajput palace ruins. Bahachur Devi is housed inside a natural cave just below the hilltop. Kalika Mata temple is the primary destination, but Devi's other manifestations also find a home in this landscape.

Not surprisingly, Shiva temples abound. The oldest, known as Lakulish (another name of Shiva) and built in the tenth century on the edge of Chassiya *talao,* is now in ruins and no longer a site of active worship. Ruins of another Shiva shrine are found inside the royal enclosure of historic Champaner and a new temple has been built adjacent to the old one. Champaner has another Shiva temple near the Maratha fortification walls, where the linga is said to have been *svayambhu* (self-manifested). At Gomukh, where the river Vishvamitri originates, is a shrine to Gupteshwar (Shiva) and below that is one to Khuneshwar Mahadev. On the pilgrim path, Shiva is worshipped as Dattashreya in a cave shrine and as Mahadev Annapurna in a built one. There is only one temple to Krishna on the pilgrim path and it is known as Ranchor-raiji mandir. There are shrines to Bhairav, who protects the site, and to local deities such as Tithariya Dev on Bhadrakali plateau. A mausoleum to the Sufi saint, Sadan Shah Pir, built above the Kalika Mata temple, attracts both Muslim and Hindu devotees.

The most imposing temples are those devoted to the Jain *tirthankaras* (prophets). In the fourteenth century, temples were built on Pavagadh hill by Jains whose wealth assured them a favored status in the Rajput court. The hill is considered to be one of the four *Siddha kshetras* (sacred regions) where *moksha* may be obtained. There are three Jain temple complexes at the base of Pavagadh hill with temples, *dharmashalas* (rest houses for pilgrims), and even an old-age home. On Pavagadh, there are seven Jain temples. Built on the remains of historic structures, the group on Mauliya plateau offers a striking composition against the hill and sky.

Like the Jain temples, Hindu *ashramas* offer pilgrim services—lodging, food, and restrooms. The *ashramas* are built and run by holy men of various sects who were attracted to Pavagadh because of Devi. By building and managing *ashramas,* they promote their sect and participate in the economy generated by the large influx of pilgrims. At the base of Pavagadh, Kabir Sahib Ka Mandir has a *samadhi* (memorial) to Dhoonawali Darbari Bapu, who is noted for curing infertility and other ailments. Adesh *ashram* was founded by Baba Balaknath, who distributed medicinal herbs found at the hill to the afflicted. Free food is given to the poor and dormitories are available for pilgrims in the *ashram,* which contains Baba Balaknath's *samadhi* and that of his successor. Disciple Khareshwar Maharaj was inspired to stand on his feet for a dozen years as an act of sacrifice until Devi gave him *darshan* in a dream and asked him to build an *ashram* at Mauliya plateau. The *ashram* he built offers overnight lodging to two hundred pilgrims at nominal rates.

It is apparent that this landscape has evolved to enable visualisation of Devi, which is the goal of the largely self-organised pilgrimage system. Temples and their *ashramas* meet the needs of over two million pilgrims each year. Established spontaneously in association with myths or renowned persons, these temple complexes are supported by the pilgrim economy. During the nine days of *Navaratri* (nine nights) festival to Devi held in September–October every year, the pilgrim flow reaches its peak. Each *ashram* functions autonomously but in similar ways, and together they meet the immediate requirements of pilgrims.

Modern pilgrims describe their beliefs about Kalika Mata in terms of *shakti* (remover of obstacles, fulfiller of wishes, one who rewards hard work). They believe that "whoever comes with faith, his work is done"; "she draws people—they walk as far away as 300 kilometers, singing *garba* (folk songs) and carrying a *ratha* (chariots) as they walk"; *shraddha* (faith) brings people here"; and "at one time all representatives of the government were women and Kali was at the head" (the last quote is from a female devotee). A few describe Kalika Mata as their *kuldevi* and claim that their belief in her will make all their work successful. Many are familiar with the myth of the hill being Sati's toe and with Kalika's displeasure with the Rajput ruler Patai Rawal. Dudhiya *talao,* which acts as a threshold to the temple, is dilapidated and unhygienic and pilgrims voice regret that in its present condition, it is difficult to bathe in its waters for physical and moral cleansing.[13]

The devotee's vision is shaped by his beliefs and conditioned by the prevalent Devi iconography. The hill appears like a yantra, conch, coconut, and even boat to those who visualize other forms of Devi on the hill. Devi iconography in the many pieces of folk art displayed in shops on the pilgrim path show her as she is seen by the devotee in her hilltop temple (*gavashka*, yantra), and also render her as a young, attractive seductress of Patai Rawal. The video "Pavagadh darshan" sold in many pilgrim shops, although refuting this myth, illustrates others—Sati's body carried by Shiva, sage Vishvamitri's penance, Mahakali (a horrific form of Kali) standing on Shiva's supine body, and Kali surrounded by the ten Mahavidyas. A pictorial map of the hill prominently displays Kalika's and Bhadrakali's temples while the site's other attractions are shown much smaller.

The landscape experience of the pilgrims is shaped by movement and vision. At Pavagadh, the hill lends the experience a dynamism that makes the journey to the top a pilgrimage in the true sense of the word. The long, arduous climb from one plateau to the next along the historic 5.28-kilometer pilgrim path, with its historic gateways, burlap-covered vendor shops, occasional shrines, and views to the valleys and plains below and hill above, is a fitting preparation for the *darshan* of Devi—a simultaneous inner and outer vision. Visionary experiences during the ascent and at the pinnacle include the phenomenal forms of Devi that the eye sees everywhere in the landscape.

CONCLUSION

At Pavagadh, the mountain cave, symbol of the archaic mother goddess, has retained its hold on the human imagination for more than four thousand years, illustrating the power of the natural archetype in the sacred landscape of the Indian subcontinent. The primeval landscape of bare rock, ephemeral springs, and layered vegetation has evolved into a cultural landscape of worship in temples and shrines, small communities that draw their sustenance from pilgrimage, and holy organisations that facilitate and manage it. Once the hill had been a sanctuary for the Rajputs, who were protected by the hill's inaccessibility and Devi. Their elaborate water-management system indicates a sophisticated understanding of ecology that was used to satisfy the utilitarian and ritualistic needs of Devi's worshippers. Kalika's and Bhadrakali's temples guarded an extensive network of fortifications that seem ingenious and formidable even in their ruined state today. Pavagadh has seen the rise and fall of Rajput and, later, Islamic rule. Although it lost its position as the moral anchor of a kingdom and capital of Gujarat a long time ago, Pavagadh shows no sign of losing its position as an archetypal symbol of faith.

NOTES

1. Thomas Coburn, "The Threefold Vision of the Devi Mahatmya," in *Devi: The Great Goddess: Female Divinity in South Asian Art,* ed. Vidya Dehejia et al. (Washington, DC: Arthur Sackler Gallery, Smithsonian Institution, 1999), 37–58.
2. See David Kinsley, *The Sword and the Flute—Kali and Krsna: Dark Visions of the Terrible and the Sublime in Hindu Mythology* (Berkeley: University of California Press, 1975), and *Hindu Goddesses: Visions of the Divine Feminine in the Hindu Religious Tradition* (Berkeley: University of California Press, 1986); John Hawley and Donna Wulff (eds.), *Devi: Goddesses of India* (Berkeley: University of California Press, 1996); Rachel Fell McDermott and Jeffrey Kripal (eds.), *Encountering Kali in the Margins, at the Center, in the West* (Berkeley: University of California Press, 2003); Alf Hiltebeitel and Kathleen Erndl (eds.), *Is the Goddess a Feminist? The Politics of South Asian Goddesses* (New York: New York University Press, 2000).
3. The *Devi Mahatmya,* also known as *Durga-Saptashati,* part of *Markendeya Purana,* was composed in the fifth or sixth century CE. See its textual analysis by

Thomas Coburn, "Devi: The Great Goddess," in *Devi: Goddesses of India,* ed. Hawley and Wulff, 31–48, and "The Threefold Vision of the Devi Mahatmya," 37–58.

4. For the history of Rajput and Islamic rule at Pavagadh-Champaner, see M. S. Commissariat, *History of Gujarat,* vol. 1 (Bombay: Longmans, Green, & Company, 1938); G. D. Patel, *Gujarat State Gazetteers: Panchmahals District* (Ahmedabad: Government of Gujarat, 1972); Herman Goetz, "Pawagadh-Champaner," *Journal of the Gujarat Research Society* 11:2 (April 1949), 1–67; R. N. Mehta, *Champaner: A Medieval Capital* (Baroda: Heritage Trust, n.d.); William Miles, "Account of the Hill-Fort of Champaner in Guzerat," in *Transactions of The Literary Society of Bombay,* vol. 1 (1819; Bombay: Bombay Education Society's Press, 1877 [reprint]), 150–156; J. W. Watson, "Historical Sketch of the Hill Fortress of Pawagadh in Gujarat," *The Indian Antiquary: A Journal of Oriental Research* 6 (1877), 1–19.

5. A *shakti pitha* derives its significance from the myth of Sati's body parts falling at the site. Sati, Shiva's wife, was not invited to the house of her father (Daksha) for the sacrificial ceremony Daksha was going to perform and neither was her husband. Angry and humiliated, she killed herself. Carrying Sati's body, the grief-stricken Shiva began the *tandav* dance (dance of destruction) until Vishnu cut up the body, allowing parts to fall to earth.

6. For a description of Vaishno Devi site, see Suraj Saraf, *Vaishno Devi, Jammu* (Jammu: Raj Mahal Publishers, 1976). The Great Goddess is worshipped as Mahalakshmi, Mahasaraswati, and Mahakali (in the form of three rocky protuberances) in a 5,200-foot-high cave with a natural spring in Trikut mountain. The sacred stream at the base of the mountain is known as Balganaga. Below on a plateau called Adh Kumari (half virgin) is a tunnel known as *garbha yoni* (womb) of the goddess where the Great Goddess hid herself for nine months from Bhairav, who was chasing after her. She finally beheaded Bhairav and threw his head in the valley named after him. Pilgrims visit the Bhairav temple only after the *darshan* of Vaishno Devi. Sati's feet are enshrined in a temple called Charan Paduka on a lower plateau.

   Kamakhya—the goddess of desire—is worshipped as a *yoni* (Sati's vulva) stone in a natural cave at the pinnacle of the Nilachal (blue) hill. The natural spring keeping the stone moist turns red, signifying menstrual blood, when the hill's mineral deposits are flushed out by the monsoon rains. The surrounding hillside has womblike caves housing shrines of the ten Mahavidyas (*tantric* manifestations of the goddess). See Brenda Dobia, "Seeking Ma, Seeking Me," in *Is the Goddess a Feminist?* ed. Hiltebeitel and Erndl, 203–238.

7. Since Yama is unable to take Kali's devotees to his kingdom in the south (Dakshina) out of fear, she is known as Dakshina-Kali, worship of whom will overcome death, according to David Kinsley, *Tantric Visions of the Divine Feminine: The Ten Mahandyas* (Berkeley: University of California Press, 1997). Kali is to be found on cremation grounds and battlefields, decapitating demons and sucking the blood out of Raktabija demon, who multiplies as each drop of his blood falls on the ground. Kali's bloodthirsty reputation demands sacrifice of heads, animal or human. At Pavagadh near the entry to the Kalika temple,

animal sacrifices are substituted with the breaking of coconuts, whose shape suggests a head.

8. Kali's yantra consists of downward-pointing triangles circumscribed by a circle that is ringed by lotus petals, all within a square with openings in the four cardinal directions. In the metallic yantras sold in Pavagadh, the number of triangles is four or five with one upwardpointing triangle. The *bindu* or the temple is in the center of the intersecting triangles that represent the hill. There are other examples of geographic yantras, such as the temples to Vindhyavasini (Mahalakshmi = sustenance), Kalikoh (Kali's cave, Mahakali = destruction), and Astabhuja (eight-armed goddess, Mahasaraswati = creation), which are believed to constitute a triangular yantra in the landscape at Vindhyachal, which is repeated in the placement of shrines in the Vindhyavasini temple complex. The yantra is experienced in the *yatra* or journey of the pilgrim, with the three apexes representing the three forms of Devi, according to Rana P.B. Singh, "Sacredscape, Cosmic Territory, and Faithscape: Goddess Territory of Vindhyachal, India" (paper presented at Pilgrimage and Complexity Conference, Indira Gandhi National Centre for the Arts, New Delhi, 1999). For a thoughtful description of Vindhyavasini, "she who dwells in the Vindhya mountains," see Cynthia Ann Humes, "Vindhyavasini—Local Goddess yet Great Goddess," in *Devi: Goddesses of India,* ed. Hawley and Wulff. Humes suggests that Vindhyavasini was originally a tribal, mountain goddess who over time became the Great Goddess of Sanskritic tradition. Vindhyavasini is worshipped in a village located at the point where the Vindhyan mountain range meets the river Ganga.

9. The goddess assumes her wind form by possessing her devotees or moving from one place to another. This form displays her power but not her full manifestation. When women devotees become possessed, their hair becomes undone from braids or buns and flies about in response to the wind that is the Devi. See Kathleen Erndl, "Seranvali: The Mother Who Possesses" in *Devi: Goddesses of India,* ed. Hawley and Wulff.

10. Shiva and Sati, it is believed, were reunited in a forest on Pavagadh hill known as Shankar vana. Sage Vishvamitri brought the river Vishvamitri (another form of the Ganga) to Pavagadh by praying to the goddess Ganga. As Ganga is present on Shiva's head, so is Vishvamitri on the head of Lakulisha in the temple on the banks of Chassiya *talao.* Vishvamitri, a *kshatriya,* prayed to Kali to grant him the status of a Brahmin. Kali appeared before him and gave him her yantra, which he placed in the Kali temple that he built at the top of the hill. Pavagadh hill was created by Himalaya's son Achal at the request of Viswamitra, whose celestial cow, Kamdhenu, fell into the valley and was able to swim to safety by filling it up with her milk. Achal filled the valley with a huge hill, one-quarter of which stood above the plain and came to be known as Pavagadh, or quarter hill. Vishvamitri cursed the demon Pavakasur for harassing the people of Pavagadh. Thereafter the demon was killed by a hillock dropped by an eagle. That hillock became the crest of Pavagadh and is known as Pavakachal. When Hanuman was flying back from Lanka carrying the mountain with the herbs that would heal Lakshmana, who had been injured in the battle between Ram and Ravan, Ravan's demons attacked him, causing him to drop one-quarter of the mountain that is known as Pavagadh. This summary is drawn from an unpublished manuscript by

Sonal Mittal Modi, "Myths and Legends of Champaner-Pavagadh" (Baroda: Heritage Trust, 2004).

11. On a festival night when Kalika was dancing the garba in the form of a beautiful woman in the temple courtyard, Patai Rawal fell in love with her and beseeched her to marry him whereupon she angrily cursed his kingdom to ruin. The story of Bhadra, the temple priest's daughter, recounts the wrath of the goddess. Patai Rawal's brother-in-law killed the temple priest when the priest refused him his daughter. It is said that Bhadra looked like Kali herself when she stabbed the culprit who then escaped. She then cursed the kingdom for the death of her innocent father and buried herself alive in a temple near the fort's gateway. Soon after, Patai Rawal followed the sound of enchanting music to a cave in a deep valley. He saw goddesses dancing around a lamp, one of whom was Bhadra. The chief goddess, Kali/Bhavani, once again foretold the ruin of the kingdom. See Modi, "Myths and Legends of Champaner Pavagadh."
12. See Ghanshyam Joshi's pamphlet, "Pavagadh Darsharn" (Pavagadh: Lalita Joshi, 1999), for the description of Pavagadh and Champaner.
13. Informal interviews with thirty people, both residents and visitors to Pavagadh, were conducted from February 14 to 18, 2004. The visitor category consisted of *darshanarthi,* those who came to obtain *darshan* from Devi, and *pravasi,* those who came for sightseeing, with the former in the majority. Residents include those living in Champaner village at the foot of Pavagadh and those on Pavagadh hill in a small settlement known as Doongar. They had mixed feelings about the prospect of future development, agreeing that it would benefit them economically but also expressing concern that their illegal ownership of land might lead to their eviction when a master plan was implemented. They faced difficulties, such as the lack of adequate and clean water, a medical dispensary, and a primary school.

PART THREE

SPATIAL ARCHETYPES

> "India's most pervasive Creation myth is not that of light. It is space that is the first and foremost phenomenon of creation, the Indian cosmogony begins with the creation of space."
>
> —**Stella Kramrisch**,
> "Space in Indian Cosmogony and in Architecture"[1]

Many design theorists believe that architectural order is born of nature, although it is not always clear precisely what "order" refers to. Does it mean that architecture, like other arts, mimics nature or that space created by design is an idealised version of natural landscape? The ability to transform natural forms into meaningful architectural shapes and space defines a civilisation. Each culture approached the task somewhat differently before modernity set in, bringing in its wake globalisation of technology and aesthetic values. Ancient Hindus believed that architecture is the re-creation of cosmos and designing is a paradigmatic act performed by gods in periodic beginnings—*illo tempore*—to be forever repeated.

In previous chapters we saw the significance of natural archetypes in grand narratives of Indic cultures and their proclivity to function as centers of sacred landscapes. Trees and caves are mimicked in the architectural forms of pillar and temple cella, their reification ensuring stability, permanence, and opportunity for human architects to repeat divine acts. The cognitive image of sacred landscape held by the pilgrim is a circular *bhu-mandala* (great round), a symbol of spatial archetype. It denotes a cyclical view of time based on solstices and equinoxes of the sun and phases of the moon, upon which the festival calendar is based. The image is reinforced in the *parikramas* (circumambulations) pilgrims are obliged to perform. The path could be around trees, mountains, rivers, regions, or even the entire subcontinent. The best known examples are the *Chaurasi* and *panch kos parikramas* of Kashi and Braj mandalas.[2] The rite is of archaic origins and was undertaken to circumscribe a sacred space or object by one's body. Very likely the inspiration was the sun's daily movement across the horizon. These perambulations around features of natural topography, practiced since prehistory, are retained in pilgrim centers and around their shrines, giving us a clue to beginnings of architectural order from ritual movement.

The key to transforming nature into the built landscape in Indic thought lies in concepts of cosmogony and cosmology. In the phenomenological framework, a place is founded by creation of space. In the overriding concern with origins, the Western distinction between space as an endless continuum and places that are invested with meaning is ignored in Indic thought. The space/place manifested in mythic time is already quartered; that is, it is directional with differential values. The circle of the cosmos is patterned into the square of measured space. It is an ideal space of cosmic proportions and classical in its regularity.

The symbol of spatial archetype—four quarters formed by a cross in a square— constitutes the basic unit of architectural vocabulary. It evolves into the elaborate grid of *vaastu purusha mandala*—employed first in Vedic sacrificial enclosures and then in temple architecture. The temple is the prototype of house and pilgrim center. Sacred architecture forms the precedent for secular structure in Indic tradition. Since the sacred and the secular are not always clearly demarcated, houses and cities alike are influenced by mandala. Its center is elaborated into the open-air courtyard—the quintessential private outdoor space of the dwelling.

Natural archetypes generate architectural form and spatial archetypes—great round and four quarters—organize space, as the following chapters show. Chapter 8 traces the antecedents of settlement forms in the treatises of medieval India. Despite the importance of spatial archetypes, built versions could differ considerably from the ideal diagrams, as seen in Jaipur, whose layout however does not strictly adhere to the prastara mandala.

Chapter 9 explains how the social order of village communities is expressed in their layouts. Village communities that spontaneously spring up do not consult *vaastu shastras*. Yet we see a consistent fourfold settlement pattern, whether the layout is nucleated or amorphous. This pattern is a reflection of the caste and lineage structure of Hindu society and assumes shapes based upon the local topography and castes.

Chapter 10 shows the significance of the courtyard in the evolution of traditional Indian dwellings. The analogy between the Hindu temple and the courtyard house may seem far-fetched—the former is a supreme expression of the Hindu faith and the latter, an ordinary dwelling shaped by day-to-day living. Yet the *vaastu purusha mandala* is the basis for both, showing the strong and persistent influence of the sacred over the secular. Although the courtyard is common to all house forms in India (with a few exceptions in the northern hilly region), the overall shape of the dwelling, its evolution, and the use of building material and technology differ.

NOTES

1. In Kapila Vatsyayan (ed.), *Concepts of Space: Ancient and Modern* (New Delhi. Abhinav Publications, 1991), 101.
2. Rana P.B. Singh, "Varanasi: Cosmic Order and Cityscape, Part III: Shiva's Universe and Pilgrimage Journeys," *Architecture + Design* (March–April 1995), 83–85, shows how *parikrama* paths constitute the spatial order of Varanasi. The outermost of five constitutes a complete circle and is called the Kashi mandala; the second and third paths are known by the pilgrim's journeys—*panchakoshi yatra* and *nagara pradakshina*. The fourth and fifth circuits involve circumambulations around the shrines of Avimukteshvara and the temple of Vishveshvara.

Chapter Eight

Design of Settlements in Vaastu Shastras

> "Ancient India's architectural monuments can be either tiny or vast; in either case they form a microcosm. Human scale is not so much a matter of size as of utility. The paradigm for architecture that India provides centres on a simulacrum of man, his world, and of the universe; but this cannot be taken as modelled on 'Adam's house,' as in the European West, but rather, perhaps, on Adam's 'heart'—that still centre of the soul."
>
> —**Michael W. Meister**, "Reassessing the Text"[1]

Urban history texts mention the mandala cities of India but give the subject cursory treatment. For example, A.E.J. Morris's *History of Urban Form* has a one-page appendix on Indian mandalas and Spiro Kostof's *The City Shaped* has only a short section on holy cities.[2] The urban history literature does not offer a clear grasp of the design philosophy behind mandala-inspired urban settlements, which reached their apogee in south India's temple cities. I will argue in this chapter that the genesis of urban form lies in a design concept well articulated in the building treatises of medieval India. As in ancient and medieval texts on architecture in other parts of the world, this design concept is based upon a family of regular geometric shapes, yet is unique because of its metaphysical basis. It is applied at all scales to the extent that settlement patterns are elaboration of architectural design at a larger scale, with a similar vocabulary of forms and their symbolic meanings, and require similar design expertise.

VAASTU SHASTRAS

Vaastu shastra, the art and science of architecture, is covered in dozens of treatises on architecture and sculpture. These compilations, collectively known as *shilpashastra (shilpa* means "art"), form one of the sixty-four branches of the divinely revealed arts. The term *vaastu* ("where immortals and mortals live") means the site; and *vaastu*, that which is designed, including ornaments, furniture, vehicles, architectural details, gateways, drains, water tanks, gardens, buildings, streets, and settlements of all sizes and types. Architectural design is thus not limited to buildings; it is a comprehensive category encompassing artifacts made at various scales. *Vaastu vidya* (study of *vaastu*) as visual art and applied astrology are considered to be the fifth and sixth *vedantas* (appendices to Veda) and *Upaveda* (a lesser Veda), attached to *Atharvaveda.*[3]

The exact number of *shilpashastras* is difficult to ascertain, as are their dates. Found in all regions of the country and written in Sanskrit, they reflect oral and textual traditions dating back to antiquity. Although varying in details, their themes are quite consistent and the later texts rely heavily on earlier ones. Their subject matter is also covered in texts on rituals (*grihya sutras*) and mythologies (Puranas and *agamas*). *Brhat samhita,* compiled by Varahamihira in the middle of the sixth century CE, is a Puranic text containing the earliest datable sources on *vaastu shastra.*[4] The *shilpashastras* were written over a period of at least one thousand years. *Manasara* was compiled between 500 and 700 CE, and *Tantrasamuccaya,* compiled by Narayanan Nambudri of Kerala, belongs to the fifteenth century.[5]

DESIGN

To design is to bring form into existence by measuring and ordering space. *Manasara* and *Mayamatam* begin with the system of measurement used in sculpture, architecture, and settlement design. The length or height is called *mana,* breadth is *prana* or *pramana,* and *parimana* is the circumference.[6] In sculpture, *talamana* is the unit of measurement based upon the length of the face. These measures derive from the root *ma,* which means "to measure" and "to build."[7] The act of measuring is the first step in bringing an object into existence. This order or measurement is based upon the human body spatially and temporally since *prana* is also the smallest unit of time and equivalent to the time needed to take a breath.[8] To measure is to bound or limit space and create a place where none existed before. Measurement also divides the whole into parts and differentiates the spatial continuum.

This organic theory of design explains why the human body is considered coterminous with designed space. In architecture and settlement design, ideal diagrams are used in spatial organisation. These diagrams were used in structures (*vedis*) for performing sacrifices in Vedic India, dating from the first millennium BCE.[9] Their plans were based upon specified forms—square, circle, triangle, wheel with spokes, *swastika,* or a bird with two wings. Their areas were equal to seven and one-half squares, the side of each square being equal to the height of a *purusha* (human figure with uplifted arms).[10]

Who is this *purusha*? In the *purushasukta* hymn of the Rigveda, he is the cosmos. When he is sacrificed by the gods, the universe with its social order is created anew.

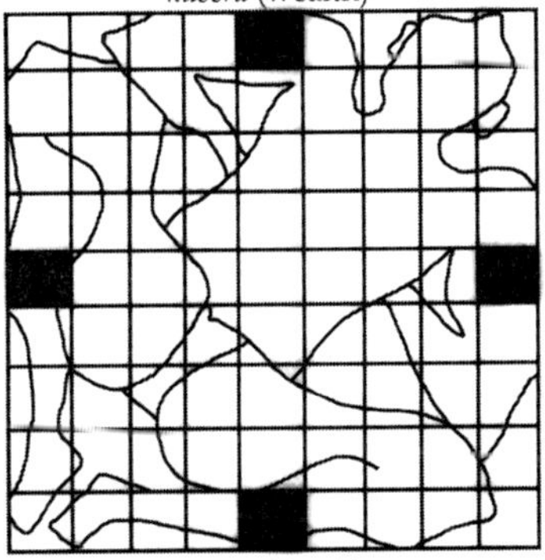

8.1: *Vaastu purusha mandala* is a spatial archetype that underlies sacred and secular architectural forms. It is the prototypes of temples, houses, and even cities.

> The Brahmana was his mouth; his arms were made into the Rajanya; his thighs were the Vaisya; and from his feet the Sudra was born.
>
> The Moon was born from his mind; from his eyes was born the Sun; from his mouth Indra and Agni; from his breath Vayu was born.
>
> From his navel was the atmosphere; from his head the sky was evolved; from his feet the earth; the directions from his ear. Thus, they fashioned the regions.[11]

Every sacrifice is the repetition of this primordial act. The sacrificer (*yajamana*) identifies himself with the *purusha* or the cosmos whose disintegration and re-creation occur during the sacrifice. The *vedi* and the *yajamana* become consubstantial with *purusha*. The *yajamana*, by building a *vedi* and performing a sacrifice, also creates himself anew and brings into existence *bhu,* the earth, that major *vaastu* that underlies all *vaastu.*[12] Every act of design that creates space and form is based on this archetypal act. The shape of the *vedi* becomes the perfect form, the archetypal plan. It signifies a microcosm and is called a mandala.

The *purusha*'s symbolic significance is not lost in architectural design and site planning. In the *vaastu purusha mandala,* which dictates temple architecture design, he is present as an anthropomorphic form fitted into a square with his head facing east or northeast. The organic form and geometric shape are coterminous. Here *purusha* lies facing downward, pressed into the earth by thirty-two gods who settle on various parts of his body. *Is purusha* a local spirit of the site, genius loci who has to be subdued so that the site can be made auspicious by the presence of gods?[13] The consecration rituals transform him into *Purusha,* the creative principle behind all existence. That which was beyond name and form, the infinite, is now delimited and manifested in concrete form.[14]

DESIGN OF SETTLEMENTS

Settlement design is an extension of architectural design. *Vaastu shastras* employ similar design principles regardless of the scale of *vaastu.* A building, village, town, and city use the same conceptual division of space, vocabulary of shapes, and units of measurement. The differences among them are quantitative rather than qualitative. Architectural details, building types, and settlement types follow a similar nomenclature.[15]

Another point of convergence between different forms of *vaastu* at various scales is the use of modules. The basic unit, the square, is congruent with the human body and other shapes, particularly the circle. The recursive division of the square in the *vaastu* mandala determines the arrangement of spaces, whether they are rooms in a building or buildings in a city.[16] In temple architecture, the width of the sanctum and the height of the door to the main shrine are determined by the height of the deity. In turn, the width of the shrine determines the size of temple enclosures.[17] The architecture of theater is another example of modular construction. According to the *Natyashastra,* the basic unit is the stage area (measuring 8 × 8 *hastas*). The sizes of other spaces are multiples of this unit (8 × 16, 8 × 32, 16 × 32). The system of division based upon square units can be traced back to Vedic altars.[18]

That settlement planning is an extension of architectural design is reinforced by the absence of a designated city planner. The *sthapati* plans settlements as he does religious and secular buildings. His capabilities in site selection, knowledge of surveying, and drafting skills come in handy in planning cities as well. His main expertise is his unique ability to create order. The divine ordination of the architect elevated him and his craft to a high status in society and imbued his actions with profound significance. In his work he mimics the primordial act of creating the universe. He is initiated into learning to draw and interpret the symbolic diagram of creation—*vaastu purusha mandala.* He is called upon when a new settlement is founded or an old one extended. He selects the site, marks the boundaries, designs the fortifications including the city walls and gates, and demarcates various quarters of the city.[19]

TRANSFORMING THE SELF AND THE SITE

Although the literal meaning of the Sanskrit word *purusha* is "male," in Upanishadic philosophy it signifies *atman* or self. The *Upanishads* also refer to the omnipresent self and source of the universe as *purusha* and *brahman*.[20] Hindu philosophy elucidates the merging of individual with universal self, *atman* with *brahman,* a process akin to the individuation that Jung believed was the realisation of the divine in man. Jung describes the self as the "thumbling in the heart" based upon *Katha Upanishad*: "That Person in the heart, no bigger than a thumb, burning like flame without smoke, maker of past and future, the same today and tomorrow, that is Self." It is *Purusha*, "smaller than small, greater than great."[21]

In mature Hindu thought, the Vedic sacrifice survives as a metaphor for actions and thoughts, leading to the disappearance of ego and birth of individuated self.[22] The ego has to die for the self to be born. This individuation occurs through sacrificing sensory impressions, thoughts, and desires and purging the archaic contents of the unconscious by bringing these thoughts to the scrutiny of the consciousness and then controlling them. *Purusha* remains the key element; self-realisation occurs in the perceptive body achieved through yogic discipline. A yantra is a symbol of this disciplined body—as a concentration tool, it enables the *yogin* to reach his center.[23] Similar to the yantra, *vaastu*, the built edifice, is the symbol of self, a projection of the owner's psychic core. The projection of self into the building is facilitated by designing with the *vaastu purusha mandala*.

The *purusha* of *vaastu purusha mandala* is a demon-like spirit of the site that must be subdued and transformed through consecration rituals and design into inhabitable spaces blessed by the presence of gods and protected from the evil of chaos. This magical-material process of transubstantiation from body to form is akin to the psychological process of transformation of self. The transformation of the site's demonic spirit into the creative impulse toward form is analogous to the sacrifice of the ego-self of the client, leading to individuation. This process entails the integration of the ego with its unresolved conflicts into a higher self, the *Purusha*. Mandala is its symbol, a projection of inner harmony into space.

CREATING CENTERS

Hindu metaphysical design philosophy is based upon a complex series of analogies and correspondences between action and form. Design or any creative act that results in material expression of measured order is mimetic of the primordial act of creation. The prototypical edifice is the Vedic altar where the disintegration and re-creation of *purusha*/cosmos occur symbolically. Its plan governs the building of temples, which are also expressions of *purusha*/cosmos. Here the *sthapati* orders space following Viswakarma, the archetypal divine architect, when he created the Vedic altar. The essence of all design, sacred as well as secular structures, lies in the order first created by the geometry of Vedic altars. Design is mimetic of the primeval act of cosmogony and, at another level, symbolic of the inner psychological processes of the client/ builder. The *purusha*/cosmos, with whom the *yajamana*/sacrificer identifies, becomes the metaphor for identifying the *yajamana*'s self/*atman* with the building. Thereby the material act of creating a physical center corresponds to the psychological discovery of one's center. Every act of building accompanied by rituals is mimetic of the primordial sacrifice, gathering the energy of cosmogony. The built edifice becomes a microcosm, a condensed, miniature replica of the whole. This association constitutes cosmological order and ensures moral order in this world as well.[24]

The *vaastu purusha mandala* regulates the plan of temples. The center is the *garbhagriha,* the womb-house or the inner sanctum of the temple complex. Small shrines to the thirty-two gods are built around the *garbha-griha,* becoming nodes in the circumambulatory rites of the worshipper. The location of doors and gateways must adhere to cardinal directions. Not only the plan but the superstructure as well is a veritable model of cosmogony, as Adam Hardy's brilliant analysis of Hindu temple form concludes. The various temple styles across the subcontinent are based upon the idea of emergence and expansion of forms from the center and their reintegration into a formless unity. The temple represents dynamism in a static structure not only as a conceptual idea but through actual composition of aedicules that project, stagger, gyrate, and split in great proliferation as they evolve from the finial downward and in the four cardinal directions.[25]

Temple architecture has influenced secular buildings. The *vaastu purusha mandala* is not explicitly used in house design, but its influence is clear in courtyard housing where the center is usually an open courtyard surrounded by rooms on all four sides. Directionality is significant in the location of rooms and entrances. The influence of the *vaastu purusha mandala* on diagrams prescribed for urban planning can be seen in the recursive division of the plot into squares for the allocation of blocks to four *varnas* and temples to various gods, with the emphasis given to the center by the location of a temple and the adjacent royal complex. Cities built accordingly become centers by virtue of their symbolic significance.

TEMPLE CITIES

Pilgrim sites in the Cauvery (known as the southern Ganga) delta in the state of Tamil Nadu have been transformed into temple cities by virtue of royal patronage over a millennium. As in numerous sites in northern India, the mandala is comprehended in the natural landscape of hills and riverbanks and enacted upon by the pilgrim through ritual circumambulations around its natural features. For example, in Tiruvannamalai the 800-meter hill, visible from twenty kilometers away, is regarded as the embodiment of Shiva. Two rocky protuberances at the hill's summit are worshipped as his feet and on the night of the festival Shivaratri he manifests himself there as a column of fire. The hill is the center of a sacred landscape with as many as twenty-seven holy spots encircling it and is marked by a tank and a shrine.[26] The Shiva temple at the base of the hill, originally a small sanctuary at a crossroads connecting different regions, grew into a large temple complex with multiple enclosures and the focus of an urban settlement. Occupying fully one-fifth of the town's total area by the eighteenth century, the temple influenced the settlement layout and the street network, which follow the concentric layout of temple enclosures. As the pilgrim circumambulates the sacred hill, he visits the main and subsidiary temples and tanks, and the deities are taken out on the "car streets" around the temple, in effect re-creating a mandala through ritual movement.[27]

The same phenomenon occurs in other temple cities such as Madurai, Shrirangam, Kanchipuram, Kumbhakonam, Tanjavur, Tiruannayanellur, Chidambaram, Tirukkalikundram, and Tirunelveli. One or more temples may form the core of the entire urban settlement, as in Madurai and Shrirangam, or temples may be the focus of a part of the town, as in Kanchipuram and Kumbhakonam. In the case of Tanjavur, a large Shiva temple called Brihadeshwara was built southwest of an existing capital by the Chola king Rajaraja in 900 CE. A processional street was built around the city for royal temple festivals and a Brahmin neighbourhood developed around the western street leading to the temple. Thus, the entire settlement, with the palace at its center, was incorporated into ritual space and blessed by the deity. Between the ninth and thirteenth centuries, the Chola kings built as many as thirty Shiva temples in the region to function as pilgrim centers, and settled Brahmins and service castes and their families around them, thereby creating temple towns. Not only streets but even agricultural fields were oriented around the temple and followed a prescribed ratio of measurements, as in Pulimangalam and Suchindram.[28]

The temple towns illustrate the incorporation and transformation of natural archetypes into built centers.[29] In these towns the mandala is a concentric diagram followed over hundreds of years as the temple complexes and towns grew in size. The seven concentric enclosures of Shrirangam's temple complex encompass most of the urban settlement. Its magnitude in area and the sheer verticality of its *gopurams* (gateways), which reach a height of sixty meters, suggest that perhaps Puranic cosmology guided its development. The idea that the cosmic center is Mount Meru, surrounded by rings of six oceans and seven continents and edged by a mountainous chain, was duplicated in Shrirangam with its temple as the center and its walls and streets as continents and oceans—the circular forms being replaced with rectangular ones. The width-to-length ratios in the four inner temple walls follow ratios of 2:3, 3:4, 5:6, and 6:7, suggesting deliberate design according to prescriptive rules.[30]

CAPITAL CITIES

In capital cities, the nexus of royal power and sacred temple in the city center implies moral and physical order. The *Arthashastra* prescribes that royal buildings should occupy one-ninth of the city and be built to the north or east of the temples in the city's center.[31] Nearly two millennia later, in the eighteenth century, Jaipur was designed by the *sthapati* Vidyadhar Bhattacharya, a Bengali architect well versed in *Manasara shilpashastra.* A fortified city with hills protecting it on the north and east, the city was the capital home of Sawai Jai Singh, the governor of Amber (in the state of Rajasthan) in the Mughal court and an astronomer. The plan of Jaipur consists of nine squares (one displaced toward the southeast as a result of a hilly outcrop), with the palace complex and the temple containing the royal patron deity occupying the center.[32] Sawai Jai Singh's interest in astronomy is reflected in the concept of the squares symbolizing the nine planets (*grahas*). Although no evidence documents that the *vaastu shastras* were consulted in laying out the city, their influence is unmistakable.[33] One of the *vaastu purusha mandalas* in the *Manasara* conforms to the original plan of Jaipur— a square evenly subdivided into nine smaller squares. Jaipur is fortified by an outer wall with gates, the palace is located in the center of the city, and the main street links its gateway with city gates.[34] The city's foundations were laid by *sthapaka* Pandit Jagannath Samrat, Sawai Jai Singh's Brahmin guru in 1727 CE. The main east-west street, the axis of the city, was built over a ridge and therefore is off by fifteen degrees from the cardinal directions. The use of modular proportions is evident in the uniform size of each side of the nine squares (2,640 feet), the ordered hierarchy in street widths (108 feet; 54 feet; 27 feet; and 13 feet 6 inches), and the

350-foot urban squares (in Jaipur called *chaupar*) at the intersections of the three north-south streets with the main east-west thoroughfare. Each square (*chowkri*) comprises eight-by-eight blocks created by a system of secondary streets.[35] The modular system in site planning extends to the architecture of buildings, as their heights and proportional arches in their elevations are related to street widths.[36]

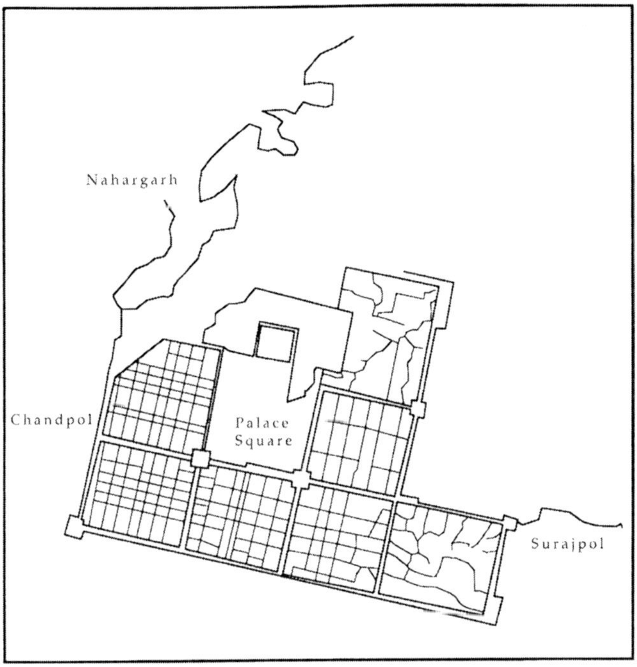

8.2: Jaipur, built in 1727 CE, is based on the *vaastu purusha mandalas* in *Manasara shilpashastra.* Its layout is a square evenly divided into nine smaller squares; however, one square is displaced toward the southeast because of a hilly outcrop, and the main east-west street built over a ridge is off by fifteen degrees from the cardinal directions (redrawn after Davar 1977).

The cohesive urban fabric of Jaipur has survived for 250 years. Indeed the quality of its civic spaces and the architectural subordination of individual buildings to an overall urban aesthetic have brought it much acclaim. In today's secular times, the codified design principles of *vaastu shastras* have not entirely lost their relevance. They outline a theory of environmental design, comprehensive in its scope and leading to a unified built environment. Architecture is considered the mother of all arts. Both architecture and urban design, its extension, demarcate place from space, emphasize centrality within a modular grid, and through building rituals identify the user/client with the structure to the highest possible degree.

Clarity in city structure, presence of an imageable center, and clearly demarcated boundaries are essential attributes of any memorable city. Clare Cooper Marcus, in her pathbreaking research on the house as a symbol of self, shows how it can chart the journey of the individual self toward psychic wholeness and individuation.[37] Cities are expressions of the collective self and their design can be a projection of beliefs about social and moral order. A city's quest to become a symbol of past tradition and future aspirations can be eased by physical order comprehensible to its citizens.

NOTES

1. In Farooq Ameen (ed.), *Contemporary Architecture and City Form* (Mumbai: Marg Publications, 1997), 89.
2. A.E.J. Morris, *History of Urban Form* (London: George Goodwin, 1979); Spiro Kostof, *The City Shaped* (Boston: Bulfinch Press, 1991).
3. Stella Kramrisch, "Patron and Practice," in *Exploring India's Sacred Art: Selected Writings of Stella Kramrisch,* ed. Barbara S. Miller (Philadelphia: University of Pennsylvania Press, 1983), 51–58.
4. The other Puranic texts include *Vishnudharmottara, Matsya, Vayu, Bhavishya, Skandha, Garuda, Agni,* and *Narada.* Three *agamas* contain *vaastu vidya*—*Kamikagama, Karanagama,* and *Suprabhedagama.* As Michael Meister points out in "Vastupurusamandalas: Planning in the Image of Man" (in *Mandalas and Yantras in the Hindu Traditions,* ed. Gudrun Buhnemann [Leiden: Brill, 2003], 251–270), Varahamihira's articulation of the *vaastu purusha mandala* in the *Brhat samhita* was the culmination of a long building tradition. In addition to the mandala's ritual and astrological uses, it was unambiguously a constructional device upon which a proportional system could be based, ushering in a new era of temple building,
5. *Sammarangana-sutradhara* by King Bhoja is attributed to the eleventh century CE and follows Vishnudharmottara, a dialogue between a king and a sage in sixth century CE. It influenced the composition of *Aparajitaprccha* more than a century later. *Aparajitaprccha* is a dialogue between Viswakarma and his son Aparajita expounding on the principles of *vaastu shastra* and committed to text by Bhuvandeva, perhaps an architect himself. Similarly *Prasadamandana vaastu shastra, Rupamandana,* and *Vaastu-Rajavallabha* are ascribed to Sutradhara Mandana, an architect employed by the king of Mewar in the fifteenth century CE. *Manasara shilpashastra* was written by sage Manasara, *Mayamatam* by Maya, *Sukranitisara* by Sukra, and *Sakalidhikara* by Agastya. Viswakarma is believed to be the author of *Visvakarmaprakasha, Vastuvidya,* and *Visvakarma-*

shilpa. See P. K. Acharya, *Indian Architecture According to Manasara Silpasastra* (London: Oxford University Press, 1928).

6. Acharya, *Indian Architecture*.
7. See Bruno Dagens (ed.), *Mayamatam—Treatise of Housing, Architecture and Iconography* (Delhi: Motilal Banarsidass Publishers, 1994). That these measures are based upon the human body is clear from the terminology. *Angula*, or the finger is the basic unit; 24 *angulas* make one *hasta*, or cubit; 26 *angulas* make one *dhanurmusti*; and 27 *angulas* make one *dhanurgraha*. Four *hastas* make one *danda* or staff and eight *dandas* are equal to one *rajju*, the cord employed in surveying. *Hasta* is used in making furniture and vehicles, *dhanurmusti* in constructing buildings, and *dhanurgraha* in planning villages, towns, and cities.
8. Stella Kramrisch, *The Hindu Temple* (Calcutta: University of Calcutta, 1946).
9. Stella Kramrisch, *The Art of India* (London: Phaidon Press, 1954).
10. The unit is called *purusha-vyama* and measures 120 *angulas*.
11. W. Norman Brown, "'The Sources and Nature of *Purusa* in the Purusasukta (Rigveda 10.91)," *Journal of the American Oriental Society* 51 (1931), 118
12. Kramrisch, *The Hindu Temple*.
13. The mythic landscape of pilgrim centers is an example of how *vaastu* at the settlement scale is considered a projection of cosmic self. The sacred land is perceived as a mandala. The *Vayupurana* reads the holy landscape of Gaya as the body of the demon Gaya Asur, who was killed by Vishnu. Various gods and goddesses reside on the demonic body, synmorphous with Gaya's topography, thereby making it a sacred land. See L. P. Vidyarthi, "Thinking About a Sacred City," *Eastern Anthropologist* 13:4 (1960), 203–215. Yet another example of landscape perceived as *purusha* is Varanasi. A prone human body representing Shiva and lying between the rivers Asia and Varuna is equated with the cosmos. The two rivers, along with a mythical rivulet joining the river Ganga at Manikarnika *ghat*, are conceived as three veins of the yogic body. The central vein terminates at the cremation *ghat* where occur physical death and possibly *moksha*. See Jonathan Parry, *Death in Banaras* (Cambridge: Cambridge University Press, 1994).
14. Kramrisch, *The Hindu Temple*.
15. Manasara describes eight kinds of villages based upon their form—*dandaka, sarvatobhadra, nandyavarta, chaturmukha, padmaka, karmuka, swastika,* and *prastara*. Terms used for timber joinery are based upon their shapes and include *nandyavarta, swastika,* and *sarvtobhadra*. These patterns are also found in perforated window screens and are named according to how many openings they have. *Mandapas* (pavilions) are called *dandaka, swastika, chaturmukha, prastara,* and *sarvatobhadra*. Rooms called *shalas* are also divided into *dandaka, swastika, nandyavarta, sarvatobhadra,* and *chaturmukha* types. See Acharya, *Indian Architecture*. The nomenclature extends to temples and palaces—the *padma* type of temple is in the form of a lotus and is only one-storied whereas the *sarvatobhadra* type has four entrances and is five-storied. See P. N. Bose, *Principles of Indian Silpasastra* (Delhi: Bharatiya Publishing House, 1978).

16. The system of measurement used is based upon the human body—24 *angulas* (fingers) are equal to four *hastas* or one *danda*. This modular conception extends to sculpture. *Talamana* (12 angulas, equal to the length of the face) is the unit for anthropomorphic deities and representation of the human body in sculpture.
17. In ancient Egypt and Greece, modularity was combined with geometry. The module would be derived from a major dimension in the building, such as the width of the inner room in an Egyptian temple. Placement of columns and piers and other dimensions of the building were determined by multiples and fractions of the module. In the case of a Doric temple, the width of the triglyph served as the module. See Kostof, *The City Shaped.*
18. Kapila Vatsyayan, *The Square and the Circle of the Indian Arts* (New Delhi: Roli Books International, 1983).
19. The architect is known as the *sthapati* (*stha* means "that which is fixed" and *pati* means "master"), the one who presides over construction of an edifice. See Ram Raz, *Essay on the Architecture of the Hindus* (Varanasi: Indological Book House, 1972). The *sthapati* is the masterbuilder and operates as the head of a team consisting of *sutragrahin, takshaka,* and *vardhakin.* The *sutragrahin* is the draftsman, who uses his knowledge of measurement by the cord (*sutra*) to lay out the building. The *takshaka* carves (*taksh*) stone, wood, and clay, and the *vardhakin* increases (*vrdh*) or adds to his work by joining parts and finishing their surfaces. Each role is crucial in architecture, from conception to overseeing the building operation, but the roles are not equal—the *sutragrahin* is the *sthapati*'s disciple and frequently his son and successor and is considered capable of completing the project should the *sthapati* die. The *vardhaki* works with the *takshaka* closely and is subordinate to him. The two obey the *sutragrahin*'s orders. In addition to this team of four, there is a priest-architect, always a Brahmin, called *sthapaka,* who acts on behalf of his patron or client, *yajamana,* and directs the *sthapati* (see Kramrisch, *Exploring India's Sacred Art*). The architectural team may consist of members of lower castes who belong to guilds called *shilpi-sangha.* They are trained as apprentices in their respective trades. The *sthapati* is required to be well versed in more than one field, including mathematics, astrology, and the Vedas. He has a generic name, Viswakarma, creator of the universe and architect of the gods. Viswakarma is considered to be the mythological ancestor of every *sthapati* and *shilpi.* The *sthapati*'s knowledge is divinely revealed by Brahma, Vishnu, or Shiva, depending upon the Puranic tradition. The *Matsya Purana* mentions eighteen sages as repositories of the sacred knowledge of *vaastu,* including Manu, Garga, Nagnajit, Parasara, Agastya, Shukra, Kashyapa, and Bhrigu. They were also the authors of texts on *vaastu shastra*. See Tarapada Bhattacharyya, *The Canons of Indian Art* (Calcutta: Firma K.L. Mukhopadhyay, 1963); and Binode Bihari Dutt, *Town Planning in Ancient India* (Calcutta: Thacker, Spink, 1925).
20. Harzer and Edeltraud, "Purusa," in *Encyclopaedia of Religion,* ed. Mircea Eliade (New York: Macmillan, 1987), 106–107.
21. Aniela Jafee, "Individuation," in *Carl Gustav Jung: Critical Assessments,* Vol. 2: *The Structure and Dynamics of the Psyche,* ed. Renos Papadopoulos (London: Routledge, 1992), 375–389.

22. Sanjukta Gupta, "The *Mandala* as an Image of Man," in *Indian Ritual and Its Exegesis,* ed. Richard Gombrich, Oxford University Papers on India 2:1 (Delhi: Oxford University Press, 1988), 32–41.
23. Mircea Eliade, *Yoga—Immortality and Freedom,* trans. Willard Trask, Bollingen Series LVI (Princeton, NJ. Princeton University Press, 1969).
24. Diana Eck, "The City as a Sacred Center," in *The City as a Sacred Center—Essays on Six Asian Contexts,* ed. Bardwell Smith and Holly B. Reynolds (Leiden: E. J. Brill, 1987), 1–11.
25. Adam Hardy, "Form, Transformation, and Meaning in Indian Temple Architecture," in *Paradigms of Indian Architecture: Space and Time in Representation and Design,* ed. G.H.R. Tillotson, Collected Papers on South Asia, no. 13 (Richmond, Surrey: Curzon Press, 1998), 107–135.
26. George Michell, "Introduction," in *Temple Towns of Tamil Nadu,* ed. George Michell (Bombay: Marg Publications, 1993), 2–17.
27. Francoise L'Hernault, "Tiruvannamalai," in *Temple Towns of Tamil Nadu,* ed. Michell, 40–57.
28. Hans-Jurgen Nitz, "Planned Temple Towns and Brahmin Villages as Spatial Expressions of the Ritual Politics of Medieval Kingdoms in South India," in *Ideology and Landscape in Historical Perspective: Essays in the Meanings of Some Places in the Past,* ed. Alan Baker and Gideon Biger (New York: Cambridge University Press, 1992), 107–124.
29. Chidambaram and Madurai are founded upon myths related to sacred groves of goddesses. Chidambaram, where Shiva is worshipped as Nataraja, king of dancers, was originally a forest of tillai trees (*Excoecaria agallocha*) inhabited by the goddess Kali. Her defeat by Shiva in a dance competition relegated her role to that of a subservient deity. See "Chidambaram" by David Smith (in *Temple Towns of Tamil Nadu,* ed. Michell, 58–75). The temple complex in the center of Madurai consists of two major shrines—that of Minakshi, the fish-eyed goddess, and that of her husband, Shiva, known as Sundareshvara. Minakshi was a Pandyan queen who was born with three breasts. When she met Shiva, her third breast vanished. They married and ruled thereafter as king and queen of Madurai. See "Madurai" by C. J. Fuller (in *Temple Towns of Tamil Nadu,* ed. Michell, 94–113).
30. Nitz, "Planned Temple Towns and Brahmin Villages."
31. Kautilya, *The Arthasastra,* ed. and trans. L. N. Rangarajan (New Delhi: Penguin, 1992).
32. Ashim Kumar Roy, "Architecture: The Dream and the Plan," *Marg* 30:4 (1977), 25–26.
33. Sawai Jai Singh's library contained a treatise by Sutradhara Mandana, an architect in the court of the ruler Maharana Kumbha of Mewar in the fifteenth century CE. See Satish Davar, "A Filigree City Spun out of Nothingness," *Marg* 30:4 (1977), 35–58.
34. See chapter 9, "Jaipur City and Palace: The Call to Order," in G.H.R. Tillotson, *The Rajput Palaces: The Development of an Architectural Style, 1450–1750* (New Haven: Yale University Press, 1987), 167–185.

35. Shuji Funo, Naohiko Yamamoto, and Mohan Pant analyzed Survey of India maps of Jaipur and found that only four squares in the center have uniformly sized blocks. Other squares have irregular street patterns, suggesting that only the core of the city rigorously followed the *shilpashastra* planning principles. See "Space Formation of Jaipur City, Rajasthan, India: An Analysis on City Maps (1925–28) Made by Survey of India," *Journal of Asian Architecture and Building Engineering* 1:1 (March 2002), 261–269.
36. Davar, "A Filigree City."
37. Clare Cooper Marcus, *House as a Mirror of Self* (Berkeley, CA: Conari Press, 1995).

Chapter Nine

Social and Spatial Order in Villages

> "For nearly three millennia caste has dominated the lives of the inhabitants of the Indian sub-continent, influencing if not determining their choice of occupation, diet and spouse, their collective rank in relation to other caste groups, and numerous other matters."
>
> —**M. N. Srinivas,** "The Caste System and Its Future"[1]

In addition to occupation, diet, spouse, and economic status, caste determines where one lives in India's villages. Territorial segregation of caste groups is a pervading factor in rural communities in all parts of the country. This division of caste groups into neighbourhoods, hamlets, or streets results in a clear reflection of the village's social structure in its layout. Space provides an important symbol for communicating the social order and anchoring the individual within it. Village layouts based on anthropological accounts reveal the ordering principles governing the territorial distribution of the different caste groups. As Chapter 8 shows, *vaastu purusha mandala,* the cosmic square underlying the ideal settlement form, allocates space to the four *varnas* in Hindu society. The mandala is a graphic representation of the universe, and each settlement becomes a microcosm, a miniature replica of the whole universe.

How far this ideal concept is translated into spontaneously formed villages can be ascertained by examining actual layouts. Archetypal forms are given shape by regional topography and local ecology. They interact with caste and kinship groupings to produce the settlement pattern. Although the influence of the caste system on village form is a pan-Indian phenomenon, availability of water, local topography, the circumstances of a village's formation, and presence of a strong dominant caste with its kinship groupings all play a role in the shape the settlement takes. This correspondence between social structure and physical form is always discernible. In this chapter we will examine this congruity between social and spatial order in village layouts from different regions.

IDEAL LAYOUTS

The *vaastu shastras* describe thirty-two types of mandalas that can be used as building plans. The numbers from one to thirty-two, in a series formed by arithmetic progression, indicate the units of division of different square mandalas. *Brhat Samhita,* containing the earliest *vaastu shastra* text, prescribes the mandalas of sixty-four squares (*manduka*) for temples and eighty-one squares (*paramasayika*) for other buildings, villages, and towns. According to the *Samaranganasutradhara,* however, the sixty-four square mandala can be used for all types of settlements.[2]

The center-periphery division of space in the mandala is reflected in a settlement's caste quarters. In the center is a temple complex and built next to it are the royal palace complex and the neighbourhood of Brahmins. All other castes are located with respect to the center in accordance with their positions in the social hierarchy. Another principle for determining settlement location is directionality—higher castes are located in the east and north or face those directions. The *vaastu shastras* give varying locations to caste quarters in settlements. Within the square, the sun's daily cycle signifies the auspicious (east and north) and inauspicious (south and west) directions.[3] This cycle becomes the basis of caste group arrangement. Brahmins reside in the north, the direction of gestation; *kshatriyas,* members of the ruling class, in the east so that they can face the rising sun; and *vaishyas* and *shudras,* in the south and the west, respectively, the directions associated with *Yama*, the god of death, and the setting sun. Thus, directionality is incorporated into the hierarchical scheme of the caste structure.

TYPES OF SETTLEMENTS

The *vaastu shastras* contain at least one chapter on designing settlements. No distinction is made among the layouts of villages, towns, and cities. Towns and cities are considered to be simply much larger versions of villages. Villages are called *gramas* and the oldest Sanskrit word for city is *pur,* derived from the Dravidian *ur.*[4] In *Manasara, Mayamatam, Aparajitaprccha,* and Kautilya's *Arthashastra*, a number of settlement types are discussed. These types are determined by form, size, natural features of the site, and inhabitants. *Manasara* describes eight kinds of villages based upon form—*dandaka* (staff), *sarvatobhadra* (quadrangular/grid), *nandyavarta* (quadrangular/concentric), *chaturmukha* (four-faced), *padmaka* (lotus), *karmuka* (bow), *swastika,* and *prastara* (conch).[5]

The street patterns in each village type determine the shapes. They divide the basically quadrangular, circular, or semicircular shape into blocks. The scheme followed here is called *padavinyas,* or division into squares. The *nandyavarta* settlement, for example, clearly displays the *sthandila* (49-square), *manduka* (64-square), and *paramsayika* (81-square) mandalas in its layout.[6] *Padmaka* and *karmuka* types of settlements have a radial-concentric organisation described by radial streets converging upon the center.

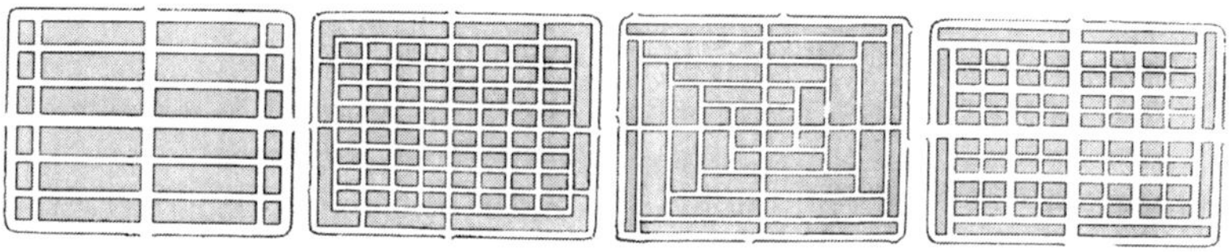

9.1: *Dandaka* (staff), *sarvatobhadra* (quadrangular/ grid), *nandyavarta* (quadrangular/concentric), and *chaturmukha* (four-faced) mandalas as described in *Manasara shilpashastras.*

In other settlements—*dandaka, sarvatobhadra, nandyavarta, chaturmukha, swastika,* and *prastara*—the center is emphasized by the intersection of cross streets. The prominence in location is buttressed by use—the center is called *brahmasthana* and is occupied by a temple. This organisation is further articulated by the number of streets and gates.[7] These six settlement types appear to be based upon the archetype of the four quarters, symbolised by the cross within a square. The forms are a physical expression of a fourfold stratified social structure. The social or dereflects the concept of cosmos as a quartered universe emanating from the power at the center.[8]

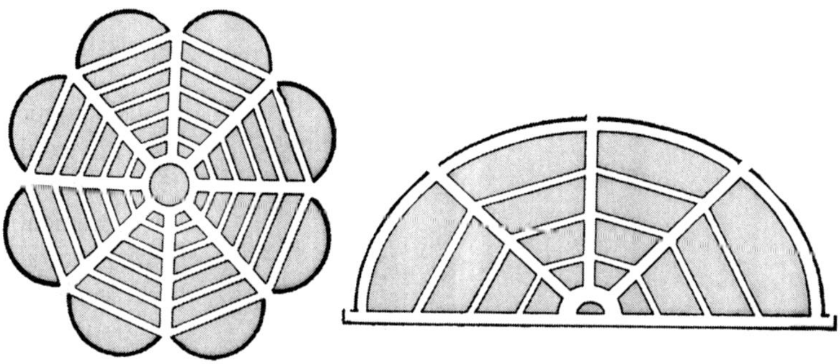

9.2: *Padmaka* (lotus) and *karmuka* (bow) mandalas as described in *Manasara shilpashastras.*

There is a high degree of geometric order and emphasis on orientation in the conception of a settlement. Do the ideal village/city plans discussed in *vaastu shastras* have any bearing on the spontaneously settled villages? Straight streets along a north-south or east-west axis, temple as focal point, and square or rectangular shapes forming around biaxial streets that bifurcate the settlement are elements of ideal layouts found in actual settlements.

I will discuss two types of nucleated settlements—symmetrical layouts of kinship groups and linear layouts of caste streets.[9] In both geometrically ordered settlement patterns and amorphous congregations of village clusters, the center-periphery distribution of castes is evident. Higher castes reside in the center of the settlement, with lower castes occupying areas farther away, depending upon their relative standing with respect to superior castes.

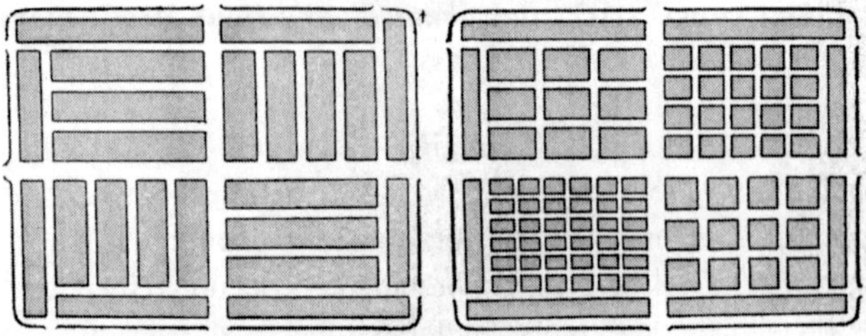

9.3: *Swastika* (solar wheel) and *prastara* (conch) mandalas as described in *Manasara shilpashastras.*

KINSHIP GROUPS

Kinship groups form territorial units in villages where large populations of a certain caste form a dominant group. Distinct subareas within caste wards are inhabited by lineages and are named after the lineage group. In the village Rampur in Punjab, studied by anthropologist Oscar Lewis, one main thoroughfare runs east-west through the village, and two or three others run in a roughly north-south direction. The houses of *jats,* the dominant caste, are clustered in the center of the village on either side of the east-west thoroughfare. The *jat* lineages and clans are grouped into units locally known as *thollas* and *panas.* The village is divided almost equally into two neighbourhoods (*panas*) known as *Dhan Singh* and *Harditt,* each of which is divided into two *thollas.*[10]

Ujariyon, a Muslim village in Uttar Pradesh, exhibited a similar pattern of patrilineage forming a spatial concentration in three neighbourhoods.[11] The village can be divided into groups of genealogical clusters traced to three brothers who are said to have founded the village about three hundred years ago. There is a strong orientation to the cardinal points in the villagers' conception of the settlement layout. In a map drawn by a villager, the layout is based upon axial roads that form a T. The main road reaches the middle of the village, called *beechgaon* (nucleus of the village), and then is bifurcated into north and south, thus dividing the village into three neighbourhoods in the east, west, and north.[12]

9.4: Aerial photograph of a nucleated village in Uttar Pradesh (Department of Landscape Architecture, University of Illinois at Urbana-Champaign collection).

In Sikh villages the thoroughfares lead to an open area where shops are clustered and/or where village meeting places are situated. Whatever actual form it may have taken over the years, Sikhs tend to think of the village as a settlement unit bifurcated in two directions by streets running north-south and east-west and thus in their minds divided into four equal sections. The meeting place becomes the center of the village at the intersection of the main streets. Conceptually Sikhs associate the four quarters with lineage clusters (*pattis*). Residents of these clusters are said to be descended from a common ancestor. Thus, the village's four lineage clusters are believed to have been established by four brothers, their descendants forming the population in each cluster.[13]

The fourfold division by biaxial streets in north Indian villages is evident when kinship groupings, rather than a caste, form a territorial unit. The renowned French structural anthropologist Claude Levi-Strauss considers a twofold division in physical and social space to be a diametric structure—an extension of cognitive duality.[14] I believe that these spatial layouts are manifestations of duality apparent in differential values attached to directions and center-periphery distribution.

CENTER-PERIPHERY DISTRIBUTION OF CASTES

The concept of ritual purity and pollution underlies the hierarchical order in the caste system. The ritual status of a caste group determines its position in the hierarchy, which is expressed in the center-periphery distribution of castes in the settlement pattern, whether linear, quadrangular, circular, or amorphous. The duality between center and periphery, reflective of the division between the ritually pure space of the Brahmins and the polluted space of the unclean and untouchable castes, is manifested clearly in village layouts. The locations of a ritually high caste group at or near the center of the settlement and of ritually lower or impure castes at the outskirts of the settlement can be seen in several villages. In eleven village communities in the Telangana region of Andhra Pradesh, the dwellings of the ritually unclean and untouchable castes are located on the settlement's periphery.[15] Such an arrangement precludes the possibility of refuse and water from the houses of the untouchable castes finding their way into the higher-caste houses and of members of the higher caste having to cross the neighbourhoods of the untouchable castes. This layout is based on the premise that space, as well as activities and people, has a ritually clean or polluting status. Movement through a polluted space can pollute the individual.

Jai Pal Singh and Mumtaz Khan's survey of four villages in northeastern Rajasthan shows that the dichotomous division of Hindu society between caste Hindus and ritually impure castes is reflected in the dual character of settlements. The dominant castes of *ahirs* in village Palawa, *jats* in Kathaiara Chauth, *gujars* in Didawali, and *meos* (who converted to Islam) in Samola occupy the main area of the settlement, which always is to the west of the area where the ritually impure castes reside. Among the ritually unclean castes, *chamars* (leather workers) and *bhangis* (sweepers) always live in the southern quarter. In this region, the social gradient of impure-pure castes is reflected along the east-west axis, at least in the original founding of the settlement.[16]

In the village Chanukhera in north-eastern Uttar Pradesh, the central location is not occupied by the caste with the highest ritual status (Brahmins) but by the dominant caste of the Rajputs, who are the local landlords. The six major caste streets slope downward to the north, south, east, and west from a central plateau on which stand the *havelis* (big houses) of the Rajputs. Adjacent to the Rajput street in the southward direction is the street of Brahmins. Adjoining its eastern flank is the street of cowherds (*ahirs*). To the north of the Rajput street is the street of merchants (*banias*), which in the northeast is adjacent to the street of blacksmiths (*lohars*), carpenters (*badhais*), and potters (*kumhars*); in the north by the street of Muslims; and to the far north-west by the streets of lower castes, such as washermen (*dhobis*) and leather workers (*chamars*). The contour of the settlement and proximity to the Rajput street marks the relative social standing of the residents.[17]

The gradation in the settlement area's ritual status in the village Kallapura in Karnataka can be understood in terms of ringlike ritual circles. The innermost circle is the temple of the village god and the progressively widening circles consist of the settlement area, threshing grounds, pastoral land, and agricultural fields. The population in Kallapura is divided into groups of original settlers and later immigrants, with the different clan groups forming nine caste divisions. The traditional agriculturists and the original settlers are the *gaudas*. The immigrants consist of relatives, agricultural labourers (*raituru*), and servants brought by the settlers and who were allowed to construct houses either on threshing grounds or in the fields. They have a lower social and religious status than the original settlers. The most sacred part of the village is the temple of the village god, and the land around it is demarcated from the rest of the village by four black stones. Lower-caste members and ritually impure objects are not allowed to enter this area. In the inner settlement area reside the village headman, the priest, and the families who are descendents of the original settlers. When the image of the village god is taken in procession, it is taken only through the inner settlement area, as are marriage processions. The area next to the inner settlement is occupied by later immigrants and other occupational groups. The area lying to the south of this outer settlement is inhabited exclusively by the untouchables.[18]

As in Kallapura, social divisions are obvious in their concentric spatial arrangement in Endavur, a Tamil village studied by anthropologist Michael Moffat.[19] The village consists of the main caste hamlet in which reside thirteen of the top castes in the local hierarchy. The untouchable hamlet (*koolini/cheri*) is located outside the village and consists of three of the five lowest local castes. Both the main caste hamlet and the untouchable hamlet are bounded by cactus hedges with two hundred yards of empty wasteland between them. The boundaries of the village are well-known and are marked by four stones.

Sometimes lower-caste groups are not located in the periphery, as in the village Potlod in Madhya Pradesh, where houses of different castes are distributed so that the village servants live in the middle of the village and are accessible to the entire community. The houses of Brahmin priests, blacksmith (*lohars*), potters (*kumhars*), tailors (*darji*), and barbers (*nai*) also are situated in the center of the village. Other castes, however, such as agricultural labourers (*balais*), cloth weavers (*bhambi*), leather workers (*chamars*), mat-weavers (*bagri*), and oil-pressers (*telis*), live in wards toward the settlement's periphery. The low-caste village sweeper (*bhangi*) lives in a hut away from the main village habitation.[20]

CASTE STREETS

Caste streets form the basic unit in villages in Tamil Nadu, Andhra Pradesh, and Orissa. Cleavages in the social structure of the rural community are represented in the caste streets. The Brahmin street (*agraharam*) is

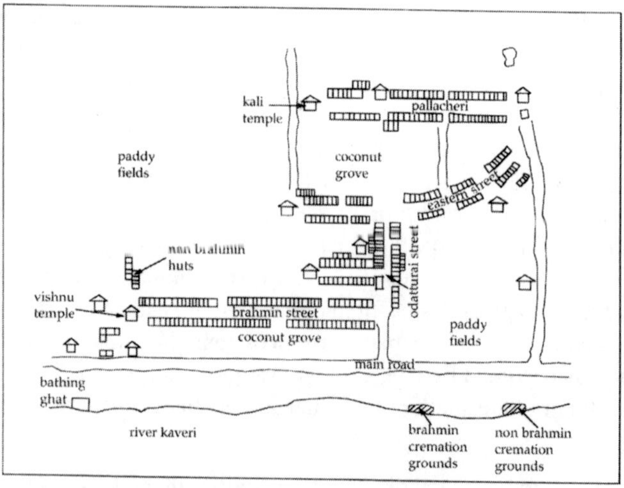

9.5: Caste neighbourhoods in Sripuram village in Tamil Nadu are laid along streets: the Brahmin street (*agraharam*), non-Brahmin street (*kudrana*), and untouchable street (*cheri*) (redrawn after Beteille 1965).

usually close to a temple of a major Hindu deity. The village Sripuram in the Tanjore district has three street neighbourhoods—the Brahmin street (*agraharam*), non-Brahmin street (*kudrana*), and untouchable (*adi-dravida*) street (*cheri*). The Brahmin street runs in an almost perfectly straight line from east to west, parallel to and near the metalled road in the village. The *adi-dravidas* are regarded as being outside Hindu society. They are permitted to reside only at the fringes of the village as entry into their space would pollute the Brahmins. There are six *adi-dravida* streets and, with only one exception, all are in the midst of paddy fields, emphasizing their social exclusion from the village. Between the Brahmin and the untouchable streets are other houses, arranged along a number of streets. Their population is larger and socially more diverse, consisting of a number of castes and subcastes.[21]

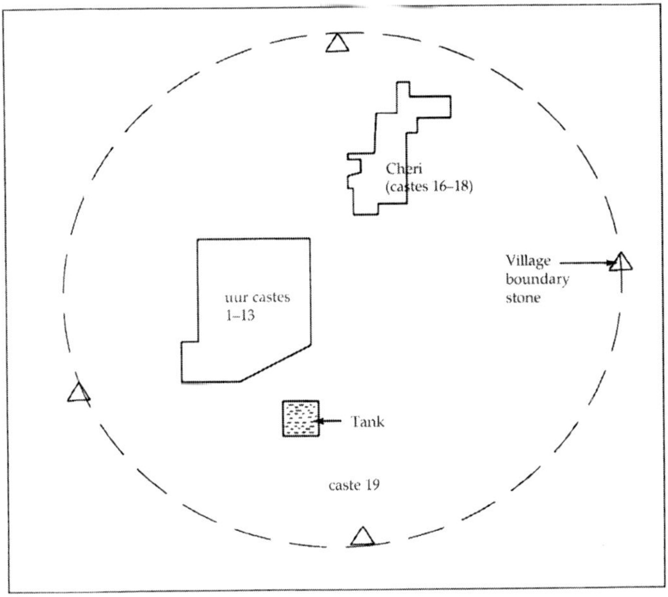

9.6: Endavur village in Tamil Nadu consists of the main hamlet of thirteen upper-caste communities and the untouchable hamlet (redrawn after Moffat 1979).

In village Kumbapettai in the Tanjore district studied by anthropologist Kathleen Gough, the *agraharam* in the northeast part of the village consists of two long rows of forty-six Brahmin houses and two temples of Vishnu and Shiva. To the south are two streets with twenty houses of cowherd (*konar*) caste. These streets also contain the village servant castes—barbers, washermen, carpenters, potters, and blacksmiths. On the eastern boundary of the village are two other non-Brahmin streets. Half a mile south across paddy fields lies an *adi-dravida* street of about eighty houses. They include *pallas* (labourers) and *paraiyas,* which is the lowest *adi-dravida* caste, whose traditional work is to remove and sell the carcasses of dead animals and to watch over the cremation grounds at night.[22]

In Devapuram in Andhra Pradesh, three spatial divisions are formed by the streets of the Brahmins (*agraharam*), agricultural labourers (*kaputuru*), and toddy-tappers (*kotturu*).[23] The *agraharam,* which is the oldest part of the village, runs parallel to the main street and faces the side entrance of Devapuram's main temple. Besides the Brahmins, the other occupants of the *agraharam* are artisan castes, such as the washermen, barber, and the potter, who perform temple services. The other two streets are populated by those with the lowest ritual status: agricultural tenants (*kapus*), later migrants, and toddy-tappers (*setti bajlis*).

TEMPLES, SHRINES AND THE BOUNDARY

Social division and territorial segregation among caste groups are accentuated by worship of different gods in temples and shrines. Temples housing the Hindu deities are maintained by a Brahmin priest and are situated close to the village center, but shrines containing village gods and other local deities are distributed throughout the settlement and are frequently located at the entrance to the village. In Sripuram, each of the village's dozen temples and shrines is used more or less exclusively by only one specific caste group in the village. The Vishnu temple, used only by the Brahmins, is situated at the western end of the Brahmin street. At the eastern end of the village is the shrine of a female deity guarding the boundaries of the village.[24] In Kumbapettai, the temples on the Brahmin street are almost exclusively used by the Brahmins although non-Brahmins (but not *adi-dravidas*) enter the outer court during festivals. The *adi-dravidas* worship their goddess in a shrine located on their street. The village shrines with crudely carved stone deities are located in the untouchable-caste sector of the village Potlod.[25] The village deity's shrine is on the banks of the stream on the southern edge of the settlement.

In Punjab, Muslim tombs and shrines and many holy places of both Sikhs and Hindus are located outside the dwelling space of the village and along its approaches, guarding the village against evil forces from beyond.[26] The village fence erected beyond the threshing grounds in the village Kallapura in Karnataka is left open only at the roads leading to neighbouring villages.

This outermost boundary is also marked by minor shrines at several places. It is a ritual, not a revenue, boundary, protecting the community from evil forces.[27]

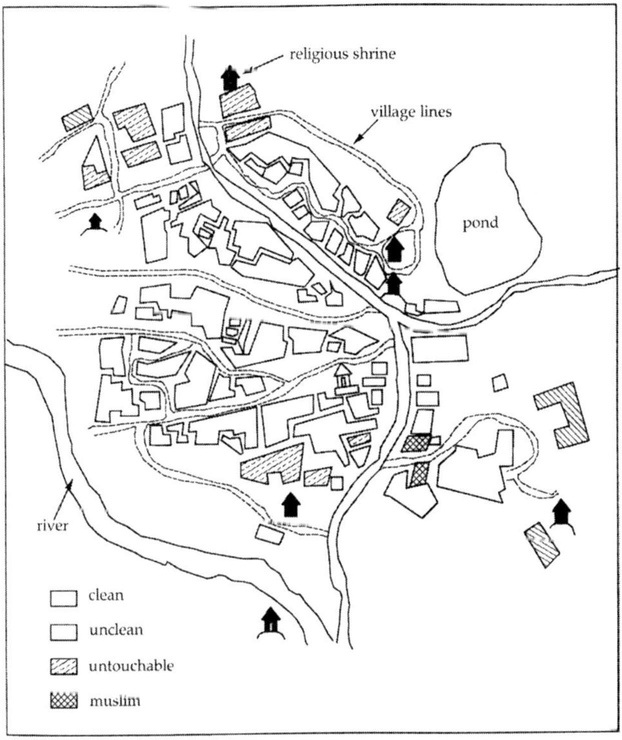

9.7. Potlod village in Madhya Pradesh has higher castes living in the center and lower castes toward the periphery (redrawn after Mathur 1964).

The significance of religious shrines at village entrances can be seen in the cognitive maps of villagers in Sri Lanka. When villagers in Kallapur in Sri Lanka were asked to draw a map of their home (*ur*), they began with the center of the village with its temple and crossroads and then marked the boundary of the village by shrines located at points where roads or the stream entered the village. These sentinel deities are located at vulnerable points in the frontier of the village, protecting it from harm from beyond. Shrines mark the conceptual boundaries of the village, emphasizing the village as a physical unit, a zone of habitation as opposed to cultivated land or forest beyond. Again this conceptual boundary does not coincide with the revenue boundary of the village.[28] Mircea Eliade's observation that a human settlement is conceived of as an island of sanctity in the midst of profane chaos is evident in these examples of ritual guarding of village frontiers.[29]

Potlod village in Madhya Pradesh has higher castes living in the center and lower castes toward the periphery (redrawn after Mathur 1964).

SPATIAL ORDER

Social divisions determined by caste structure govern every aspect of life—from occupation, rules of behaviour, observances of religious customs and taboos, to what one eats and where one lives in rural India. Residence in a particular location in turn defines relationships among castes, with social distance expressed in space. Founding a settlement is an act of not only delineating the order of the sacred from the chaos of the profane but also ascribing value within the demarcated territory. The scale of ritual purity that underlies caste structure is extended to space. The simple twofold duality of sacredness and profanity, analogous to purity and impurity, order and disorder, is differentiated into elaborate social categories and expressed in space.

As physical symbols of social hierarchy, the ritual status of caste neighbourhoods is derived from that assigned to its residents—from ritually pure to unclean. Although strict territorial segregation between caste neighbourhoods does not always exist, the mixing of castes in a neighbourhood is limited to those who are not separated greatly in the social hierarchy. In G.N.R. Mudiraj's study of eleven villages, in 69 percent of mixed-caste neighbourhoods, the caste groups were close in terms of ritual status.[30] There was not a single instance of members of castes at opposite ends of the hierarchy (for example, a Brahmin and an untouchable) living side by side. In 73 percent of the cases of mixed neighbourhoods, either a caste group was numerically too small to have its own distinct neighbourhood or was too large to be able to confine itself to one location.

In the center-periphery distribution of caste groups from the highest at the center to the lowest at the periphery, the gradation does not always follow the caste hierarchy. Certain lower artisan castes in the service of temples or village headman are found closer to the village nucleus even though their status may be lower than those of other agricultural castes residing farther away. Among the villages discussed, Potlod in Madhya Pradesh and Devapuram in Andhra Pradesh exhibit this pattern.

In the map of a village, its history can be read. When the village needs the service of certain castes, they are invited to settle down. A village can grow from a hamlet that has fissioned from its parent village. It may be a unicaste settlement consisting of a number of kin groups (with a few other castes providing support services) or it may consist of more than one caste, all of whom have demarcated distinct neighbourhoods for themselves.

Is caste the most meaningful unit in understanding the pattern of village settlement? That is not always the case; kinship or clan groupings may be a more useful basis for understanding settlement patterns, especially when a caste group is large and important enough to be a dominant force. Villages in northern India have neighbourhoods formed by exogamous clans, symmetrical along a major axis such as a street. Hierarchical arrangement (in the form of center-periphery distribution) of caste groupings also exists alongside these neighbourhoods.

A pertinent question to ask is whether caste neighbourhoods, with their own temples and shrines, ponds and wells, cremation grounds, and social territory out-of-bounds for some caste groups, introduce a divisive factor in the unity of the village. Untouchable hamlets situated outside the village are not recognised as an integral part of a village and there may even be confusion as to which village they belong. In southern India, the Brahmins count only the residents of their own street as members of the village. Economic interdependence between the castes, however, is not affected by their spatial segregation and there may be ritual events that bring the whole village together.

Caste neighbourhoods are duplicated in urban areas as well as seen in both traditional and colonial cities and metropolises of modern India. In Jaipur, residential districts divided by streets known as *rasta* or *marga* are also caste neighbourhoods. Higher castes live near the royal complex at the center, which is reflected by the preponderance of large *havelis* (mansions with courtyards) close to the palace.[31] In the core of older cities, caste guilds form homogenous, segregated neighbourhoods, such as *katra* and *mohalla* in northern India and *pol* in western India. Owen Lynch has identified as many as two hundred *mohallas* in Agra with names derived from the caste of their inhabitants.[32] The walled city of old Delhi has numerous *katras* (derived from the Sanskrit term *karvata,* meaning "market town") that are also caste neighbourhoods. *Pols* in Ahmedabad and other towns in Gujarat are homogeneous along caste lines with gateways and a hierarchical street network of spinal streets segmenting into cul-desacs.[33] These neighbourhoods reflect the rural settlement pattern of north Gujarat where families of the same caste and kin live in two rows of housing around a common space that is both a street and a yard. The walled neighbourhood is entered through a gateway known as *khadki.* The urban *pols* can contain more than one caste, but in the overall urban pattern the higher castes of traders and financiers reside in the central area while the periphery is occupied by the lowest caste of artisans.[34]

Caste neighbourhoods continue to play a significant role in the ecology of Indian cities, especially in their core areas. Because of acute housing shortages and the appeal of living close to extended family, or even because of general socioeconomic immobility, the population turnover is low. Residential distribution of caste groups in Poona over the last 150 years shows the distinctive patterns of segregation and centralisation of higher castes to have remained unchanged despite the city's growth.[35] A 1968 survey of Bangalore revealed that residential segregation is based on caste, with lower castes inhabiting the city outskirts.[36] A high degree of spatial separation existed between the Brahmins and the untouchables. This duplication of rural center-periphery distribution of castes in urban areas shows continuities in tradition and the meaninglessness of a strict rural-urban dichotomy.[37]

CONCLUSION

The key to understanding the spatial order of the village lies in its social order. A village layout is not a random agglomeration of houses. There is a logic in the distribution of neighbourhoods since the social structure is reified in space. This spatial reification adds to the social stability. The rural landscape bears the imprint of ideal settlements discussed in *vaastu shastras*. The village can be interpreted as a microcosmic replica of the ordered cosmos, a divine creation in which every caste is assigned its place in the social and spatial hierarchy.

The social structure of the village is expressed in different ways—in caste streets, amorphous clusters of houses, and symmetrical arrangements of kinship groups around axial streets. The caste gradation is expressed in physical terms, with the center occupied by higher castes, the fringes by lower castes, and outside the village by the untouchables, whose exclusion from Hindu society is physically expressed by their exclusion from the village. As the village boundaries are conceptual, so is the center. The temple to prominent Hindu deities marks the focal point of the village, which may not coincide with the geometric center. The role of directionality in the territorial distribution of caste and kinship groups is not always clear, but generally south and west are regarded as inauspicious locations and inhabited by lower and untouchable castes.

NOTES

1. In *Village, Caste, Gender, and Method: Essays in Indian Social Anthropology* (Delhi: Oxford University Press, 1996), 121.
2. Stella Kramrisch, *The Hindu Temple* (Calcutta: University of Calcutta, 1946).
3. Brenda Beck, "The Symbolic Merger of Body, Space, and Cosmos in Hindu Tamil Nadu," *Contributions to Indian Sociology* 10:2 (1976), 213–243.
4. Amita Ray, *Villages, Towns and Secular Buildings in Ancient India* (Calcutta: Firma K.L. Mukhopadhyay, 1964). Villages are also named after their inhabitants in the *Jatakas—kevatta gama* (fishermen's village), *kammara gama* (smiths' village), *vaddhaki gama* (carpenters' village), *nalakara gama* (basket-makers' village), *kheta* (village of *sudras*), and *agraharam* (Brahmins' village). Villages are classified by their size and location as well. For example, *gamaka* is a small village; *nigama gama* is a village that has grown into a town; *dvara gama* is a village formed at the edge of a city; *pachchanta gama* is a frontier or border village located away from the settlement. See Binoy Ghosh, *Primitive Indian Architecture* (Calcutta: Firma K.L. Mukhopadhyay, 1953).
5. P. K. Acharya, *Indian Architecture According to Manasara-Silpasastra* (London: Oxford University Press, 1928).
6. See Ram Raz, *Essay on the Architecture of the Hindus* (Varanasi: Indological Book House, 1972); Binode Bihari Dutt, *Town Planning in Ancient India* (Calcutta: Thacker, Spink, 1925).
7. Bruno Dagens (ed.), *Mayamatam—Treatise of Housing, Architecture and Iconography* (Delhi: Motilal Banarsidass Publishers, 1994); Dutt, *Town Planning in Ancient India.*
8. Another way to categorize settlements is by location, function, and inhabitants. *Pura, nagara, nagari,* and *rajadhani* refer to cities, bigger in size than other settlements. This typology is drawn from Kautilya's *Arthashastra* dating back to the fourth century BCE. It contains a clearly formulated hierarchical system of the organisation of a kingdom. The smallest unit is the village; a group of ten villages is governed by the *sangrahana*; two hundred villages are governed by the district headquarters called the *karvatika*; four hundred villages, by a *dronamukha,* or divisional headquarters; and eight hundred villages, by *sthaniya,* or provincial headquarters. See L. N. Rangarajan (ed.), *Kautilya—The Arthashastra* (New Delhi: Penguin Books, 1992).
9. Social anthropologist David Mandelbaum has identified three main types of settlements: nucleated, linear, and scattered isolated hamlets or clusters of houses. See David Mandelbaum, *Society in India* (Berkeley: University of California Press, 1970). The nucleated village may consist of an agglomerate of shapeless clusters with winding streets, defining the assemblage of discrete clusters, or the village may be a square or rectangular cluster with straight streets running parallel and at right angles to each other. A linear village consists of straight streets between parallel rows of houses along transport routes or bodies of water. A linear cluster may grow into a rectangular or square village as streets are added at right angles to the old streets. The scattered type of village has isolated clusters of houses strung out with no definite boundary indicating the limits of

any one village. Geographers have identified these village types with different regions in India. The nucleated village is found in the fertile Gangetic plain (Uttar Pradesh and Bihar), Malwa plateau, river valleys in Tamil Nadu, and portions of Maharashtra. The linear types of villages are found in the coastal districts of Orissa, Andhra Pradesh, Gujarat, Kerala, Konkan, and in the Bengal delta. The scattered homesteads are found in hill areas, as in the Himalayan foothills, highlands of Gujarat, the Satpura range in Maharashtra, the Vindhya hills, and where there are numerous water sources, such as Kerala. The ecological zones of fertile plains, coastal districts, and mountainous regions not only have distinct settlement patterns, but also have a profound effect on the structure of social relations in the community. In all three forms of settlements— nucleated, linear, and isolated clusters—caste or kin group is the defining factor in the internal composition of the village or the hamlet.

10. The Brahmins in the northern end of the village, the leather workers (*chamars*) and potters (*kumhars*) live in the northeastern section, sweepers (*bhangis*) form a block in the southwestern end, and the washermen (*dhobis*) are in the southern part. See Oscar Lewis, *Village Life in Northern India* (New York: Vintage Books, 1965).

11. Marion Smith, "Social Structure in the Punjab," in *India's Villages,* ed. M. N. Srinivas (Bombay: Asia Publishing House, 1960), 161–179.

12. The caste system is still practiced among Muslims in India as a result of continuing social practices of converted Hindus. It has, of course, no religious or ideological basis in Islam. The four *Ashraf* castes—*Sayyads, Sheikhs, Mughals,* and *Pathans*—claim higher status than non-*Ashraf* castes on the basis of foreign descent. They are distinguished by their claimed relationship to the Prophet or other religious figures, and are similar in status to the higher Hindu castes. They do not follow any specific occupations and are landowners claiming ritual supremacy over the service castes. The non-*Ashraf* castes are allegedly Hindu converts and their hierarchy is based on their occupations. They include weavers, washermen, barbers, and butchers. Their occupations endow them with impure status similar to that of lower Hindu castes.

13. There is also a cluster of houses in the south belonging to outsiders who have married into the village and settled there. Significantly, there was no settlement originally in the south, which in the Hindu tradition is an inauspicious direction associated with *Yama,* the god of death. The village graveyard is located in the south and is the site of the battle with the Hindu king in which the clan of the founders of the village was destroyed. See Amita Sinha, "Environmental and Social Change in the Home and Neighbourhood in Northern India" (unpublished Ph.D. dissertation, University of California, Berkeley, 1989).

14. Claude Levi-Strauss, *Structural Anthropology* (New York: Basic Books, 1963). He discusses Bororo village in South America, which is divided into two moieties by an east-west axis dividing the eight village clans into two groups of four exogamous units. This axis is crosscut by another, perpendicular to the first and running north-south. The north-south axis splits up the eight clans into other groups of four called "upper" and "lower" or, when a village is located on a watercourse, "upstream" and "downstream."

15. G.N.R. Mudiraj, "Spatial Differentiation of Castes: Analysis of a Regional Pattern," *Man in India* 53:1 (January–March 1973), 24–37.
16. Jai Pal Singh and Mumtaz Khan, "Hindu Cosmology and the Orientation and Segregation of Social Groups in Villages in Northwestern India," in *Mythical Space, Cosmology, and Landscape: Towards a Cultural Geography of India* (New Delhi: Manak Publications, 2002), 86–120.
17. Yogendra Singh, "Chanukhera: Cultural Change in Eastern Uttar Pradesh," in *Change and Continuity in India's Villages*, ed. Karigondar Ishwaran (New York: Columbia University Press, 1970).
18. Gurumurthy Gowdra, "Ritual Circles in a Mysore Village," *Sociological Bulletin* 20:1 (March 1971), 24–38.
19. Michael Moffat, *An Untouchable Community in South India* (Princeton, NJ: Princeton University Press, 1979).
20. K. S. Mathur, *Caste and Ritual in a Malwa Village* (New Delhi: Asia Publishing House, 1964).
21. Andre Beteille, *Caste, Class and Power* (Berkeley: University of California Press, 1965).
22. Kathleen Gough, "The Social Structure of a Tanjore Village," in *India's Villages*, ed. M. N. Srinivas (Bombay: Asia Publishing House, 1960), 90–102.
23. Y. S. Subramanyam, *Social Change in Village India: An Andhra Case Study* (New Delhi: Prithvi Raj Publishers, 1975).
24. Beteille, *Caste, Class and Power.*
25. Gough, "The Social Structure of a Tanjore Village."
26. Smith, "Social Structure in the Punjab."
27. Gowdra, "Ritual Circles in a Mysore Village."
28. Valentine E. Daniel, *Fluid Signs—Being a Person the Tamil Way* (Berkeley: University of California Press, 1984).
29. Mircea Eliade, *Cosmos and History: The Myth of the Eternal Return* (New York: Harper Torchbooks, 1959).
30. Mudiraj, "Spatial Differentiation of Castes."
31. Shuji Funo, Naohiko Yamamoto, and Mohan Pant, "Space Formation of Jaipur City, Rajasthan, India: An Analysis on City Maps (1925–28) Made by Survey of India," *Journal of Asian Architecture and Building Engineering* 1:1 (March 2002), 261–269.
32. Owen Lynch, "Rural Cities in India: Continuities and Discontinuities," in *India and Ceylon: Unity and Diversity*, ed. Philip Mason (London: Oxford University Press, 1967), 142– 157.
33. Harish Doshi, *Traditional Neighborhood in a Modern City* (New Delhi: Abhinav Publications, 1974).
34. V. S. Pramar, *Haveli: Wooden Houses and Mansions of Gujarat* (Ahmedabad: Mapin Publishing, 1989).
35. Surinder K. Mehta, "Patterns of Residence in Poona, India, by Caste and Religion: 1822–1965," *Demography* 6:4 (November 1969), 473–491.

36. Noel Gist, "The Ecology of Bangalore, India: An East-West Comparison," in *Urbanism in World Perspective,* ed. Sylvia Fava (New York: Thomas Y. Crowell, 1968), 177–188.
37. Caste quarters are found in newer areas of Bangalore, Bombay, and Calcutta, attesting to the group and caste-oriented migration patterns. The large-scale rural-to-urban migration to cities such as Bombay and Calcutta has resulted in the formation of neighbourhoods in which caste along with language has played a decisive role. Caste, kinship, and place of origin are the most important factors in the migrant's choice of a residential area in Bombay. See William Rowe, "Caste, Kinship, and Association in Urban India," in *Urban Anthropology: Cross Cultural Studies of Urbanisation,* ed. Aidan Southall (New York: Oxford University Press, 1973), 211–247. Caste associations, which are responsible for things such as cooperative housing, help in extending the rural caste ecology into the city and represent an adaptation of the traditional social structure to the requirements of urban life.

Chapter Ten

The Void as Center: Courtyard Dwellings

> "The house is indeed a mirror of the self if we can learn to interpret what we see, comprehend what it means, and act on what it seeks to communicate."
>
> —**Clare Cooper Marcus**,
> *House as a Mirror of Self: Exploring the Deeper Meaning of Home*[1]

The enclosure of open space within a built structure is a common form found in courtyard dwellings in many parts of the world, including the Near East, the Mediterranean, South Asia, and China. In widely different cultures and varying climatic zones, it belies any deterministic theories on spatial organisation. Although it satisfies sociopsychological needs of privacy and security and is climatically suitable in hot, dry regions, its meaning in Indian society goes beyond surface functionality.

The symbolic meaning of home as a symbol of self is projected from a deep layer of the psyche. Deeply held psychological patterns of meanings can only be understood by the conscious mind in the form of symbols. The archetype "self" is associated with a common pattern of psychological meanings, which acquire specificity within a particular cultural context. Thus, the self archetype, part of every human psyche, finds particular expression in each given culture. Its constancy should not be confused with rigidity, since one of its symbols—the home—evolves as it is created, adapted, and destroyed or abandoned.

Archetypal symbols or spatial archetypes are not static entities, and for their dynamic character to be understood, a process-centered approach is necessary. The process of evolution may be broadly classified into differentiation and segmentation. Differentiation enables places to become associated in use and connotative meanings with increasing specificity. Segmentation allows for reproduction of places (to use a biological metaphor) to occur through fission.

The courtyard, with its arrangement of units around a central open space, is a spatial archetype marked by strong centrality with its inward focus creating a strong edge condition. The integration of outdoor space in a building describes a dialectical relationship between architecture and landscape. Open space is contained within a building set within a context of streets and other open spaces. The courtyard boundaries mark the beginnings of a place by demarcating it from the continuum of space, whether in a religious structure or an ordinary dwelling. The evolution of the place continues with the differentiation of the building structure into areas associated with different functions. Further segmentation of spaces with similar functions occurs in parallel with household needs.

GENESIS OF THE COURTYARD PLAN

An open enclosed area within the dwelling is found in almost all parts of the Indian subcontinent with the exception of the northern hilly areas. The wide prevalence of this form implies that cultural tradition, rather than environmental forces, availability of certain building materials, or building technology, is the primary determinant dictating building form. Sanskrit treatises on architecture—*shilpashastras*—mention *chatushala* (an open quadrangle surrounded on all four sides by rooms; *chatu* means "four" and *shala* is a structure with a longitudinal span) as an ideal form for a building.[2] The social stratification in Hindu society was reflected in the houses prescribed for each caste—Brahmins, *kshatriyas*, *Vaishyas*, and *shudras* occupying *chatushalas, trishalas* (*tri,* three), *dvishalas* (*dvi,* two), and *ekashalas* (*eka,* one), respectively.[3]

As discussed in the *shilpashastras,* the inner court of the building is called *antarmandala*. Pillared roofed structures (*mandapas*) and verandahs (*alinda*) are other characteristic features found in both temples and secular buildings to this day. The open quadrangle is seen in the Buddhist monasteries (*viharas*), which consist of a row of cells around a courtyard, and in series of concentric enclosures in the Hindu temple complexes in south India.

Vaastu purusha mandala, a microcosmic version of the universe, underlies these building types. The square form with its network of lines of forces running north-south and east-west contains a void in the center, symbolizing not emptiness but concentrated energy. The *vaastu purusha mandala* is divided into a square grid, each quarter designating the place of a god, with the central square (*brahma-sthana*) left empty. In a temple plan based on *vaastu purusha mandala,* the center is considered a void within the shrine (*garbha-griha*) in which the deity is placed.[4]

In a house, the sacred basil plant (*tulsi*) is found in the courtyard. At the level of body-house-cosmos analogy, the void at the center represents the cave in the heart in which the soul or *atman* resides. Thus, the void is not synonymous with emptiness or devoid of energy, but filled with it. The *purusha* or the primeval male, an anthropo-morphic symbol of site, lies with his head facing the north-east and his feet south-west in the mandala. The areas of the square grid in these directions acquire varying degrees of sanctity and, therefore, are associated with different aspects of daily life.

HOUSE FORM AND SETTLEMENT PATTERN

The traditional Indian house is essentially a courtyard dwelling. It can be traced back in time to the Indus Valley civilisation that thrived in the third millennium BCE. The excavated city of Mohen-jo-daro (now in Pakistan) had houses with one or more courtyards within a gridiron urban layout. In traditional Indian villages, courtyards appear in all guises but the underlying unity of form is apparent. The village layouts can be compact or dispersed, depending upon the distances between individual houses or their cluster. The cluster itself could be amorphous, nucleated, or linear, depending upon the region in which it is found. This regional location, together with the household's economic standing, influences the courtyard's size and

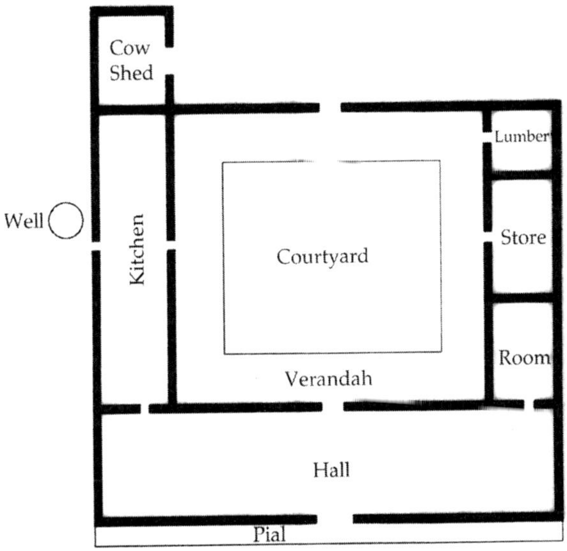

10.1: The traditional house in Tamil Nadu has a courtyard in the center surrounded by a verandah (*kudam*) behind which are rooms.

location within the dwelling. In more defensive clusters, the private and secure courtyard forms the largest expanse of open space with correspondingly smaller public outdoor spaces.

In Kerala, where the water table is high, eliminating the need to cluster around the available water sources, dispersed households are the norm. A *Namboodri illam* or a *Nayar taravad* is a self-sufficient structure that contains living quarters, a bathing tank, cremation spot, and snake grove. The house itself is based upon a *Nalupura* plan with wings around the four sides of a courtyard, deriving their names from the directions in which they are located around the central space.[5]

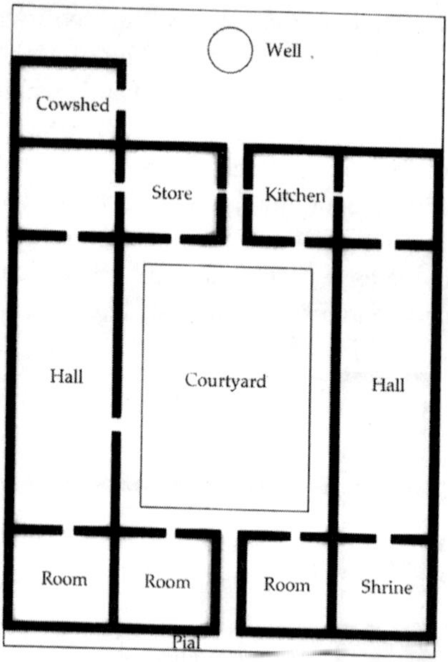

10.2: Traditional courtyard house in Andhra Pradesh.

In neighbouring Tamil Nadu, where the houses are oblong-shaped and arranged in a linear cluster, courtyards are smaller but the houses have open verandahs (*kudams*) around them. Sky wells in the courtyard allow rainwater to be collected in troughs. The courtyard house in Andhra Pradesh is called *manduva illu* (four-roomed house) and is built by the well-to-do.[6] Coastal regions of Andhra Pradesh and the southern part of Orissa with their linear fishing villages also present a variation of courtyard arrangement, with the open space located behind the living quarters and the street forming a community space. In a linear settlement pattern such as this, the size of the courtyard shrinks as the street becomes a shared community courtyard.

The villages in the eastern region of India have huts surrounding an enclosure containing a cattle shed and a bathing tank (*pukur*). Initially two huts might be placed parallel to and facing each other to organize the space rectangularly, later reinforced with the addition of two more huts to complete an inner rectangle. The farmstead in West Bengal is always an assemblage of several huts organised in this manner and in Assam has a bamboo fence surrounding it to further accentuate the pattern.[7]

In most of northern India, villages are compact and nucleated with narrow, winding bylanes fronted by blank walls behind which lie spacious courtyards. The ideal house in a Haryana village is a *chowk-band ghar* (house with a central court), granting its owner considerable social status. A rectangular dwelling, the *chowk-band ghar* is a six-bay-deep structure with the third bay consisting of an open court (*chowk*) surrounded by verandahs (*dalanis*) on all sides.

In the north Gujarat house, the *chowk* separates the outer room (*khadki*) from the living rooms (*ordo* and *parsal*) at the back. The *chowk* is adjacent to rooms for kitchen and water storage and is also edged by a verandah.[8] In the desert region of Rajasthan, houses are built close together, sharing walls and creating a cellular structure in which the courtyards break up the mass.

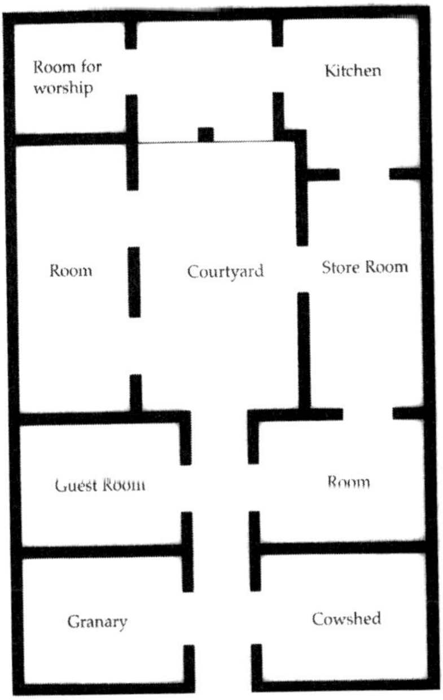

10.3: Traditional courtyard house in Orissa.

The compact structure reduces exposure to the excessive solar radiation while the open space within the built structure allows movement of air for a cooling effect.[9]

No sharp distinction exists between traditional rural and urban houses. They share the same pattern of internalised open space, creating involuted garden cities. In Old Delhi, 25 percent of open space is devoted to private courtyards, but only 10 to 15 percent is given over to public streets.[10] The urban morphology consists of neighbourhood clusters based upon caste or place of origin. These clusters have a defensive layout and may be walled, as in the *katras* of Lucknow or *pols* of Ahmedabad. The street hierarchy ranges from wide-open commercial areas to narrow, shaded, residential cul-de-sacs within a cluster. The courtyard thus forms a segment of the continuum of open spaces ranging from public to private. Interestingly *chowk* is applied to open spaces within the street network and is used for the courtyard, suggesting that square open space is a prototypical ideal form within and between buildings, in residential and urban design.

DIFFERENTIATION AND SEGMENTATION

The dwelling evolves from the courtyard, which remains the focal point of the house. In northern India, the first step in building a residence is to enclose the land with a boundary. Thus, a courtyard is born and, usually rectangular in shape, its size and form change as the house grows and the building is constructed from the outside in. The building tradition is additive and open-ended. The form and construction techniques allow changes (both divisions and increments) to be made easily.

Cardinal directions play an important role in differentiating place once it is demarcated by means of a ritual or physical boundary from the continuum of space. The archetypal mandala underlying the built form represents the elements (fire, earth, wind, and water) and forces (sun, rain, life, and death) of the cosmos. East is a favourable direction because of its association with the rising sun. South and west are believed to be directions of malign forces. The human body, dwelling, and settlement should be correctly oriented within this cosmic square for the sake of health and well-being.[11] Thus, an entrance should be on the east side of a dwelling because entrances are vulnerable points, but the east is associated with benevolent forces.

The economic standing of the household is another factor that allows differentiation and rooms for specialised functions to be built. In rural areas, separating livestock from human areas is the first step. Living areas are then differentiated into sleeping and storage spaces, a kitchen, and a shrine for the household god. In Madhya Pradesh, even the nomenclature of dwelling types clearly indicates the dwelling's size and, therefore, economic standing of the owner. The house of the wealthy landowners, known as *kelu,* has separate rooms for men and women, a granary, storeroom, kitchen and outbuilding for cattle. The *ora* is the average-sized house of the cultivator and has only two rooms—one for cooking and eating and the other for storage, sleeping, and the household god. The house of poor menials is known as *tapra* and consists of a single room, which serves as a combined kitchen, storeroom, bedroom, and cowshed.[12]

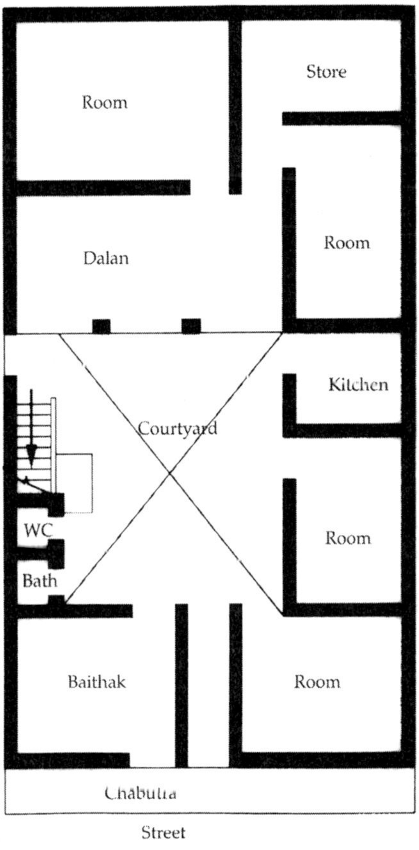

10.4. Traditional courtyard house in Uttar Pradesh with chabutra fronting the street.

Similarly, in southern Gujarat the individual houses of the Koli community are large spaces housing the family and cattle. The cattle are kept in the center, the front is used by male family members to do their work and receive visitors, and the back is used for cooking and activities requiring privacy. With prosperity and enhanced social status, the large space is sub-divided by internal partitions, the cattle are removed to an Traditional courtyard house in Uttar Pradesh with *chabutra* fronting the street. outbuilding, the front of the house has a verandah, and the loft becomes a second story. In urban areas, this evolvement also included the addition of more rooms and a verandah in the front along with a backyard for cooking, bathing, and washing.[13]

In Uttar Pradesh, as the family grows in number, rooms are added on all four sides of the courtyard. The courtyard's open space and the living rooms are mediated by a semi-open verandah, which is roofed but has no walls. Ideally the rooms surrounding the courtyard should be fronted by the verandah, which later may be enclosed to form another room, if necessary. Similarly, fission in the household structure (that is, the breakup of the extended family into several nuclear families) results in the courtyard being divided by a wall. In Uttar Pradesh, courtyards may be shared by two or more households that have separate living rooms and cooking hearths. The courtyard dwelling form allows this segmentation of spaces to occur easily.

There is further differentiation of space in the form of segregation between male and female areas, which are more sharply demarcated in northern India than in the rest of the country. In the *jat* villages of Haryana, the segregation takes an extreme form as men's quarters (*baithak*) are built on a separate plot of land (usually on the outskirts of the village) away from the main house (*ghar*) where the women of the family live.[14]

In Rajasthan, the *havelis* (mansions) in urban areas contain separate courtyards, an outer and an inner one, for male and female members of the household, respectively. The word *haveli,* which is of Persian origin and means "enclosed space," came to denote a residential block three to five stories high and situated around an open court in medieval towns. A *haveli* would accommodate several families, the high-density occupation balanced by an open court with a well, a space for washing and drying clothes and socialising, and a play space for children. An expansion of this form is the *char-chowk haveli,* which is a mansion with four courtyards arranged symmetrically around two axes, much like an urban settlement.[15]

COURTYARD AS CENTER AND AXIS

Space is invested with the sacred or polluting character of the activities associated with it. For example, the kitchen is considered a pure area because food is cooked and consumed there. In contrast, defecation is a polluting activity to be followed by a cleansing wash. In Uttar Pradesh's rural housing, the activities of preparing food and cooking spill out into the courtyard, because the kitchen itself may be quite small. The place for defecation is little more than a roofless, walled structure with a hole in the ground and connected to a septic pit. These areas are separated by the courtyard, which serves as a pollution-purity axis.[16]

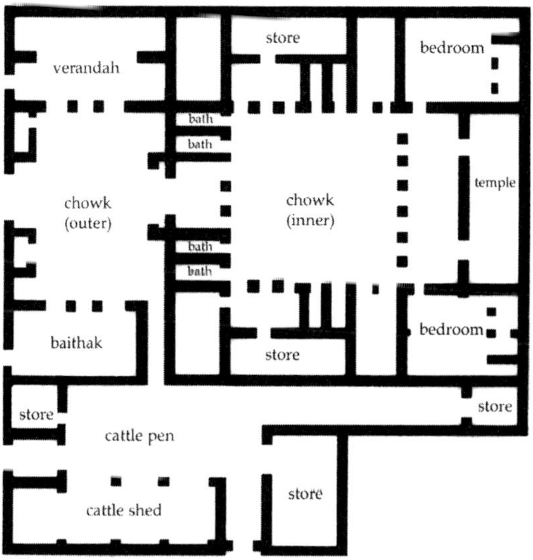

10.5: A *haveli* (mansion) in Rajasthan has more than one courtyard, with the more private one in the interior (redrawn after Wacziarg and Nath 1982).

Because of the arrangement of rooms around it, the courtyard becomes the locus of all circulation within the house. It is a place with a high degree of visibility. Most daily household activities, including washing, drying, and gossiping, take place in the privacy of the courtyard. It is very much a woman's domain, with the men seldom intruding into it. Not only do spontaneous gatherings occur at any time of day, but the extended family also gathers in the courtyard on ceremonial occasions to celebrate rites of passage. It is the site of *mandapa* where weddings take place around the *havan kunda* (sacred fire pit). The courtyard thus serves as a family and communal hearth on important occasions, acting as a symbol of unity in partitioned families.

As an internal open space that is a physical and ceremonial center, the courtyard is usually connected to the public outdoors through a narrow chamber, symbolising a dark, narrow passage to the center. This entry also allows for direct access to the courtyard from the outside and is flanked by rooms used primarily by male family members and guests. The entry threshold is always marked by a bench, verandah, or low sitting platform—*pial* in Tamil Nadu, *jagali* in Karnataka, *otlo* in Gujarat, *osari* in Maharashtra, *modh* in Rajasthan, and *chabutra* in Uttar Pradesh. Men use this space to interact with the public. This area serves as a site for threshold rituals and is often decorated with carved brackets, balustrades and pillars, niches for lamps, colourful patterns on walls and floor, and sometimes a Ganesha (elephant-headed god) icon for protection from evil forces.

EVOLUTION

Courtyard housing in India derives meaning from an approach emphasizing the role of center and boundary in the making of place and the evolving processes of differentiation and segmentation. In the context of Indian vernacular dwellings, the origin of their form can be traced back to traditional texts. The house evolves by marking a boundary on the land and then adding structures that enclose an open quadrangle. The spatial configuration allows this kind of evolution to take place. Other configurations (such as corridor-axial or grid) have their own patterns of evolving.

Religious and social associations play a role in differentiation of space. Symbolizing cosmic forces, cardinal directions determine locations for entrances, the household shrine, and areas where polluting activities are performed. The structure of the family, including relationships between men and women, elders and young, segregate areas within the house. For the residential structure to be congruent with the family's life cycle, change in the form of segmentation must occur. As the extended family fissions into smaller units, courtyards are divided or, if space allows, contiguous courtyards are built.[17]

The relationships between dwellings vary depending upon the settlement layout in different regions, but the essential idea—the center as a void—remains constant. The functional purposes of courtyard housing—privacy and security—are intertwined with metaphysical connotations of the void. In a religious structure, such as the Hindu temple, the center-void is the seat of divine essence; in a residential structure, the religious symbolism is vestigial and social uses are dominant.

The use of courtyard forms in vernacular dwellings and religious architecture is widespread on the Indian subcontinent. But why does this particular form symbolize this region's cultural tradition? Its presence in other parts of the world, including China and the Middle East, suggests that it is a universal archetypal symbol that found expression in the pre-industrial, patriarchal societies. In India, the philosophical tradition of Hinduism forms a religious sub-stratum over which the social structure rests, the courtyard being an appropriate symbol for the entire edifice. Spatial introversion becomes a symbol of social introversion. The more rigid the codes banning women from public life, the more difficult it is to gain access to the interior courtyards and the greater is their enclosure.

NOTES

1. (Berkeley: Conari Press, 1995), 17.
2. P. K. Acharya, *Indian Architecture According to Manasara-Silpasastra* (London: Oxford University Press, 1928).
3. Binod Behari Dutt, *Town Planning in Ancient India* (New Delhi: New Asian Publishers, 1977).
4. Building rituals reenact the myth of cosmogony, reinforcing the conception of building as microcosm. The foundation ceremonies for houses involve pegging down a golden snake to stabilize the site in a hole. In Hindu mythology, snakes are supporters of the terrestrial world and are depicted as such in religious iconography. The foundation stone above the snake has an eight-petaled lotus carved on it, again symbolizing the primeval waters on which the earth floats like a lotus leaf. See Ismet Khambatta, "The Meaning of Residence in Traditional Indian Society," in *Dwellings, Settlements and Tradition,* ed. Jean-Paul Bourdier and Nezar AlSayyad (New York: University Press of America, 1989).
5. Joan Mencher, "Kerala and Madras: A Comparative Study of Ecology and Social Structure," *Ethnology* 5:2 (1966), 135–171.
6. K. M. Subrahmanyam, "Four Main House Types in South India," *Journal of Madras Geographical Association* 13:2 (1938), 168–175.
7. Ashok Mitra, "Rural House Types and Village Settlement Patterns," in *India: Cultural Patterns and Processes,* ed. Allen Noble and Ashok Dutt (Boulder, CO. Westview Press, 1982), 105–124.
8. Interestingly, the *chowk* appears in urban areas in northern Gujarat. It is added to separate inner and outer areas of the house, which were built to accommodate functions related to trade and manufacture. In rural settlements, the house is a simple tripartite structure: two rooms fronted by a verandah. The open space of the *khadki*—that is, the cluster of houses inhabited by related families—is used by children and men daily and by the families for marriages and religious festivals occasionally. *See* V. S. Pramar, "The North Gujarat House," in *Havelt: Wooden Houses and Mansions of Gujarat* (Ahmedabad: Mapin Publishing, 1989), 59–121.
9. Kulbhushan Jain, "Jaisalmer: Architecture of a Desert Town," in *Stones in the Sand: The Architecture of Rajasthan,* ed. Giles Tillotson; *Marg* 52:4 (June 2001), 90–101.
10. Rory Fonseca, "The Walled City of Old Delhi," *Landscape* 18:3 (Fall 1969), 213–243.
11. Brenda Beck, "The Symbolic Merger of Body, Space, and Cosmos in Hindu Tamil Nadu," *Contributions to Indian Sociology* 10:2 (1976), 213–243.

12. K. S. Mathur, *Caste and Ritual in a Malwa Village* (New Delhi: Asia Publishing House, 1964).
13. See the chapter "Sociology and Planning of the South Gujarat House," in Pramar, *Haveli: Wooden Houses and Mansions of Gujarat,* 139–151.
14. A. B. Mukerji, "Jats—A Study in Human Geography," *Geographical Review of India* 16:2 (1984), 12–31.
15. Francis Wacziarg and Aman Nath, *Rajasthan—The Painted Walls of Shekhavati* (New Delhi: Vikas Publishing House, 1982).
16. Amita Sinha, "Participant Observation: A Study of State-Aided Self-Help Housing in Lucknow, India," in *Housing the Poor in the Developing World: Methods of Analysis, Case Studies and Policy,* ed. A. Graham Tipple and Kenneth Willis (London: Routledge, 1991), 16–34.
17. The courtyard form is remarkably resilient in the face of social, political, and economic changes in society, as Jyoti Hosagrahar's study of *havelis* in nineteenth-century Delhi reveals. After the failure of the 1857 mutiny, when the landed aristocracy on the side of the Mughal emperor lost their land and means of livelihood, their neighbourhood-like *havelis* were fragmented into smaller houses and tenements. Toward the end of the nineteenth century, the new merchant class built much smaller *havelis* with a single central courtyard using new materials and technology. See Hosagrahar, "Mansions to Margins: Modernity and the Domestic Landscapes of Historic Delhi, 1847–1910," *Journal of Society of Architectural Historians* 60:1 (March 2001), 26–45.

PART FOUR

ARCHETYPES AND DESIGN

> "The recurring motifs offer a rich and satisfying treasure of new/old forms to draw upon in design, but they are more than a mere stylistic repository. Because they originate in our deep past, dating to thousandsofyearsago,these forms activate a deeply buried archetypal stratum in our psyches, a powerful, potentiating inner Buried Treasure waiting to be discovered to enrich our understandingandpractice of architecture."
>
> **—Mimi Lobell,**
> "The Buried Treasure: Women's Ancient Architectural Heritage"[1]

A comprehensive narrative of landscapes of India is temporally and spatially beyond the scope of this book. What I have attempted in these pages is to interpret the meanings of significant landscape patterns and trace them to a common pattern of symbols. The first two chapters discussed views of nature and the framework for interpretation of cultural landscapes. The second part of the book explored natural archetypes and their built versions in the context of epic narratives of Hinduism and legends of the Buddha's life. In these stories, myriad meanings are attached to trees, water, and hills, including meanings related to origin, creation, *axis mundi, shakti,* purification, and regeneration. Natural archetypes, individually and together, have contributed to the creation of sacred landscapes in pilgrim centers associated with Rama, Krishna, Devi, and the Buddha. These landscapes have supported more than one myth through time; indeed, royal patronage in medieval India supplanted Shiva worship with the Rama cult at many pilgrim sites. Meanings too have shifted as we saw the tree of life transformed into the tree of wisdom with prehistoric goddess worship giving way to newer gods and goddesses.

The third part of the book focused on landscapes constituted by cities, villages, and their housing—largely secular realms of everyday life. I believe that the genesis of their forms lies in the mandala—the spatial archetype of four quarters and its symbols represented by courtyards, a cross within a square, and grid patterns. In all parts of India these basic forms are found time and again at various scales of habitation. They acquire specificity in their regional expressions: villages can be nucleated or amorphous, courtyards can be at the center of the dwelling or at the back, cities may have only a few *chowks* and show a gridded layout in some neighbourhoods. There are many other factors that finally shape an urban or rural landscape—climate, topography, building materials, available technology, and even habitual patterns of daily life. The idealised form of archetypal symbols is therefore considerably modified by site exigencies.

The persistence and widespread presence of archetypal symbols in the traditional Indian landscape are an extraordinary phenomenon meriting close attention. These symbolic landscapes have a strong hold upon the hearts and minds of millions, drawing them as pilgrims from near and far. They are highly valued as spiritual destinations and are examples of place attachment that develops not simply from years of domicile or a lifetime of memories, but from resonance with archetypal thought structures. The natural landscape of the Indian sub-continent impressed its scale and magnificence upon its human inhabitants over eons. Its spectacular sites, probably the earliest cult spots of mother-goddess worship, were later incorporated into Indo-Aryan mythology. Myths of cosmogony, sagas of epic heroes and their struggle against nature's demonic forces, and revelations of divinity to sages endowed the associated landscapes with immanence and the possibility of transcendence.

Landscape representations in oral legends, verbal texts, and iconography are based upon the seemingly universal duality of wilderness and pastoral settings. *Lila,* the play about the great drama between good and evil, was understood as a nature allegory. Gods and demons, celestial beings and those of the underworld, were at some level personifications of natural forces, capable of both good and evil. Text about and images of landscapes in epics and their illustrated manuscripts express conceptual categories of the sublime and picturesque as formulated in the Indian context. Ancient gardens imitated sacred groves and represented nature perfected, its ugliness and terror banished to give humans pleasure. Landscape representations are based upon the aesthetic theory of *rasa* celebrating resonance between human emotions and nature.

Actual landscapes—such as Mount Kailash, the meeting of river streams at Prayaga, Bodhi trees and their environs, the groves of Vrindavan, *shakti-pithas*—draw their power from grand mythic narratives. As the narratives are told and retold in oral traditions and written texts, the settings may shift to wherever believers want them to be. Some, such as Ayodhya, Dwarka, and Kishkindha, became capitals of great empires. And even after those empires fell, temple-building at these sites continued. Despite structural similarities in their configuration of hills and rivers, these pilgrim sites are not alike. Their landscapes exhibit variety and dynamism, evolving and transforming in response to rising and falling empires and shifting allegiances to gods.

Natural archetypes are abstracted in built forms. The Hindu craftsman/builder styled himself after Viswakarma, the divine architect, whose actions he mimicked in creating space ever anew. Mimesis extended from actions to forms; natural archetypes were reproduced in cosmic pillars as trees, temples as built mountains, tanks as oceans. The family of forms inspired by nature took shape within the quartered space of a mandala. In pilgrim complexes nature was conceived in the image of a mandala; pilgrim movement shaped the landscape, and circumambulatory paths in turn organised the pilgrim's experience of space and time. The mandala governed the architectural edifice of the Hindu temple and the Buddhist stupa while their structures read metaphorically as built versions of the cosmic mountain. The gridded and modular structure of the mandala is very much a human creation, abstracting nature's energy and forms and subduing the destructive aspect of nature, signified by the *vaastu purusha mandala* diagram. The void as center is analogous to the inner space in the heart where divinity dwells. Thus, the geometric and the organic are reconciled by considering the mandala an icon of *purusha.* Codified in design manuals, mandalas as a basis for design are not limited to buildings and settlements. This spatial archetype is found in the vernacular landscape where it has become an intrinsic part of social practice, gender and kinship relations, and caste structure. This pervasiveness explains its longevity and strong hold over traditional ways of life.

Natural and spatial archetypes are analogous to word roots in the landscape vocabulary. They may be considered building blocks of the landscape edifice. Over the course of time they acquire many layers of cultural meanings and patterns of use. They resonate with deeply embedded archetypal structures in the collective psyche and can evoke profound experiences. For a modernising society in transition, they offer an anchor, communicating continuity and stability. Some of their connotations, such as caste and gender segregation, no longer conform to acceptable practices, yet enough associations with other healthy social practices remain to make them viable for design. By honoring natural archetypes in planning and design, the reintroduction of environmental consciousness is possible.

A landscape history of the Indian sub-continent is largely unwritten except for publications on Mughal gardens. Natural and spatial archetypes offer a point of departure for exploring how cultural landscapes evolved over time. The architectural history of the Indian subcontinent, first written during the colonial era, should be updated by situating buildings in their landscape context.[2] By focusing on buildings alone, architectural historians run the risk of ignoring the true meaning of forms. Sacred sites tell us the story of nature veneration, mythology, royal patronage, pilgrim circulation, settlement patterns, and architectural styles. In addition to temples, other building types include forts, palaces, guild halls, and water structures, which can also give us insight to the cultural past.

Local and regional pilgrim sites generate religious tourism on a large scale and are widely recognised and revered landscapes. Some are truly natural splendors, revealing nature at its most spectacular, while others evoke awe because of their architectural magnificence. Many have historic relics, which need protection and conservation. Pilgrimage has historically been mostly a self-organised phenomenon involving institutions and individuals working autonomously, but professional intervention is increasingly necessary to ensure that pilgrim sites are protected and managed. Unsightly commercial development, environmental degradation, and lack of facilities detract from the pilgrim experience. Planning and design expertise, therefore, is required for proper infrastructure development and heritage protection of these sites.

In what ways can the study of cultural landscapes contribute to the ongoing debate between tradition and modernity that informs any new development in India? Public landscapes evolve as a result of many small uncoordinated actions over time. An environmental designer must coordinate needs with the existing landscape and should deliberate upon the consequences of her actions—will her plans lead to radical rupture or harmonious coexistence with what is already there? Should the past always inform the present and shape the future, or should it be dismissed as a retrograde vestige of no consequence? There are no easy answers to the dilemmas faced by modernizing societies anxious to adopt global values of efficiency, standardisation, and consumerism but suffering from pangs of unresolved identity conflicts. Globalisation also brings in its wake homogenisation—landscapes begin to look the same no matter where they are if local history, technology, and culture are ignored. This homogeneity brings about a loss of unique identity, cultural memory, and place value.

In drawing upon natural and spatial archetypes for designing habitats of the future, architects, landscape architects, and urban designers may be able to reverse this trend. A special issue on landscape architecture of India's widely read design magazine, *A+D,* points to the necessity for finding indigenous models for theory and practice in these fields.

> With over 250 practicing professionals now in the field, there ought to be enough collective experience to take some tentative first steps towards marking out a philosophical common ground of aesthetic and ecological values, firmly rooted in our own tradition and history.
>
> Another cornerstone of our theoretical foundation is therefore, a concern for rediscovery of Indian tradition, about, for example, relation with land, water, and vegetation, including the ancient wisdom of site planning contained in the *vaastu shastra*.[3]

Traditional vocabulary used in innovative ways can result in a physical environment possessing a clear identity and rooted in the past. *Identity* is, however, a loaded term, and there are many kinds of identities, distinct or overlapping, to which one may simultaneously belong—cultural, local, regional, and national. Which kind of collective identity does the physical environment express and promote? Who is excluded by that act of expression? In a land of many faiths and traditions, who is not represented? I advocate neither revivalism nor traditionalism for its own sake, nor a pastiche of motifs borrowed indiscriminately from various sources, as the postmodernists do, but an open-ended language of forms that embody in the deepest sense an inclusive sense of collective selfhood.[4] This self emerges not from exclusive boundaries drawn on caste or sectarian lines, but from spiritual ideals and environmental consciousness.

Chapter-11 describes the design implications for sacred sites and promotes an environmental ethic derived from the religious worldview. Chapter-12 examines the dialectic between social and environmental change in rural and urban housing and in urban structure. Chapter-13 looks at contemporary Indian architecture and the use of archetypal design vocabulary as a legitimating device in the architectural discourse searching for a cultural identity.

NOTES

1. In Ellen Perry Berkeley and Matilta McQuaid (eds.), *Architecture: A Place for Women* (Washington, DC: Smithsonian Institution Press, 1989), 151.
2. For a critical historiography of Indian architectural history, see Amita Sinha, "Architecture and Identity in Colonial Discourse," *Journal of the Indian Institute of Architects* 66:10 (November 2001), 21–25, and "Indian Architectural History: A Post-Colonial Perspective," *Journal of the Indian Institute of Architects* 68:7 (December 2003), 46–49.

3. Mohammad Shaheer, "Landscape Architecture—Where We Are: Where We Should Be," *Architecture+Design* 13:3 (May–June 1996), 17–19.
4. Jon Lang, Madhavi Desai, and Miki Desai, in their book *Architecture and Independence: The Search for Identity—India 1880–1980* (Delhi: Oxford University Press, 1997), describe the tussle among modernism, traditionalism, and revivalism in Indian architecture. They feel that a true identity cannot emerge from building types and details drawn from monumental architecture of the past, yet they offer no alternatives.

Chapter Eleven

Implication for Pilgrimage Sites

> "Hindu pilgrimage often involves a self-conscious attempt to cultivate a rapport with Indian geography that establishes, reaffirms, or transforms one's religious identity. As in Australian Aboriginal tradition, the divine and heroic narratives that are basic to the Hindu textual and oral traditions are stamped in the landscape. The landscape is numinous with transformative, redemptive tales that can be read and appreciated by those initiated into its secrets."
>
> —**David Kinsley,**
> "Learning the Story of the Land: Reflections on the Liberating Power of Geography and Pilgrimage in the Hindu Tradition"[1]

The pilgrim encounters natural archetypes in the holy waters, sacred hills, small shrines, and large temples as he was walks the *parikrama* (circumambulatory) path, takes a dip in the river, or climbs a hill. Shady *pipal* and banyan trees, long *ghats* bathed by the flowing river, and temple courtyards provide vivid kinesthetic and visual experiences. The significance of these natural archetypes is enhanced by their role in the well-known stories listened to or read in the *sthala puranas* (site histories) sold on the spot. Could the experience be made even more meaningful for the devout? Unsightly development, refuse, and the detritus of ever-increasing numbers of visitors take their toll in diminishing the sacred ambience. The structure of the pilgrim landscape constituted by circumambulatory paths, temples and *ghats* on riverbanks, ponds and groves, temples and *dharmashalas* (rest houses) can be clarified and made legible through minor design interventions.

REDESIGNING SARNATH

Sarnath, located on the outskirts of Varanasi, was chosen by the Buddha for his first sermon and establishing the Buddhist *sangha*. The site's sacred importance is attested to by the large number of religious monuments built and rebuilt over the ages. The ancient ruins of Sarnath are interspersed with more recent structures, forming pockets in a largely agricultural landscape.

The earliest relics at the site can be traced to the third century BCE and consist of three stupas. There are ruins of seven monasteries, which were built over hundreds of years, and numerous small stupas built in the tenth and eleventh centuries CE by devotees wishing to commemorate their pilgrimages. They were destroyed by Islamic invasions in the thirteenth century, but the last two centuries have witnessed a revival. In recent years, Buddhist monks and nuns from Japan, Thailand, Myanmar, Sri Lanka, Tibet, and Thailand have constructed their monasteries and temples. Now Sarnath attracts many visitors, ranging from pilgrims to visitors from Varanasi and abroad. The peace and tranquillity required for religious worship and meditation are disturbed by the recreational use of open space where the ruins lie. Vendors, noisy traffic, and new housing disrupt the religious ambience of the site.

The Department of Landscape Architecture at the University of Illinois at Urbana Champaign proposed a landscape plan in 1990–1991, parts of which have been implemented.[2] In a bid to restore the environment and design for increasing numbers of visitors, we developed a project that created a cultural heritage district centered on the archaeological ruins. The cultivated fields of wheat and mustard around the archaeological site were preserved, new groves of trees were planted, steps to water bodies were built, wetlands were retained, and Buddhist-style architectural structures were designed for the visitors center and meditation complex. The site plan enhanced local wayside shrines, provided designated areas for vendors, limited vehicles, and unified the site with railings and pillars. Two 5.4-meter-high pillars mark the entry to the cultural heritage district, and the main entry route to ancient ruins is demarcated with pillars and railings. The visitors center, with its small auditorium and display spaces, was designed in the Buddhist architectural style. Its vaulted roof with *chaitya* windows, colonnade, extended plinth, ornate lintels, and paneled wooden doors recalls traditional Buddhist prayer halls.

At the archaeological site, a hierarchical pathway system separates the primary pathways of devotees from the secondary ones for tourists. The secondary path system circumvents the fragile ruins, allows for panoramic views, and contains seating and interpretive plaques. The primary path penetrates the site and provides physical access to the religious structures. North of the ruins, a meditation center was built in relative isolation. The approach to it is gradual on a woodland path through a deer park along a narrow stream. The buildings, situated on terraces overlooking the deer path, consist of an entry structure with facilities for group dining, a hall for group meditation, and four monasteries with cells for resident monks.

They were designed in the form of a traditional Buddhist monastery with a row of cells around a courtyard. Between buildings, plantings create outdoor meditation spaces. The group meditation hall is an open, vaulted structure, enclosed on one end by a semicircular wall in the manner of a Buddhist apsidal chapel. The complex also had a stepped bathing tank for ablutions. The natural ambience is similar to that of the traditional living quarters of Buddhist monks in the parks and tree groves of ancient India.

PAVAGADH HILL AS A CULTURAL SANCTUARY

The Department of Landscape Architecture at the University of Illinois at Urbana Champaign has proposed a landscape management plan that would ensure protection of Champaner-Pavagadh's cultural heritage.[3] This heritage is broad, ranging from historic buildings and relics of historic urban infrastructure to recently built temples. It includes not only material artifacts but also living cultural traditions that inspire veneration toward landscape design. The design goal of Pavagadh Cultural Sanctuary is to interpret cultural narratives of the past and present while ensuring preservation of historic sites. Presently the archaeological remains of Pavagadh and Champaner are neglected and not a popular stop for pilgrims whose knowledge of the past is derived from timeless mythology. The 5.28-kilometer-long historic pilgrim path, snaking its way up the hill, can serve as a spine from which secondary heritage trails can lead to historic sites at various elevations on the hilly terrain. The visceral experience of climbing the steep steps of the pilgrim path and partaking of the visual delights at moments of rest has inspired the design of *vishram sthals* where heritage sites can be viewed in all their precarious glory.

In this dry, drought-prone land with only one small river flowing down the hill, the survival of fortified communities rested upon careful management of this precious resource. Its symbolic significance was even greater; temple worship required the presence of large water bodies for ritual purification. The Rajputs set about harnessing the flow of monsoon rainfall on the hill in the innumerable cascades and ephemeral streams through an ingenious system of macroand micro-catchments and conveyance. This occurred along two watersheds: one from the top of Pavagadh hill through the northeastern side of historic Champaner to the large Wada *talao* on the plains, and the other to the northwest. Dudhiya, Chassiya, Annapurna, Teliya, and Medhi *talaos* on the former watershed collect water and have wells on their periphery to purify and extend scarce water supplies. A parallel system to the west collects storm overflows from the macro-catchment basins in Mauliya *talao* and directs them to the three reservoirs—Ganga, Yamuna, and Saraswati—built at the edge. Farther down, three tributaries drain water from the hillside into one stream that is diverted through a tunnel to supply water to Kasbin *talao,* a large, square tank just outside the city gates. This elaborate rainwater catch and conveyance system ensured that plentiful water was available all year, but five centuries later water is still a scarce commodity and the historic tanks and *talaos* are empty most of the year. As a result, the potential of water—its religious, utilitarian, and aesthetic uses—remains unfulfilled at the site. The dilapidated state of reservoirs and channels calls for conservation measures, such as rebuilding and extending *ghats* on upper *talaos* for access to water by pilgrims and resident communities, removing sediment from *talao* basins, and planting their edges with trees for more shade.

AN ENVIRONMENTAL AGENDA

India is crisscrossed by a vast network of sacred sites, some of local or regional importance, others of pan-Indian significance. These could prove to be exemplary sites where an environmental ethic based upon nature veneration is visible and enacted upon. Here the mythic framework affords a transcendental experience of the mundane landscape to those who are open to the experience. Sacred trees, water, hills, and the land itself are perceived to have a purifying effect on the body and spirit. The concept of harmony among nature, animals, and human beings guides behaviour, ritual and otherwise.

Temples can take the lead in environmental conservation and education. Sri Venkatesvara Devasthanam at Tirupati has set an example followed by other Hindu temples in supporting tree planting programmes. Today many programmes are attempting to restore the ecological health of pilgrim sites. The World Wildlife Fund undertook the reforestation and cleaning of the *parikrama* path in Vrindavan, a town in the sacred Braj *kshetra.*[4] Large-scale deforestation has destroyed many sacred groves associated with Krishna, leading to decreased water flow in the river Yamuna, a reduced water table in the region, and the consequent drying up of wells and tanks. The river has changed its course, no longer flowing by the *ghats* and temples. It is also highly polluted with industrial effluents and raw sewage, making bathing a hazard. The project has promoted planting along the entire eleven-kilometer *parikrama* path by devotees and local residents, who get the tree saplings from a nursery maintained by the International Society of Krishna Consciousness (ISKON). ISKON has also bought Raman Reti, a grove where young Krishna and his brother Balarama played, so that it can be protected from real estate development.

Another example is the Kanak Vrindavan valley in Rajasthan, where the rebuilding of Govind Deoji temple has spearheaded the environmental restoration of the surrounding region. The valley is surrounded by the Aravali hills and contains the Mansagar lake created by damming the river Darbhavati. Since the walled city of Jaipur was built in the early eighteenth century, the valley has progressively deteriorated. In the twentieth century, city sewage and toxic waste flowing into the lake from factories in the city led to water pollution. The reduced green cover caused soil erosion, siltation in the lake, air pollution, warmer temperatures, and gradual elimination of area wildlife. Since 1978 the rebuilding of temples in the valley according to a master plan has been accompanied by re-introducing flora typical of the region. Kanak bagh, the garden attached to Govind Deoji temple and buried under two feet of soil, has been restored. The portion of the valley known as Kanak ghati, which is north of the temple complex and spreads over two square kilometers, was reforested, attracting wildlife and reducing soil erosion. Rainwater was intercepted, collected, and recycled through pools, increasing the water table. The master plan also treated the valley as a symbolic Krishna's landscape, reminding one through sculptural depiction of episodes in his life at various points.[5]

Such sites hold within themselves the potential for sustaining biological diversity and can constrain human greed and abuse of the natural environment. An example is the sacred groves precinct amidst a cultivated landscape found in many parts of India.[6] One such grove in coastal Orissa, which lies amidst rice fields cultivated for centuries, contains the temple of goddess Harchandi on top of a wooded hill by a meandering river.[7] Ancient tamarind and neem trees on the hilly slopes overlook the casuarina pine groves next to the cultivated land. In the goddess's grove, no tree is felled, animal killed, or plant cultivated. The grove is considered akin to the goddess's body and is celebrated in the festival of her menses, which is attended by people from sixty villages in a twenty-kilometer radius. In the Uttara Kannada region of Karnataka, sacred groves known as *kans* are cult spots of local deities, worshipped by villagers in the form of crude stones or termite mounds. Over time and under brahmanic influence, the mother goddesses became identified with Hindu goddesses and were housed in temples or small shrines. Now greatly reduced in number, these sacred groves are fragmented specimens of living ecosystems and centers of biodiversity, which can serve as "gene banks" for restoration of natural ecosystems in the adjacent region.[8]

Many religious texts promote ecological sustainability and prohibit harm to the natural world. *Arthashastra, Bhagavata Purana, Vishnupurana,* and *Manusmriti* contain dictums against cutting down trees, killing animals, and polluting rivers.[9] Devi Mahatmya in the *Markanda Purana* celebrates the earth as the material form of the Goddess. In the *tantric* tradition there are 108 *pithas* (holy seats) where the mother goddess lives with her consort and which serve as major pilgrimage centers. This may have been an aboriginal, proto-Indian custom, a relic of prehistoric goddess worship.[10]

Could an environmental ethic based upon a reconstructed goddess ecology find resonance in contemporary India? Vandana Shiva argues that recovering the feminine principle in nature and society is absolutely essential to combat large-scale environmental problems caused in part by technology that seeks to exploit nature by building dams, using forestation programmes for timber yield and high-yield seeds that require chemical fertilisers.[11] Such enterprises have diminished the concept of nature as *prakriti* and obliterated the role of women in creating sustainable communities. They have desacralised the landscape and destroyed the delicate web of ecology that enabled humans to live in harmony with their environment.

It could be argued that the recovery of a pre-industrial way of life is neither possible nor desirable. It could also be argued that nature veneration by itself cannot check its despoliation, especially when such issues lie beyond the scope of a small community in the anonymous public realm. In the eyes of the faithful, divine nature can absorb any number of shocks, waste, pollution, and sin. The Clean Ganga Campaign in Varanasi, without local participation and involvement, is a good case in point. Residents of the Dasasvamedha *ghat* believe that the Ganga is not affected by partially or fully uncremated bodies. Distinguishing between physical cleanliness and sacred purity, they do not worry too much about an unclean Ganga.[12]

Given the scale of environmental problems facing India today, any resources that can aid ecological action should be harnessed. An environmental movement has a better chance of succeeding if it is grounded in local faiths and belief systems instead of being couched only in scientific terminology or cast in ideological frameworks derived from a non-indigenous worldview. Moral imperatives work best when referenced to cultural narratives. That these narratives are incomplete without the archetypal landscape can only help the environmental cause.

NOTES

1. In Lance Nelson (ed.), *Purifying the Earthly Body of God: Religion and Ecology in Hindu India* (Albany: State University of New York Press, 1998), 228.

2. Department of Landscape Architecture at the University of Illinois at Urbana-Champaign, *Sarnath: A Master Plan for Tourism Development* (New Delhi: Thomson Press, 1989), and *Sarnath: Design Guidelines and Case Studies for Tourism Development* (New Delhi: Thomson Press, 1990). The project is featured in Amita Sinha, "The Conservation of Sacred Sites: Sarnath, a Case Study," *Landscape Research* 16:3 (Winter 1991), 23–30, and Amita Sinha, "On Holy Ground," *Landscape Design* 235 (November 1994), 34–36.
3. For details, see *Champaner-Pavagadh Archaeological Park* and *Champaner-Pavagadh Cultural Sanctuary,* cooperative projects in 2001 and 2003, respectively, by Department of Landscape Architecture, University of Illinois at Urbana-Champaign, USA, and Heritage Trust, Baroda, India.
4. See Ranchor Prime, *Hinduism and Ecology: Seeds of Truth* (London: Cassell, 1992).
5. Rajiv Khanna, "Kanak Vrindavan Valley, Jaipur," *Architecture+Design* 12:3 (May–June 1996), 55–65.
6. Madhav Gadgil and Ramachandra Guha report that in Uttar Kannada (in the state of Karnataka) as much as 6 percent of the land was once a sacred habitat and has now decreased to 0.3 percent in a 5-km-by-5-km area. There are fifty-two sacred groves in the area containing remnant pockets of the rain forest and refuge for many species. See their *Ecology and Equity: The Use and Abuse of Nature in Contemporary India* (New Delhi: Penguin Books, 1995).
7. Frederique A. Marglin and Puran Chandra Mishra, "Sacred Groves: Regenerating the Body, the Land, the Community," in *Global Ecology. A New Arena of Conflict,* ed. Wolfgang Sachs (London: Zed Books, 1993), 197–207.
8. M. D. Subash Chandran and J. Donald Hughes, "Sacred Groves and Conservation: The Comparative History of Traditional Reserves in the Mediterranean Area and in South India," *Environment and History* 6 (2000), 169–186.
9. See Vasudha Narayanan, " 'One Tree Is Equal to Ten Sons': Hindu Responses to the Problems of Ecology, Population, and Consumption," *Journal of American Academy of Religions* 65:2 (June 1997), 291–332.
10. See Agehananda Bharati, "Pilgrimage in the Indian Tradition," *History of Religions* 3:1 (Summer 1963), 135–167.
11. Vandana Shiva, *Staying Alive: Women, Ecology, and Development* (London: Zed Books, 1991).
12. Kelly Alley, "Idioms of Degeneracy: Assessing Ganga's Purity and Pollution," in *Purifying the Earthly Body of God,* ed. Nelson, 297–330.

Chapter Twelve

Implication for Environmental Design

> "As the common space of a house, appropriate to the climate and the social habits of the occupants, the internal courtyard is a simple device for maximizing transactions with one's immediate relatives and family. As a personal space, it compensates for the anonymity and stress of urbanism. As private space, one identifies with it, and with a little care (requiring no more than the daily household waste water) it nourishes a small garden or a tree. Finally, as a gathering place it facilitates the fulfillment of private and public ritual. By contrast, the open space in the new developments is public, impersonal, outside the sphere of daily life of an Indian household and costly to maintain. For lack of adequate irrigation, these spaces remain dry and dusty through most of the year, provide grazing areas after the monsoon for the insatiable goats and dhobis' donkeys of Delhi—or attract squatters, who ultimately must be evicted."
>
> —**Rory Fonseca,**
> "The Walled City of Old Delhi: Urban Renewal and an Indigenous Community"[1]

In traditional societies whose way of life remains unchanged for centuries, cultural norms regarding appropriate spatial layouts and their use are internalised by every member. The inhabitant has control over building design and production, open spaces have agreed-upon civic rules for use as community gathering areas, and religious architecture embodies cultural beliefs about cosmos and man's position in it. Societies, however, rarely remain static; social change caused by internal and external agents is inevitable. When violent disruption in society is caused by revolution, invasion, or colonisation, the landscape is radically altered. Large-scale demolition and rebuilding may take place in cities; new means of transportation and communication may bring farflung areas under central control; existing means may be disrupted, causing fragmentation of the state; or new systems of revenues and land division may alter the agricultural landscape. In such situations, archetypal symbols lose their clarity of meaning. Alien symbols, representing other cultures and ways of life, are imposed or may be voluntarily adopted.

In the last millennium the Indian sub-continent has been buffeted by many disrupting agents of change—Islamic invasions, European colonisation, as well as the onset of modernity. Modernisation changes the way individuals view themselves in relation to society. It fundamentally alters person-environment relations. Space becomes commodified, no longer reflecting a society's past, social ideals, and religious traditions. Male and female, sacred and profane, private and public—these psychosocial dualities become diffuse with consequences for the way in which the physical environment is organised and experienced. The transformation in the spatial archetype from the nucleated village to the orthogonal grid of new housing colonies in postcolonial urban India has far-reaching social implications.

COURTYARD HOUSING

The house has been described as a symbol of self, indicator of identity, and setting for ritual. It can also assume an active role as an agent of change to the existing social order. A novel built form requires adjustments of lifestyles and habits that affect the way in which individuals view themselves in relation to the society and ultimately the social structure itself.

The long tradition of courtyard housing in India shows signs of disappearing with modernisation. With European colonialism, a new housing type—the bungalow—was introduced. In this housing type, the building does not contain open space but is surrounded by it in the tradition of the English country villa.[2] This exteriorisation reduces the privacy and security that enclosed courtyards offer. Because places act as a catalyst for changes occurring in gender roles, family composition, and social networks, adoption of the new bungalow prototype is a sign of social change in Indian society. Evidence of the link between social and environmental changes is seen in the impact of government-built housing in places such as Lucknow in northern India.[3] The new housing, both the process and product, is a professional endeavour. The process lies in a state agency selling a constructed house to a family at a subsidized rate. It includes the government acquiring the land, designing and constructing the houses, and providing this subsidized housing to low-income families. Many of the residents are rural migrants or those who have moved from the inner city with its traditional courtyard housing.

The very fact that housing is a state responsibility and is designed by professionals is a facet of modernisation. It represents a change from a non-professional design process in vernacular dwellings and settlements undertaken by the user-builder to housing by professionals who are not necessarily residents of the environments they design. The architects and planners are responsible for introducing innovations in the built environment that have far-reaching impacts on the lifestyle of its inhabitants.

The organisation of spaces in the housing colony influences family structure, modes of privacy, and the role of women in the family. The design of these houses is derived from the bungalow model, which is a detached house set in open space and consisting of special-purpose rooms and attached bath and toilets. There are many reasons for the adoption of this housing model in urban areas— identification with modernity, high population density precluding the construction of traditional dwellings with large courtyards, and architects trained in the Western idiom.

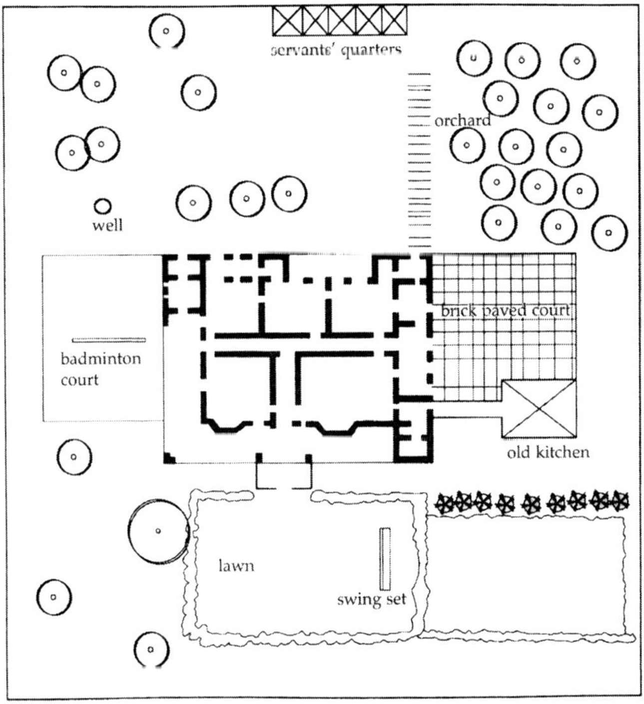

12.1: A bungalow with sloping tiled roof, large manicured lawn, and badminton court in Lucknow cantonment.

The bungalow's small size makes it unsuitable for any family but nuclear. In a survey of low income housing in Indira nagar, out of fifty households three-fourths were nuclear families. As a result of the dwelling's small size and the high density of occupancy, the family is brought closer together. The spatial segregation of male and female realms is no longer possible. Since the family is predominantly nuclear, behavioural restraints fostered by the presence of the family elders and the extended kin group disappear, resulting in closer interaction between husband and wife, and father and children. Thus, privacy boundaries are drawn, encompassing the nuclear family and excluding the larger, extended family, unlike in traditional society where decision-making takes place at the level of the extended family unit.

The changed spatial configuration of houses and their smaller size, together with changing relationships in the nuclear family structure, have wide implications for behavioural norms governing women's activities. In northern India, observances of *purdah,* which dictates separate areas for men and women, become difficult, if not impossible, in a one or two-roomed house. And behavioural restraints created by the presence of in-laws and other elderly members of the extended family are considerably relaxed in a nuclear family. Although a semblance of courtyard is included in new housing, its size is too small to be used for socialising by women with their neighbours or other visitors as in the traditional courtyards. Many women thus use the front step to sit and talk, adding vitality to the street life. The street in housing colonies is no longer an exclusively male domain.

In contrast to avoiding a display of individual status as in vernacular housing, modern housing types in the colony have a drawing room containing items such as a television, sofa, refrigerator, toys in a display case, and calendars. Residents make a conscious attempt to display identity and status by means of objects. Materialistic cues become important indicators of one's position in a changing society. The house becomes an economic commodity because of the acute housing shortage and the social and spatial mobility of the urban dwellers. The front room is frequently rented out to supplement the family income. Extensions to the house, beyond what is built by the housing authority, are considered investments. Buying and selling houses is seen as a business enterprise. This represents a change from the traditional view that the dwelling is a shelter for the extended family. The changing meaning of the house causes it to become a status symbol and a sign of individual rather than collective accomplishment. It marks the transition from a collective to an individuated identity as reflected in shrinking privacy boundaries, material objects signifying purchasing power, and unique styles of decoration and furnishings.[4] I had studied this housing colony in the late 1980s when it was less than a decade old. Long-term adaptation by its inhabitants might show tradition reasserting itself. Rosin's longitudinal study of a residential colony in a Jaipur suburb shows that after two generations of incremental construction, the bungalow-style houses have become more like *havelis* found in the old city ward. To accommodate family expansion or segmentation, an additional suite of rooms is built; to procure domestic service by servants, shacks are built in the compound or rooms are added under staircases; to generate income by renting out rooms, alterations like the building additions in courtyard housing are made. The courtyard at the back shrinks and the front garden is transformed into the outer courtyard of the traditional *haveli*. In the struggle between the modern view of home as an expression of class through styles of consumption and leisure and the more traditional view of home as a container for the extended family and a productive site of their long-term economic interests, tradition appears to be winning.[5]

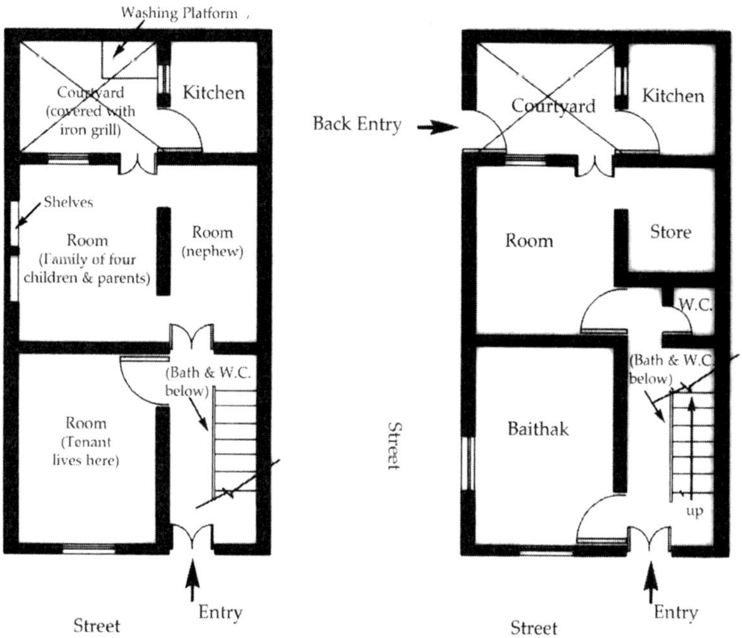

12.2: Low-income houses in Indira Nagar, Lucknow built in the early 1980s by the State Housing Board have small rear courtyards.

In a recent survey of bungalows in Lucknow cantonment, I found that home-owners treated their houses like traditional courtyard houses despite the bungalow's compact form, absence of internal outdoor space for segmentation, and the cantonment's restrictive policy regarding alterations. While the army officers lived in nuclear families, the civilian families were either joint (two brothers and their families living under the same roof) or extended (grandparents, parents, and their children). In two cases the bungalow had been divided along the center (this division was aided by the bungalow's symmetrical design) for two families and, in one bungalow, rooms had been divided among seven siblings. In yet another bungalow the central rooms remained common spaces (drawing, dining, and multipurpose rooms) and dressing rooms on the periphery had been converted into bedrooms for children, grandparents, and the parents. The front verandah had been enclosed by decorative grillwork and the back verandah had been converted into two kitchens (for vegetarian and non-vegetarian cooking). Two *chabutras* (terraces) had been added, including one at the back for washing and drying clothes, and for pickles, and serving a purpose similar to that of a courtyard.[6]

URBAN STRUCTURE

The meaning of home derives, in part, from its neighbourhood setting. In cities, courtyard houses are found in older neighbourhoods where the grid, if ever used, has long been distorted into an organic pattern of winding streets narrowing into labyrinthine residential lanes and blind cul-de-sacs. Medieval cities such as Ahmedabad, Lahore (now in Pakistan), Lucknow, and Shahajanabad are oriented toward the interior of the building but are extroverted within because of the presence of community squares or *chowks*.[7] Civit as exists, albeit dissipated, within the multinucleated systems of *katras, ganjs,* and *pols* (caste neigbourhoods). Informal rules of negotiation enable public use despite the strongly territorial nature of urban space. In the nineteenth-century colonial era, as European communities established themselves in civil lines and cantonments, where the bungalow, surrounded by open space on all sides, ruled, novel forms of public spaces appeared as malls, race courses, botanical and zoological gardens, and parks. Lacking walls, a seemingly ordered and extroverted urban pattern came into existence, cheek by jowl with the historic precolonial city.

I will illustrate the dichotomy between indigenous and colonial using Chowk and Hazratganj in Lucknow as an example.[8] In the eighteenth century, Lucknow grew rapidly along the banks of the river Gomti when a series of fort complexes was built by Shia Nawabs. Chowk (a Sanskrit term referring to the space at the junction of crossroads), the main marketplace to the southeast, had existed as a linear marketplace, linking trade routes to other cities in the province before the beginning of Nawabi rule in Lucknow. The nobility built *ganj* with houses, bazaars, and mosques, attracting craftsmen and traders. A *ganj,* therefore, formed the urban tissue and the unit of urban growth. Ideally a *ganj* would have a square built around crossroads with two main gates and two smaller ones built at the end of each street. The streets were lined with shops that had private residences at the rear. Thus, each *ganj* contained a *chowk* at its center. As the city center became increasingly

12.3: Chowk, the oldest street in Lucknow, feels like an elongated courtyard carved out of a dense building mass (courtesy Rajat Kant).

populous and affluent, the main Chowk gathered not only commerce but also institutions of religion and learning and, most colorful of all, houses of courtesans known as *kothas*. The main street was bounded between two gateways known as Akbari and Gol darwazas. The riverbank, occupied by palaces of Nawabs, was developing its own street network for the passage of elite on elephants and carriages, and processions on state occasions. One of these, Hazratganj, which became the center of British Lucknow, was a wide thoroughfare leading from Farhat Bakksh, the palace of Nawab Saadat Ali Khan, to his country retreat, Dilkusha, on the city outskirts. After the 1857 mutiny, it became the center of colonial Lucknow with European shops and cinemas, hotels, and restaurants. In proximity to spacious bungalows of civil lines, it slowly changed to a Western-style boulevard, serving as the public realm of the city's European section.

In the old city, the urban fabric is tightly knit so that Chowk feels like an elongated courtyard carved out of a dense building mass. With the width varying between 12 and 18 feet, the horizontal-to-vertical ratio of street width to building height increases from 2:3 to 1:2 as one moves down the street. Slight meanders of the street obstruct views down its length. A strong sense of enclosure makes Chowk kinesthetically stimulating. Other senses are assailed by the vibrant colours, rich aromas, and numerous sounds of this tactile space rich for the proximate senses. The main street is always thronged with people making things, buying and selling, eating delicacies, and hanging out. Its high perceptual density keeps the visitor alert and curious.[9]

Hazratganj, which overtook Chowk as the main commercial center sometime in the twentieth century, provides a study in contrast with its European colonnaded architecture, spaciousness, automobile traffic, and Western feel. Although predominantly a commercial center, it has attracted many corporations and government institutions, such as Town Hall building (now housing a bank), Municipal Corporation, Civil Hospital, and General Post Office. The straight and wide stretch of the street allows for distant views and automobile traffic. With the street width between 75 and 90 feet, the horizontal-to-vertical ratio of building height to street width is 1:3. Off the main street are enclosed markets, such as Halwasiya and Janpath, with tiny shops facing inward.

Which of the two models, indigenous or colonial, should be a precedent for urban design? The colonial model has long been seen by planners as the only appropriate solution to the problems of city planning. The considerable strengths of the indigenous model are forgotten or ignored—its seamless connection with residential areas, conservation of space with no wasted no-man's-land (ill-maintained by municipal organisations with stretched

12.4: Hazratganj was the center of British Lucknow and, thoughbuilt by Nawab Saadat Ali Khan, had the feel of a Westernstyle boulevard that it still retains to some degree (courtesy Rajat Kant).

resources) and subtle gradations in size of spaces, sunlight, noise levels, and perception of crowdedness as one moves from the primary bazaar street to tertiary residential lanes. Hazratganj shows many signs of an involuted pattern taking over in its smaller markets where space is shaped by the considerable informal economy of small scale enterprises and vendors who cannot afford large rental shops. The tenacity of the older form is revealed in its revival in new residential developments, such as Indiranagar where small scale and ease of proximity to the clientele work to its advantage.

RURAL PLANNING

Existing research on rural and urban Indian landscape shows caste to be the single most important variable ordering the settlement pattern. An unbroken tradition rooted in religion dating from ancient India continues, with strong conservative forces in society, resisting attempts to restructure it along secular lines. What are the possibilities of change in the rural landscape in which the social and physical have such a remarkably clear correspondence to each other? As long as caste stratification remains the basic unit of rural Indian society, the physical structure is not likely to change on its own. Social change occurs slowly in rural Indian society. As landownership patterns change, the caste hierarchy may shift, losing its social relevance in the process. Schools and primary healthcare centers are secular venues of social mixing where caste is not the basis of social interaction. The rural development schemes initiated by the state provide an opportunity for new forms of layout that need not duplicate the patterns of caste segregation. When assistance is given in the form of financing, land, or building materials, recipient households belonging to different castes may find themselves next to each other.

Village demarcation into caste neighbourhoods allows for certain caste groups to be targeted as victims in the event of caste factions, as is increasingly the case in rural areas, especially in northern India. In upgrading rural settlements, a housing policy should be adopted that ensures that untouchables are not relegated to the outskirts of a settlement or form floating hamlets in the midst of fields, unattached to any particular village. Their incorporation in a village or a mixture of castes in neighbourhoods may not promote intercaste solidarity, but it will reinforce the village identity and may help to break down existing strong religious taboos against commensalism and community relations.

In the newly constructed housing schemes in urban areas initiated by development authorities and housing boards, division into different income groups results in clear class distinctions in these neighbourhoods, mostly found on the fringes of expanding cities where land is available. Caste is no longer a factor, though the corelation between caste and class cannot be ruled out.

In conclusion, in the evolving landscape of Indian villages and cities, the clarity of archetypal symbols is losing ground as society modernises and secular thinking in the workplace and public sphere replaces religiously ordained tasks. Alien symbols such as the grid (a sign of efficiency and standardisation) in settlement layouts and single-activity zonal planning, however, rarely have staying power since they do not reflect cultural ethos. For the environmental designer the implications are mixed. He can work for positive environmental changes by adopting alien forms to remedy social injustice and inequity. Landscape design by itself cannot obliterate gender and caste discrimination, but it can and does act as a catalyst in social change.

NOTES

1. In *Landscape* 18:3 (Fall 1969): 25.
2. See Anthony King's exhaustive cross-cultural analysis of the bungalow form in colonial India and elsewhere in *The Bungalow: The Production of a Global Culture* (New York: Oxford University Press, 1995). From a single-room structure with a verandah, the bungalow evolved in response to climatic conditions, was influenced by Palladian symmetry, and was embellished with features of the prevailing architectural styles in Great Britain. As Swati Chattopadhyay points out in her study of nineteenth-century bungalows in colonial Calcutta, the Palladian classicism of English residences was altered by organizing the interior so that the central hall could be a focal point of gathering and give access to the individual rooms around it in the manner of an Indian courtyard house with rooms surrounding a central open space. See Chattopadhyay, "Blurring Boundaries: The Limits of 'White Town' in Colonial Calcutta," *Journal of Society of Architectural Historians* 59:2 (June 2000), 154–179.
3. See Amita Sinha, "Participant Observation: A Study of State-Aided Self-help Housing in Lucknow, India," in *Housing the Poor in the Developing World*, ed. Graham Tipple and Kenneth Willis (New York: Routledge, 1991), 16–34.
4. James Duncan, "From Container of Women to Status Symbol: The Impact of Social Structure on the Meaning of the House," in *Housing and Identity: Cross Cultural Perspectives*, ed. James Duncan (New York: Holmes and Meier Publishers, 1981).
5. R. Thomas Rosin, "Garden Suburb into Olde City Ward: A Longitudinal Study of Social Process and Incremental Architecture in Jaipur India" (manuscript submitted for publication in *Journal of Material Culture*, July 2000).
6. Amita Sinha, "Bungalows of Lucknow Cantonment, India," *Open House International* 24:2 (1999), 56–63.

7. Vivek Nanda, "Urbanism, Tradition, and Continuity in Ahmedabad," *Mimar* 38 (March 1991), 26–36.
8. For a comprehensive discussion, see Amita Sinha and Rajat Kant, "Urban Evolution and Transformation in Lucknow, India: A Comparative Study of Its Streets," *Open House International* 23:1 (1997), 34–42.
9. Tim Edensor, "The Culture of the Indian Street," in *Images of the Street: Planning, Identity, and Control in Public Space,* ed. Nicholas Fyte (London: Routledge, 1998), 205–221, calls to attention the heterotopic order of the Indian street with its apparent disorder characterised by rich "olfactory geographies," "haptic geographies," and diverse soundscapes. The street supports a diverse range of activities—public and private, work and leisure, holy and profane—in a series of overlapping micro-spaces. He contrasts it with the colonial attempt to demarcate single-purpose spaces where Europeans could retreat from the perceived urban chaos of the native quarters.

Chapter Thirteen

Visions for the Future

"In India, the sky has profoundly affected our relationship to built form, and to open space. For in a warm climate, the best place to be in the late evenings and in the early mornings is outdoors, under the open sky. Such spaces have an infinite number of variations: one steps out of a room…into a verandah…and thence on to a terrace…from which one proceeds to an open courtyard, perhaps shaded by a tree…or by a large pergola overhead. At each moment, subtle changes in the quality of light and ambient air generate feelings within us—feelings which are central to our beings. Hence to us in Asia, the symbol of Education has never been the Little Red School house of North America, but the guru sitting under the tree. True enlightenment cannot be achieved within the closed box of a room—one needs to be outdoors, under the open sky."

—**Charles Correa,** "The Blessings of the Sky"[1]

Current Indian architectural and urban design discourse revolves around morphologies and typologies of buildings and urban spaces but neglects to explain how conjunctions of forms and functions come about. More importantly, meanings of landscape symbols are largely avoided. Archetypes provide us with a framework for their exploration. Let us examine how symbols, which I believe are basic constituents of Indian landscapes—trees, water, courtyards, a cross within a square, and cosmic architecture—appear in the work of contemporary designers and are attributed secular meanings in the twenty-first century.

Trees provide shade and shelter and act as nodes in rural and urban landscapes. They are outdoor public shelters giving refuge from the relentless sun to the weary. Often they are surrounded by public spaces if they are at crossroads or act as neighbourhood courtyards in a dense urban mass. They are loci of activities—children playing, old men snoozing on *charpoys* (string cots), neighbours meeting, and vendors selling their wares. Occasionally an impromptu shrine containing a Shiva linga, Hanuman, or goddess springs up and devotees may be seen circumambulating the tree and performing *puja.* Within temple precincts, trees are found at the entry to the complex, near the main shrine, and at the four gateways as in temple of Pandharpur, marking the sacred center and its entry thresholds.[2] Trees are frequently associated with water in wells or tanks. The tree-water dyad brings life to a public space, offering respite from heat in the pleasant microclimate it engenders.

13.1: Well under a tree in a temple courtyard in Hardwar.

The significance of water in the Indian landscape surpasses that of other natural elements. The hot, dry climate of most of the Indian sub-continent parches the land before the arrival of monsoons; access to water is precious indeed in those months. A picturesque landscape vocabulary of *ghats, kunds,* and step wells has evolved over millennia to give shape and access to water for religious rituals and pragmatic use. *Ghats,* or steps, at the edge of water, especially along rivers, are ubiquitous, allowing people to draw water, bathe, wash, worship, and cremate their dead. The body of water is lined with stone steps, circular or polygonal terraces (*burjes*), pavilions (*chattris*), shrines, and trees. Those in pilgrim cities, such as Varanasi, Hardwar, Mathura, and Ayodhya, acquire added significance as part of a pilgrimage circuit and sites of ritual bathing. The *ghats* are lined with temples, their towers forming an arresting skyline of spiky silhouettes.

Kunds mark sacred sites, and usually temples are built in their vicinity. The body of water, fed by a natural spring, is given a square, rectangular, polygonal, or circular shape by building steps and terraces around it.

In pilgrim towns, such as Pushkar (near Ajmer) and Mishrikh (near Lucknow), *ghats*, temples, *dharmashalas* (rest houses for pilgrims), and residences have sprung up around the large *kund*, making it the center of settlement.[3] A tight-knit urban fabric with winding alleyways surrounds the spacious body of water. The contrast heightens the feelings of restfulness and serenity. Some *kunds*, such as Banganga at Walkeshwar (in Mumbai) and Pushkar, contain a wooden pole symbolizing the *axis mundi*—Mount Meru arising from the cosmic ocean.[4]

Kunds and wells traditionally make for elaborate water buildings in the western states of Gujarat and Rajasthan where the low water table caused acute water scarcity until the advent of piped water. They date back to the seventh century CE when they were first excavated out of rock and then built structurally for the next twelve hundred years in Hindu and later Islamic kingdoms. Stepped ponds consist of diagonal stairs in a triangular formation all around the tank. The architecture of step wells consists of linear stepped terraces reaching down more than 150 feet from the ground level to the source of water. They were public structures, built as acts of philanthropy by the town's royalty and wealthy citizens on its outskirts within parks and along caravan routes for thirsty travelers. They were and still are used by men and women for drawing water, bathing, resting in cool shade, and meeting people. Some have small mother-goddess shrines worshipped by women, undoubtedly a continuation of traditional practices.[5]

DESIGNING WITH NATURE

Landscape architecture in postcolonial India has not carved out an independent professional niche and lies within the purview of architects practicing architecture or neighbourhood and urban design. It is interesting to see that natural archetypes—such as trees and water—are the focus of projects by several well-known architects. Charles Correa draws on the symbolism of traditional landscapes in Surya Kund (New Delhi) and the JN Centre for Advanced Scientific Research. The geometry of the *kund* and its stepped form is retained in a meeting place for think tanks in the solar energy farm of a futurologist. It is precisely oriented to the cardinal directions as the *vaastu purusha mandala* with its center is marked by *Shri yantra*. Sages (*rishis*) have retreated to forests for meditation since ancient times, and Correa plays upon this nature metaphor in his design of a long, curving granite wall that frames access to a grove of trees in the Centre for Advanced Scientific Research. From the built world of research labs and offices, the scientist (a modern *rishi*) steps out into pristine nature mimicking the ancients in their search for enlightenment.[6]

13.2: Surya kunda in Delhi, designed by Charles Correa, is an outdoor meeting place for members of a think tank group (courtesy Charles Correa).

The hallmark of Joseph Allen Stein's long career in India is his sensitivity to the interaction of architecture and landscape, especially in the many projects that he has designed in South Delhi. Between India International Centre and Ford Foundation Headquarters lies the exquisitely designed memorial plaza to Mahatma Gandhi and the Reverend Martin Luther King Jr., which overlooks the historic Lodhi Gardens. A simple gesture of four granite blocks inscribed with quotations from the two leaders is lent authority by the two flanking ficus trees in the manner of *akshaya vata,* the eternal trees.[7]

Nature's presence in the public realm modifies the microclimate and makes the space more comfortable, thereby ensuring its use. Contemporary Indian urbanism with its widespread neglect of public open space will be much improved if traditional patterns are employed. The huge, grassy lawns in *maidans* (large open space), public parks, and boulevards—the landscape legacy of colonialism—are not maintained well. They need water and care—resources often lacking in financially strapped municipal bodies. What if indigenous patterns were used, presenting a different face of nature, one that is bound up with traditional values of veneration and familiar customs? Instead of urban wastelands of dumped garbage, there could be terraced platforms around large, shade-giving *pipal* and banyan trees in brick-paved courtyard plazas. Water would enliven the space not in the form of clogged fountains but through horizontal sheets in tanks shaded by trees where children could splash and all people could wash and congregate.

COURTYARD DESIGN

Courtyards are a widely prevalent spatial archetype in the vernacular landscape of the Indian sub-continent. Traditionally found in rural and urban housing, they now appear in institutional buildings designed by architects wishing to draw upon an indigenous spatial pattern. This pattern denotes introversion, an orientation toward the private realm, and a defensive posture. It implies a high level of enclosure, visual surveillance, and territoriality, well suited to meet the requirements of an extended family. When employed outside the familial situation, its success as a spatial pattern should not be taken for granted. Architects have employed it imaginatively in housing, campuses, and museums. Without post-occupancy evaluations, however, we do not know if these courtyards function beyond mere visual spaces and passive solar building elements; if they do indeed become extensions of indoor spaces and bring together their unrelated residents in a community.

Perhaps the best known housing layout designed around a courtyard-like common space is Charles Correa's Belapur artists' village in New Bombay. Not only are seven free standing houses clustered around a central open space, three such clusters form a unit and define a larger open space. Again three such units are combined to form the largest open space that is curvilinear along a local stream in Belapur. A hierarchy of open spaces mirrors a gradient of privacy, the smallest court being the most intimate in scale with the greatest potential for social interaction among residents. A portion of the open space could be utilised for adding to the house as the family increases in size or its economic situation improves. Here the courtyard design allows for incremental additions, flexibility in construction, and a fine grain of open space–built structure ratio.[8]

Raj Rewal's projects in New Delhi are based on the idea that courtyards and roof terraces create a porous architecture that draws upon the vernacular desert townscape of Rajasthan as well as Mughal fort-palaces, such as Fatehpur Sikri. In the Asian Games village, semi-public courtyards punctuate the dense mass of residential buildings (each unit has either a courtyard or a terrace) and are linked by narrow pedestrian streets framed by entrance gateways. The network of open spaces is dynamic with a sense of continuity and high enclosure creating an intimate feel. Similar imagery pervades the National Institute of Immunology and Central Institute of

Educational Technology with their courtyards linked by shaded pathways. Both institutional (such as the laboratories, lecture hall complex, and faculty lounge) and residential buildings (such as the senior and junior staff housing) in the National Institute of Immunology are built around central open spaces. The Institute of Educational Technology has two linked courtyards, including one at the entry leading to the main space with a pre-existing banyan tree. The open-air amphitheater makes it a central meeting place and a visual focal point of the corridors and terraces on the upper two floors.[9]

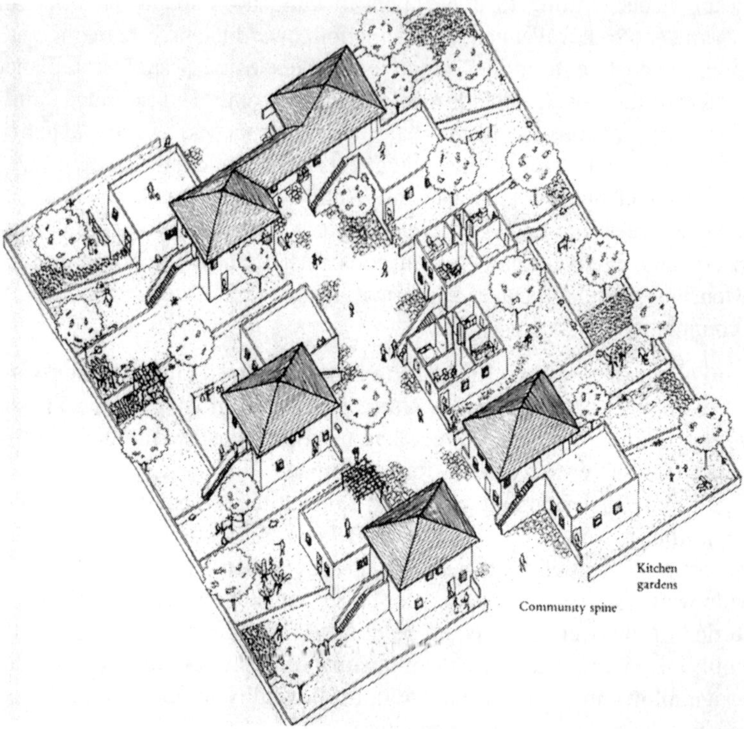

13.3: Belapur Housing in New Bombay, designed by Charles Correa, is designed around a hierarchy of open spaces that foster community life (courtesy Charles Correa).

The success of the courtyard in various building types makes it a powerful spatial archetype, one that works at many levels—symbolic, climatic, and social. For an open space to function effectively and act as a courtyard in the true sense of the word, it should be appropriately scaled; that is, it should not be so large as to lose its sense of enclosure and thereby definition. For it to act as an extension of indoor space, transitions are needed, whether verandahs or *chabutras* (terraces). In the traditional Uor square-shaped housingprojects, the interior space should have activity nodes, such as play equipment for children, garden plots for individual residents, and shaded hardscaped spaces with benches for outdoor seating, instead of being green areas devoid of activities as is too often the case.

URBAN SQUARE AND STREET

The courtyard denotes a private open space and its use in the public realm results in an introverted urban structure. Traditional urbanism on the Indian sub-continent, especially in settlements displaying organic growth, is considered to be involuted and dendritic in pattern, with public spaces as leftover areas, irregular in outline and accidentally produced. Yet, there exists an ancient urban prototype, the *chowk* (square at the crossroads). The first settlements grew at crossroads, and over time the pattern, a symbol of the spatial archetype of four quarters, was incorporated in the mandalas recommended in the *shilpashastras*.

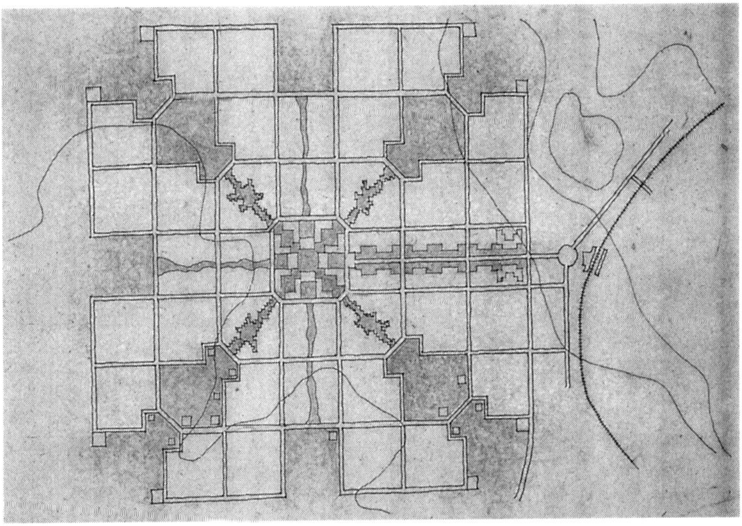

13.4: Charles Correa's design for the new town of Bagalkot in Karnataka is based on a mandala pattern (courtesy Charles Correa).

Chowk also refers to the residential courtyard in northern and western India. The urban *chowk,* however, is a diametric contrast to the residential one. It is extroverted in its orientation and dynamic in feel, flowing into the linear open spaces of the streets. The cross-axial street pattern, akin to the *cardo* and *decumanus* of Roman military camps and colonies, is oriented along north-south and east-west axes and entered through gateways. The crossroads, the most public space of a settlement, is a logical space for commerce. A cohesive and coherent streetscape exists in the planned *chowks* of Jaipur and Shahajanabad. They are highly symmetrical and regular and embody the classical approach to urban design.

Architects have employed the *chowk* motif in the design of public spaces in new communities. Balkrishna Doshi has incorporated the traditional urban spine in his Electronics Corporation of India township in Hyderabad and low-cost housing project in Indore. It is in Vidhyadhar Nagar—a satellite town of Jaipur—that we see the main axis of commerce and public buildings intersected by streets leading off to residential sectors whose geometry is derived from the eighteenth-century layout of Jaipur.[10] Charles Correa's scheme for the new town of Bagalkot in Karnataka is an interesting variation on the nine-square plan of Jaipur and concentric mandala patterns of temple cities, such as Shrirangam. He locates the main *chowk* in the very center of the town. A *kund* in its center leads to smaller *chowks* containing shops and offices in the four corners. Diagonal bazaar streets oriented to the northeast, southwest, southeast, and northwest may be entered from the *chowks* through gateways. Here the idea of *chowk* at crossroads achieves its fullest expression.[11]

New commercial centers in Indian cities can achieve a harmonious integrity in their layouts and architectural fabric if they adopt the timeless symbol of cross within a square. The streetscape can be continuous and unified if a consistent architectural vocabulary is used. The ratio of street width to building height can be manipulated (ranging between 1:1 and 2:1) to achieve a human scale. The urban square at the street intersection could be nucleated with trees, *kunds,* and public art. It could be framed by gateways at street ends. Vendors can be accommodated in the colonnades lining the shops or in the linear plaza with shade trees in the middle of the street. This urban node could be fully pedestrian with provisions for parking private and public transport in entry plazas located near the gateways.

VAASTU DESIGN

Although *vaastu* design has always guided temple architecture, over the last decade it has enjoyed a renaissance of sorts in non-religious buildings. Indeed, some professionally trained architects have become instant "*vaastu* experts." In some ways, this current *vaastu* design practice is akin to planning according to fêng shui principles. It represents a creative adaptation of medieval knowledge, minus its philosophical profundities, to contemporary needs. The explanation for this newfound popularity lies perhaps in the superstitious beliefs of clients, who are anxious to reap the benefits, material and spiritual, accrued from appropriate selection of site to right placement of openings and furniture.[12] Non-traditional building types, such as offices, hotels, apartment buildings, and factories, are covered in a spate of recently published handbooks. They offer *vaastu* designs based on orientation principles, which promise to bring prosperity and good fortune to the owners and residents.[13] *Vaastu vidya* (knowledge of *vaastu*) is treated as a mystical process governing the location of building uses and equipment in auspicious directions, according to the *vaastu purusha mandala*. A complex system of associations among directions, planets, elements, zodiac signs, body parts and sensations, seasons, colours, and shapes is taken into account in designating auspicious temporal and spatial uses. The householder's horoscope is consulted when building his house to locate openings based upon the position of the sun in various zodiacs.

Can *vaastu* design articulate a theory and grammar of architecture that are uniquely Indian? The *vaastu* expert and the architect, a product of the modern system of the professional education, do not always see eye to eye. The former has access to closely guarded mystical knowledge resting upon age-old tradition while the latter is shaped by values of modernism that stress innovation in forms, building materials, and technology. Yet *vaastu* design strikes a resonant chord for architecture in search of Indian identity.[14] It also holds the clue to interpreting architectural history according to canonical tradition. For this reason alone it should be an integral part of design education.

VISIONARY ARCHITECTURE

Visionary architecture offers the opportunity for expressing cosmological and cosmogonic motifs that have consistently appeared in the long history of Hindu sacred landscapes. These archaic symbols have withstood the passage of millennia; their timelessness could be attributed to them being expressions of archetypes embedded in the collective unconscious. They evoke a sense of grandeur, fascination, and mystery and reaffirm kinship with a larger entity. They hold clues in our search for cultural identity. As Romi Khosla says:

> While looking at the work of a contemporary Indian architect, by listening to him talking or by reading about him, it becomes abundantly clear that many architects share the same entry point. One is looking at a single entry point that reveals a shared state of mind and not the architectural style. Indeed the style of the built form seems to be irrelevant because such a multiplicity of styles from someone like Charles Correa would send any critic trying to comprehend it on a

wild goose chase. This *supra* entry point through which our architects are seeking recognition and realisation is an overriding need to *invent authenticity*.[15]

Charles Correa's highly imaginative designs are drawn upon archetypal symbols, especially of *imago mundi*. He is fascinated with the idea of buildings as microcosms and with using iconic imagery in building details and artwork. His Jawahar Kala Kendra in Jaipur, housing the arts, mimics the city of Jaipur in its plan, complete to the disjointed square forming the

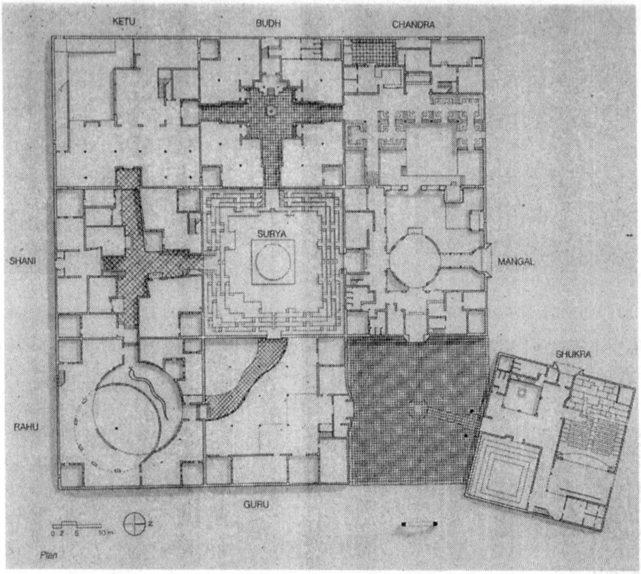

13.5: Jawahar Kala Kendra in Jaipur, designed by Charles Correa, mimics the nine square mandala plan of Jaipur (courtesy Charles Correa).

entry point. The squares named after the nine planets represent a programme (display of textiles, weaponry, library, performing arts) consistent with planetary associations. The central square, as in many other projects by Correa, is named after the sun (*surya*) and is called Surya kunda, the symbol of the sun arising out of the primeval ocean. Surroun ded by *ghat*-like steps, the central square is laid out as a gathering place. The cosmic symbolism is strengthened by planetary icons of inlaid stone in the walls surrounding each square. The building in its symmetry, massing, volumes, iconography, materials, and colour is a powerful expression of the ancient concept of cosmos in secular terms. In the Inter-University Center for Astronomy and

Astrophysics on the Pune University campus, Correa designed two concrete columns at the entry (painted blue at the top to suggest their merging with the sky) as *axis mundi,* beyond which lies the *kund*—in this case, a grassy square with diagonal stone paving— in the image of centrifugal forces of our expanding universe.[16]

Two more examples will suffice to show that visionary architecture built in the last two decades can draw upon cosmic imagery of the past and yet be powerful in its impact on contemporary society. Matrimandir in Auroville (an *ashram* in Pondicherry), designed by Roger Anger, is a cosmic egg floating on the primeval waters. The flattened sphere contains a meditation chamber accessed by a pair of spiral steel ramps and with a crystal globe lit by a heliostat as the single source of illumination. The entire structure is supported by four pairs of sickle-shaped piers rising out of a water tank.[17] Iranian architect Fariburz Sahba's Baha'i Temple in New Delhi is another instance when a cosmogonic motif, in this case a lotus rising out of the waters, has been employed with startling effect. The structure consists of three layers of concrete lotus petals clad with marble rising out of nine reflecting pools. The outermost layer forms canopies over nine entrances while the inner layers surround a domed hall. Its magnificent space is lit with skylights while exterior lighting gives the illusion of a lotus emerging out of the waters.[18]

13.6: Matrimandir in Auroville is an example of visionary architecture and symbolizes the cosmic egg floating on the primeval waters (courtesy Surinder Bagha).

These examples celebrate a cosmic vision in the service of institutions devoted to societal progress and well-being. The buildings possess clarity of form and uniqueness that grant them iconic status and universal appeal. A relevant question is whether their meanings remain unchangingly metaphysical; in other words, are the forms read by the general populace in ways similar to those promoted by architectural discourse? In the words of their designers, they resonate with images buried in the substratum of collective memory. From this point of view, they may be seen as the most recent efforts in a three-thousand-year history of transforming the natural order into a built one. I believe that the use of traditional forms is more than a legitimizing device to authenticate the design by connecting it to the time-honored past. It represents resistance to global trends that tend to homogenize landscapes by repeated use of currently trendy styles and logos, irrespective of regional and cultural differences.

NOTES

1. In *Charles Correa,* with an essay by Kenneth Frampton (London: Thames and Hudson, 1996).
2. Jan Pieper, "Arboreal Art and Architecture in India," in *Concepts of Space—Ancient and Modern,* ed. Kapila Vatsyayan (New Delhi: Abhinav Publications, Indira Gandhi National Centre for the Arts, 1991), 333–342.
3. Anil K. Verma, "Mishrikh," *Architecture and Design* 11:4 (July–August 1994): 79–85, based upon detailed documentation, outlines a master plan for renovating the landscape of Mishrikh *kund.* The large *kund* at Pushkar has fifty-two *ghats* around its edge and has more than a hundred temples—the most significant one is dedicated to Brahma who performed a *yajna* at the site. The mythic explanation for the existence of fresh water at this site is that the lotus falling from Brahma's hands struck the land at three spots, causing three *kunds* to spring up. The geographic explanation is that the Pushkar basin on the edge of the great Thar desert, enclosed on the northeast and southeast by hilly ranges, has sand dunes blocking the valley and impeding drainage of the headwaters of Luni river. Small lakes are created and sustained by dams. Temples to Brahma's wives—the goddesses Savitri and Gayatri—on top of two hills are clearly visible from the main *kund.* Nearby is the Naga hill and *kund,* believed to cure pilgrims of snakebites. See Ranjani Mishra, *Holy Pushkar: A Pilgrim's Journey in Quest of Lord Brahma* (New Delhi: Kanishka, 1999).
4. Eric Parry, "Ritual of the City," *Architectural Review* 181:1081 (1987), 14–23.
5. Morna Livingston's "The Stepwells and Stepped-Ponds of Western India," *Asian Art and Culture* 8:2 (Spring 1995), 3–19, is an excellent overview of their phenomenal experience and architectural qualities. For details see Jutta Jain-Neubauer's *The Stepwells of Gujarat* (New Delhi: Abhinav Publications, 1981).
6. Correa, *Charles Correa.*
7. Stephen White, *Building in the Garden: The Architecture of Joseph Allen Stein in India and California* (Delhi: Oxford University Press, 1993).

8. Correa, *Charles Correa.*
9. Raj Rewal, "The Use of Tradition in Architecture and Urban Form," in *Contemporary Architecture and City Form: The South Asian Paradigm*, ed. Farooq Ameen (Mumbai: Marg Publications, 1997), 52–63.
10. William Curtis Jr., *Balakrishna Doshi: An Architecture for India* (New York: Rizzoli International, 1988).
11. Correa, *Charles Correa.*
12. See Kathleen Cox, *Vastu Living: Creating a Home for the Soul* (New York: Marlowe and Company, 2000). The book is a how-to guide for designing homes, offices, and gardens in accordance with *vaastu* principles. Cox bases her designs on the client's disposition as identified in the Ayurvedic medical system.
13. Vibhuti Chakrabarti mentions ten books on *vaastu* design published in the last decade in her *Indian Architectural Theory: Contemporary Uses of Vastu Vidya* (Richmond, Surrey: Curzon Press, 1998).
14. *Ibid.*
15. Romi Khosla, "Current Architecture in India," *Mimar* 11:4 (December 1991), 20–25.
16. Correa, *Charles Correa.*
17. Sarbjit Bagha, Surinder Bagha, and Yashinder Bagha, *Modern Architecture in India: Post-Independence Perspective* (New Delhi: Galgotia Publishing, 1993).
18. *Ibid.*

Glossary

aarti	ritual obeisance
adharma	non-righteousness
akasha	sky
akshayavat	eternal tree
amalaka	fruit symbol on temple crest
amrta	elixir of immortality
anjan	kohl
apsaras	female celestial spirits
arama	garden
ashram	hermitage for ascetics
asura	demon
atman	individual soul
avatara	reincarnation
bhairava	form of Shiva
bhakta	devotee
bhakti	devotion
bhav	emotion
bodhisattva	one who is on the way to attaining Buddhahood
Brahma sutras	aphorisms of *vedanta* philosophy
brahman	universal soul
Brahmin	priestly caste
chaitya griha	hall for assembly of congregation
chaudahkos	pilgrimage circuit measuring 14 *kos*
parikrama chattravali	royal umbrella
dan	charity
dandauti parikrama	circumambulation done with prostrations
darshan	sighting
dharma	religious creed and code of conduct
gandharva	nature spirit

garbha-griha	temple shrine
ghats	steps lining the edges of a water body
giri-pradakshina	circumambulatory tour of mountain
grama devata	village deity
harmika	altar with railing on top of a stupa
jhula	swing
Kali yuga	fourth and present epoch of Hindu mythology
kalpa vriksha	wish-fulfilling tree
karawka mandala	bow-shaped auspicious form
karma	action
karsevak	volunteer for religious duties
kinnara	nature spirit
kirtan	devotional swinging
kshatriya	warrior caste
kshetra	sacred site
kshetrapala	guardian of *kshetra*
kumbha	water pot
Kumbha Mela	festival held every twelve years at a pilgrim site
kund	water tank
kunj	bower
lila	divine play
linga	aniconic symbol of Shiva shaped like a phallus
madhurya	sweet love
mandala	auspicious form
maya	illusion
moksha	liberation from the cycle of birth and death
naga	serpent
nagakal	stone slab with entwined snakes motif
nagapanchami	snake festival
niikunj	arbor
panch kos parikrama	five-*kos* pilgrimage circuit
papa	sin
paribhajaka	sect of wandering philosophers
parikrama	pilgrimage circuit
pishacha	evil spirit

prakriti	nature
pralaya	apocalypse
punya	spiritual merit
Puranas	mythological texts
purusha	primeval man
Purusha	brahman
rakshasa	demon
rasa	essence
ras lila	dance drama with Krishna mythology as the theme
ras mandala	circular performing arena
rasoi	kitchen
sadhu	holy man
sakyamuni	the Buddha
sangha	Buddhist congregation
sangharama	monastic complex
sansara	mortal world
saptapuri	the seven holy cities—Ayodhya, Dvarka, Hardwar, Mathura, Kanchi, Ujjain, and Varanasi
sarovar	lake
Shesh-naga	serpent king supporting the earth
shakti	feminine principle
shastra	sacred knowledge texts
sharavan	monsoon season
shikhara	mountain crest
stambha	pillar
svayambhu	self manifested
tantric	religious texts and practice revealed by Shiva; specific to present age of *Kali yuga*
tapas	austerity
tapovana	forest where asceticism is practiced
tila	mound
tirtha	sacred center signifying fords or crossings
Treta Yuga	third epoch of Hindu mythology
trikona	triangle
tulsi	basil plant, symbol of goddess Lakshmi

Upanishads	speculative treatise concerned with the nature of man and the universe, forming latter part of the Vedic literature, dating from the eighth century CE
vaastu	designed objects and space
vaastu purusha mandala	archetypal symbol
varnas	social stratification system—progenitor of caste structure
Vasuki	serpent-demon
Vedas	four ancient canonical collections of hymns, prayers, and liturgical formulae composed between 1500 and 1000 BCE—Rigveda, Samaveda, Yajurveda, and Atharvaveda
vedanta	system of monastic philosophy based upon an investigation of the latter part of Vedas
vedika	sacred altar
vidhyadhars	nature spirits
viharas	monasteries
vinaya	one of three divisions of Buddhist canon in Pali
Vrtra	demon
yaksha	nature spirit
yantra	magical diagram
yojanas	measurement of distance equal to 3.5 km
yoni	icon in the shape of female sex organ, signifies *shakti*

Bibliography

Acharya, P. K. *Indian Architecture According to Manasara-Silpasastra.* Calcutta: Oxford University Press, 1927.

Alley, Kelly. "Idioms of Degeneracy: Assessing Ganga's Purity and Pollution." In *Purifying the Earthly Body of God: Religion and Ecology in Hindu India,* ed. Lance Nelson, 297–331. Albany: State University of New York Press, 1998.

Appleton, Jay. *The Experience of Landscape.* London: John Wiley, 1975.

Asher, Frederick. "Gaya: Monuments of the Pilgrimage Town." *Marg* 40:1 (1989): 45–60.

Bahga, Sarbjit, Surinder Bahga, and Yashinder Bagha. *Modern Architecture in India: Post-Independence Perspective.* New Delhi: Galgotia, 1993.

Bakker, Hans. *Ayodhya.* Groningen: Egbert Forsten, 1986.

———. "The History of Hanumat Worship at Ayodhya." In *Pilgrimage Studies: Text and Context,* ed. D. P. Dubey, 127–135. Allahabad, India: The Society of Pilgrimage Studies, 1990.

Banerjee, Priyatosh. *The Blue God.* Bombay: Lalit Kala Series of Indian Art, 1981.

Baumer, Bettina. "From Guha to Akasa: The Mystical Cave in the Vedic and Saiva Traditions." In *Concepts of Space: Ancient and Modern,* ed. Kapila Vatsyayan, 105–122. Indira Gandhi National Centre for the Arts, New Delhi: Abhinav Publications, 1991.

Beck, Brenda. "The Symbolic Merger of Body, Space, and Cosmos in Hindu Tamil Nadu." *Contributions to Indian Sociology* 10:2 (1976): 213–243.

Beteille, Andre. *Caste, Class and Power.* Berkeley: University of California Press, 1965.

Bharati, Agehananda. "Pilgrimage in the Indian Tradition." *History of Religions* 3:1 (Summer 1963): 135–167.

Bhardwaj, Surinder. *Hindu Places of Pilgrimage in India.* Berkeley: University of California Press, 1973.

Bhattacharyya, Tarapada. *The Canons of Indian Art.* Calcutta: Firma K.L. Mukhopadhyay, 1963.

Blackburn, Stuart. "Creating Conversations: The Rama Story as Puppet Play in Kerala." In *Many Ramayanas—The Diversity of a Narrative Tradition in South Asia,* ed. Paula Richman. Berkeley: University of California Press, 1991.

Bloss, Lowell. "The Buddha and the Naga: A Study in Buddhist Folk Religiosity." *History of Religions,* 13:1 (August, 1973): 36–53.

Bose, Atindra Nath. "Oldest Indo-Aryan Cities." *Journal of Indian History,* Madras, 21 (April 1942): 60–82.

Bose, Phanindra N. *Principles of Indian Silpasastra*. Delhi: Bharatiya, 1978.

Brill, Mike. "Archetypes as a 'Natural Language' for Place-making." In *Ordering Space—Types in Architecture and Design,* ed. Karen Frank and Lynda Schneekloth, 61–78. New York: Van Nostrand Reinhold, 1994.

Brown, W. Norman. The Sources and Nature of *purusa* in the Purusasukta (Rigveda 10.91). *Journal of the American Oriental Society,* 51 (1931): 118.

Buhnemann, Gudrun. "Mandala, Yantra, and Cakra: Some Observations." In *Mandalas and Yantras in the Hindu Traditions,* ed. Gudrun Buhnemann, 13–56. Leiden: Brill, 2003.

Chakrabarti, Vibhuti. *Indian Architectural Theory: Contemporary Uses of Vastu Vidya.* Richmond, Surrey: Curzon Press, 1998.

Chandran, M. D. Subash, and J. Donald Hughes. "Sacred Groves and Conservation: The Comparative History of Traditional Reserves in the Mediterranean Area and in South India." *Environment and History,* 6 (2000): 169–186.

Chattopadhyay, Swati. "Blurring Boundaries: The Limits of 'White Town' in Colonial Calcutta." *Journal of Society of Architectural Historians,* 59:2 (June 2000): 154–179.

Coburn, Thomas. "The Threefold Vision of the Devi Mahatmya." In *Devi, The Great Goddess: Female Divinity in South Asian Art,* ed. Vidya Dehejia et al., 37–58. Washington, DC: Arthur Sackler Gallery, Smithsonian Institution, 1999.

Commissariat, Manekshah S. *History of Gujarat.* Bombay, 1 (1938).

Condon, Patrick. "A Built Landscape Typology: The Language of the Land We Live In." In *Ordering Space—Types in Architecture and Design,* ed. Karen Frank and Lynda Schneekloth, 79–94. New York: Van Nostrand Reinhold, 1994.

Coomaraswamy, Ananda. *Buddha and the Gospel of Buddhism.* New York: Harper and Row, 1964.

———. "Early Indian Architecture." *Eastern Architecture,* 2 (1930): 209–233.

———. *Elements of Buddhist Iconography.* Cambridge, MA: Harvard University Press, 1935.

———. *Yakshas,* Smithsonian Miscellaneous Collections, 80:6. Washington, DC: Smithsonian Institution, 1928.

Cox, Kathleen. *Vastu Living: Creating a Home for the Soul.* New York: Marlowe and Company, 2000.

Csikszentmihalyi, Mihaly. *Flow—The Psychology of Optimal Experience.* New York: Harper and Row, 1990.

Curtis, William, Jr. *Balakrishna Doshi: An Architecture for India.* New York: Rizzoli International, 1988.

Dagens, Bruno, ed. *Mayamatam—Treatise of Housing, Architecture and Iconography.* Delhi: Motilal Banarsidass, 1994.

Dallapiccola, Anna. "The City of Vijayanagara: Kiskindha, the Monkey-Kingdom." In *The Legend of Rama: Artistic Visions,* ed. Vidya Dehejia, 61–72. Bombay: Marg Publications, 1994.

Daniel, Valentine E. *Fluid Signs—Being a Person the Tamil Way.* Berkeley: University of California Press, 1984.

Das, Jithendra. *The Buddhist Architecture in Andhra.* New Delhi: Books and Books, 1993. Davar, Satish. "A Filigree City Spun out of Nothingness." *Marg* 30:4 (1977): 35–58.

Dewan, Jatin. "Development of Land-water Interface: Ayodhya." Unpublished B.Arch. Thesis, Chandigarh School of Architecture, 1990.

Dimmitt, Cornelia, and J.A.B. van Buitenen, eds. *Classical Mythology in the Sanskritic Puranas.* Philadelphia: Temple University Press, 1978.

Dimock, Edward. "Lila." *History of Religions* 29:2 (1989): 159–173.

Dobia, Brenda. "Seeking Ma, Seeking Me." In *Is the Goddess a Feminist? The Politics of South Asian Goddesses,* ed. Alf Hiltebeitel and Kathleen Erndl, 203–238. New York: New York University Press, 2000.

Doshi, Harish. *Traditional Neighborhood in a Modern City.* New Delhi: Abhinav Publications, 1974.

Dubey, D. P., and Rana P.B. Singh. "Chitrakut: The Frame and Network of the Faithscape and Sacred Geometry of a Hindu Tirtha." In *The Spirit and Power of Place: Human Environment and Sacrality,* ed. Rana P.B. Singh, pub. 41, 301 332. Varanasi: National Geographic Society of India, 1994.

Duncan, James. "From Container of Women to Status Symbol: The Impact of Social Structure on the Meaning of the House." In *Housing and Identity: Cross Cultural Perspectives,* ed. James Duncan, 36–59. New York: Holmes and Meier Publishers, 1981.

Dutt, Binode Bihari. *Town Planning in Ancient India.* Calcutta: Thacker, Spink & Company, 1925.

Dutt, Sukumar. *Buddhist Monks and Monasteries of India.* London: George Allen & Unwin, 1962.

Eck, Diana. *Banaras: City of Light.* New York: Alfred Knopf, 1982.

———. "The City as a Sacred Center." In *The City as a Sacred Center—Essays on Six Asian Contexts,* ed. Bardwell Smith and Holly B. Reynolds, 1–11. Leiden: E. J. Brill, 1987.

———. "Following Rama, Worshipping Siva." In *Devotion Divine: Bhakti Traditions from the Regions of India,* ed. Diana Eck and Francoise Mallison, 49–71. Egbert Forsten, 1991.

———. "The Goddess Ganges in Hindu Sacred Geography." In *Devi: Goddesses of India,* ed. John Hawley and Donna Wulff. Berkeley: University of California Press, 1996.

———. "The Imagined Landscape: Patterns in the Construction of Hindu Sacred Geography." *Contributions to Indian Sociology* 32:2 (1998): 165–188.

———. "India's Tirthas: 'Crossings' in Sacred Geography." *History of Religions* 20:4 (May 1981): 323–344.

Edensor, Tim. "The Culture of the Indian Street." In *Images of the Street: Planning, Identity, and Control in Public Space,* ed. Nicholas Fyte, 205–221. London: Routledge, 1998.

Eliade, Mircea. *Cosmos and History: The Myth of the Eternal Return.* New York: Harper Torchbooks, 1959.

———. *Patterns in Comparative Religion.* New York: World Publishing, 1963.

———. *The Sacred and the Profane.* New York: Harvest Books, 1959.

———. *Yoga—Immortality and Freedom,* trans. Willard Trask. Bollingen Series 56. Princeton, NJ: Princeton University Press, 1969.

Entwistle, Alan W. *Braj—Centre of Krishna Pilgrimage.* Groningen: Egbert Forsten, 1987.

Erndl, Kathleen. "Seranvali: The Mother Who Possesses." In *Devi: Goddesses of India,* ed. John Hawley and Donna Wulff, 173–194. Berkeley: University of California Press, 1996.

Fonseca, Rory. "The Walled City of Old Delhi." *Landscape* 18:3 (Fall 1969): 213–243.

Forman, Robert. "The Hindu Temple: The Metaphysical Architecture of the Kandariya Mahadeva." *Man in India* 65:2 (June 1985): 154–176.

Foucher, Alfred. *The Life of the Buddha According to the Ancient Texts and Monuments of India,* trans. S. B. Boas. Westport, CT: Greenwood Press, 1963.

Frampton, Kenneth. *Charles Correa.* London: Thames and Hudson, 1996.

Fritz, John. "Vijayanagara: Authority and Meaning of a South Indian Imperial Capital." *American Anthropologist* 88:1 (March 1986).

———, and George Mitchell. "Interpreting the Plan of a Medieval Hindu Capital, Vijayanagara." *World Archaeology* 19:1 (June 1987): 105–129.

Frye, Northrop. *Anatomy of Criticism.* Princeton, NJ: Princeton University Press, 1957.

Fuller, Chris J. "Madurai." In *Temple Towns of Tamil Nadu,* ed. George Michell, 94–113. Bombay: Marg Publications, 1993.

Funo, Shuji, Naohiko Yamamoto, and Mohan Pant. "Space Formation of Jaipur City, Rajasthan, India: An Analysis on City Maps (1925–28) Made by Survey of India." *Journal of Asian Architecture and Building Engineering* 1:1 (March 2002): 261–269.

Gadgil, Madhav, and Ramachandra Guha. *Ecology and Equity: The Use and Abuse of Nature in Contemporary India.* New Delhi, India: Penguin Books, 1995.

Gallant, Christine. *Tabooed Jung: Marginality as Power.* New York: New York University Press, 1996.

Gamble, John. "Landscape in Motion." In *Landscape in America,* ed. George Thompson, 251–260. Austin: University of Texas Press, 1995.

Gangoly, Ordhendra C. *Landscape in Indian Literature and Art.* Calcutta: University of Lucknow, 1963.

Ghosh, Binoy. *Primitive Indian Architecture.* Calcutta: Firma K.L. Mukhopadhay, 1953.

Gist, Noel. "The Ecology of Bangalore, India: An East-West Comparison." In *Urbanism in World Perspective,* ed. Sylvia Fava, 177–188. New York: Thomas Y. Crowell, 1968.

Goetz, Herman. "Pawagadh-Champaner." *Journal of the Gujarat Research Society* 11:2 (April 1949): 1–67.

Goldman, Robert. "A City of the Heart: Epic Mathura and the Indian Imagination." *Journal of American Oriental Society* 106:3 (1986): 471–483.

———. Introduction and Translation of *The Ramayana of Valmiki—An Epic of Ancient India*. Vol. 1: *Balakanda,* 1–118. Princeton, NJ: Princeton University Press, 1984.

———, and Sally Sutherland. Introduction, Translation, and Annotation of *The Ramayana of Valmiki*. Vol. V: *Sundarakanda,* 3–98. Princeton, NJ: Princeton University Press, 1996.

Gough, Kathleen. "The Social Structure of a Tanjore Village." In *India's Villages,* ed. M. N. Srinivas, 90–102. Bombay: Asia Publishing House, 1960.

Gowdra, Gurumurthy. "Ritual Circles in a Mysore Village." *Sociological Bulletin* 20:1 (March 1971): 24–38.

Growse, Frederic S. *Mathura: District Memoir,* 3rd ed. Ahmedabad: New Order Book Company, 1978.

Gupta, Sanjukta. "The *Mandala* as an Image of Man." In *Indian Ritual and Its Exegesis,* ed. Richard Gombrich, 32–41. Oxford University Papers on India 2:1. Delhi: Oxford University Press, 1988.

Gussow, Alan. "Beauty in the Landscape: An Ecological Viewpoint." In *Landscape in America,* ed. George Thompson, 223–240. Austin: University of Texas Press, 1995.

Haberman, David. *Journey Through the Twelve Forests: An Encounter with Krishna.* New York. Oxford University Press, 1994.

Hardy, Adam. "Form, Transformation, and Meaning in Indian Temple Architecture." In *Paradigms of Indian Architecture: Space and Time in Representation and Design,* ed. G.H.R. Tillotson, 107–135. Collected Papers on South Asia 13. Richmond, Surrey: Curzon Press, 1998.

Hardy, Friedhelm. "Krnaism." In *Encyclopaedia of Religion,* ed. Mircea Eliade, 384–392. New York: Macmillan, 1987.

Harzer, Edeltraud. "Purusa." In *Encyclopedia of Religion,* ed. Mircea Eliade, 106–107. New York: Macmillan, 1987.

Hawley, John Stratton. *Krishna, the Butter Thief.* Princeton, NJ: Princeton University Press, 1983.

Herman, Phyllis. "Sita in the Kitchen: The *Pativrata* and *Ramarajya.*" *Manushi: A Journal About Women and Society* 120 (September–October 2000): 5–11.

Hiltebeitel, Alf, and Kathleen Erndl, eds. *Is the Goddess a Feminist? The Politics of South Asian Goddesses.* New York: New York University Press, 2000.

Hosagrahar, Jyoti. "Mansions to Margins: Modernity and the Domestic Landscapes of Historic Delhi, 1847–1910." *Journal of Society of Architectural Historians* 60:1 (March 2001): 26–45.

Humbert, Elie. "Archetypes." In *Carl Gustav Jung: Critical Assessments.* Vol. II: *The Structure and the Dynamics of the Psyche,* ed. Renos K. Papadopoulos, 307–317. London: Routledge, 1992.

Humes, Cynthia Ann. "Vindhyavasini—Local Goddess yet Great Goddess." In *Devi: Goddesses of India,* ed. John Hawley and Donna Wulff, 49–76. Berkeley: University of California Press, 1996.

Huntington, John. "Sowing the Seeds of the Lotus—A Journey to the Great Pilgrimage Sites of Buddhism." Part 1. *Orientations* (November 1985): 46–61; Part II. *Orientations* (February 1986): 28–43.

Irwin, John. "The Ancient Pillar-cult at Prayaga (Allahabad): Its Pre-Asokan Origins." *Journal of the Royal Asiatic Society* 2 (1983): 253–280.

———. "Ashokan Pillars: A Reassessment of Evidence." *The Burlington Magazine* 115:848 (November 1973): 706–720.

———. "The Axial Symbolism of the Early Stupa: An Exegesis." In *The Stupa—Its Religious, Historical and Architectural Significance,* ed. Anna Dallapiccola, 12–37. Wiesbaden: Franz Steiner Verlag, 1980.

———. "The Stupa and the Cosmic Axis: The Archaeological Evidence." In *South Asian Archaeology,* Vol. 2, ed. Maurizio Taddei, 799–837. Naples: Instituto Universitario Orientale, 1979.

Isacco, Enrico, and Anna Dallapiccola, eds. *Krishna, the Divine Lover—Myth and Legend Through Indian Art.* Bombay: B. I. Publications, 1982.

Jackson, John B. "In Search of the Proto-Landscape." In *Landscape in America,* ed. George Thompson, 43–50. Austin: University of Texas Press, 1995.

———. *A Sense of Place, A Sense of Time.* New Haven, CT: Yale University Press, 1994.

———. "The Word Itself." In *Discovering the Vernacular Landscape,* 3–8. New Haven: Yale University Press, 1984.

Jafee, Aniela. "Individuation." In *Carl Gustav Jung: Critical Assessments,* ed. Renos Papadopoulos. Vol. 2: The Structure and Dynamics of the Psyche, 375–389. London: Routledge, 1992.

Jain, Kulbhushan. "Jaisalmer: Architecture of a Desert Town." In *Stones in the Sand: The Architecture of Rajasthan,* ed. Giles Tillotson. Marg Publications, 52:4 (June 2001): 90–101.

Jain-Neubauer, Jutta. *The Stepwells of Gujarat.* New Delhi: Abhinav Publications, 1981.

Jayakar, Pupul. *The Earth Mother.* San Francisco: Harper and Row, 1990.

Johnston, Edward H. *Asvaghosha's Buddhacharita or Acts of the Buddha.* Delhi: Motilal Banarsidas, 1984.

Jung, Carl. "The Philosophical Tree." In *The Collected Works of C. G. Jung,* Vol. 13, ed. Herbert Reed, Michael Fordham, and Gerhard Adler and trans. R.F.C. Hull. Princeton, NJ: Princeton University Press, 1967.

Kakar, Sudhir. *The Inner World: A Psycho-Analytic Study of Childhood and Society in India,* 2nd ed. Delhi: Oxford University Press, 1981.

Kaplan, Rachel, and Steve Kaplan. *The Experience of Nature: A Psychological Perspective.* Cambridge: Cambridge University Press, 1989.

Kellert, Stephen. "The Biological Basis for Human Values of Nature." In *The Biophilia Hypothesis,* ed. Stephen R. Kellert and Edward O. Wilson. Washington, DC: Island Press, 1993.

Khambatta, Ismet. "The Meaning of Residence in Traditional Indian Society." In *Dwellings, Settlements and Tradition,* ed. Jean-Paul Bourdier and Nezar Al Sayyad. New York: University Press of America, 1989.

Khanna, Rajiv. "Kanak Vrindavan Valley, Jaipur." *Architecture and Design* 12:3 (May–June 1996): 55–65.

Khosla, Romi. "Current Architecture in India." *Mimar* 11:4 (December 1991): 20–25.

King, Anthony. *The Bungalow: The Production of a Global Culture.* Cambridge: Oxford University Press, 1995.

Kinsley, David. *Hindu Goddesses: Visions of the Divine Feminine in the Hindu Religious Tradition.* Berkeley: University of California Press, 1986.

———. *The Sword and the Flute—Kali and Krsna, Dark Visions of the Terrible and the Sublime in Hindu Mythology.* Berkeley: University of California Press, 1975.

Koshambi, Damodar D. "At the Crossroads: Mother Goddess Cult Sites in Ancient India." *Journal of the Royal Asiatic Society of Great Britain and Ireland* (1960): 17–31, 135–144.

———. *Myth and Reality.* Bombay: Popular Prakashan, 1962.

Kostof, Spiro. *The City Shaped.* Boston: Bulfinch Press, 1991.

Kramrisch, Stella. *The Art of India.* London: Phaidon Press, 1954.

———. *The Hindu Temple.* Calcutta: University of Calcutta, 1946.

———. "Patron and Practice." In *Exploring India's Sacred Art: Selected Writings of Stella Kramrisch,* ed. Barbara S. Miller, 51–58. Philadelphia: University of Pennsylvania Press, 1983.

———. "Space in Indian Cosmogony and in Architecture." In *Concepts of Space: Ancient and Modern,* ed. Kapila Vatsyayan, 101–104. Indira Gandhi National Centre for the Arts, New Delhi: Abhinav Publications, 1991.

———. "The Temple as Purusa." In *Studies in Indian Temple Architecture,* ed. Pramod Chandra, 40–46. New Delhi: American Institute of Indian Studies, 1975.

Lang, Jon, Madhavi Desai, and Miki Desai. *Architecture and Independence: The Search for Identity— India 1880–1980.* Delhi: Oxford University Press, 1997.

Lannoy, Richard. *The Speaking Tree: A Study of Indian Culture and Society.* New York: Oxford University Press, 1971.

Lefeber, Rosalind. Introduction, Translation, and Annotation of *The Ramayana of Valmiki.* Vol. 4: *Kishkindhakanda.* Ed. Robert Goldman, 55–57. Princeton, NJ: Princeton University Press, 1994.

Leoshko, Janice. "The Case of Two Witnesses to the Buddha's Enlightenment." *Marg* 39:4 (1988): 39–52.

Levi-Strauss, Claude. *Structural Anthropology.* New York: Basic Books, 1963.

Lewis, Oscar. *Village Life in Northern India.* New York: Vintage Books, 1965.

L'Hernault, Francoise. "Tiruvannamalai." In *Temple Towns of Tamil Nadu,* ed. George Michell, 40–57. Bombay: Marg Publications, 1993.

Ling, Trevor O. "Bodhi-Tree." In *A Dictionary of Comparative Religion,* ed. S.G.F. Brandon, 145. New York: Scribner, 1970.

———. *The Buddha.* London: Temple Smith, 1973.

Livingston, Morna. "The Stepwells and Stepped-Ponds of Western India." *Asian Art and Culture* 8:2 (Spring 1995): 3–19.

Lobell, Mimi. "The Buried Treasure: Women's Ancient Architectural Heritage." In *Architecture: A Place for Women,* ed. Ellen Perry Berkeley and Matilda McQuaid, 139–157. Washington, DC: Smithsonian Institution Press, 1989.

———. "Spatial Archetypes." *Re-Vision: A Journal of Consciousness and Change* 6:2 (Fall 1983): 69–82.

Lutgendorf, Philip. *The Life of a Text: Performing the Ramacaritmanas of Tulsidas.* Berkeley: University of California Press, 1991.

Lynch, Owen. "Rural Cities in India: Continuities and Discontinuities." In *India and Ceylon: Unity and Diversity,* ed. Philip Mason, 142–157. London: Oxford University Press, 1967.

Malandra, Geri. "The Mahabodhi Temple." *Marg* 40:1 (1989): 9–28.

Malville, John M. "Astronomy at Vijayanagara: Sacred Geography Confronts the Cosmos." In *The Spirit and Power of Place: Human Environment and Sacrality,* ed. Rana P.B. Singh, pub. 41, 171–188. Varanasi: National Geographical Society of India, 1994.

Malville, McKim. "Astrophysics, Cosmology, and the Interior Space of Indian Myths and Temples." In *Concepts of Space: Ancient and Modern,* ed. Kapila Vatsyayan, 123–144. Indira Gandhi National Centre for the Arts, New Delhi: Abhinav Publications, 1991.

Mandelbaum, David. *Society in India.* Berkeley: University of California Press, 1970.

Marcus, Clare Cooper. "Designing for a Commitment to Place: Lessons from the Alternative Community of Findhorn." In *Dwelling, Seeing, and Designing: Towards a Phenomenological Ecology,* ed. David Seamon, 299–330. Albany: State University of New York, 1993.

———. *House as a Mirror of Self: Exploring the Deeper Meaning of Home*. Berkeley, CA: Conari Press, 1995.

Marglin, Frederique A., and Puran Chandra Mishra. "Sacred Groves: Regenerating the Body, the Land, the Community." In *Global Ecology: A New Arena of Conflict,* ed. Wolfgang Sachs, 197–207. London: Zed Books, 1993.

Marriott, McKim. "The Feast of Love." In *Everyday Life in South Asia,* ed. Diane Mines and Sarah Lamb, 249–260. Bloomington: Indiana University Press, 2002.

———, ed. *Village India. Studies in the Little Community.* Chicago: University of Chicago Press, 1955.

Marshall, Anne, Rana P. B. Singh, and John McKim Malville. "Pilgrimage, Death, and the Sun at Gaya." In *Proceedings of the Conference on Pilgrimage and Complexity.* New Delhi: Indira Gandhi Center for the Arts, 1999.

Masson, Jeffrey L. "The Childhood of Krsna: Some Psychoanalytic Observations." *Journal of the American Oriental Society* 94:4 (1974): 454–459.

Mathur, K. S. *Caste and Ritual in a Malwa Village.* New Delhi: Asia Publishing House, 1964. McDermott, Rachel Fell, and Jeffrey Kripal, eds. *Encountering Kali in the Margins, at the Center, in the West.* Berkeley: University of California Press, 2003.

Mehta, R. N. *Champaner: A Medieval Capital.* Baroda: Heritage Trust, n.d.

———, and Rasesh Jamindar. "Urban Context." In *Ahmadabad,* ed. George Michell and Snehal Shah, 16–29. Bombay: Marg Publications, 1988.

Mehta, Surinder K. "Patterns of Residence in Poona, India by Caste and Religion: 1822–1965." *Demography* 6:4 (November 1969): 473–491.

Meing, Donald W. "The Beholding Eye: Ten Versions of the Same Scene." In *The Interpretation of Ordinary Landscapes,* ed. Donald W. Meing, 33–50. New York: Oxford University Press, 1979.

Meister, Michael. "Vastupurusamandalas: Planning in the Image of Man." In *Mandalas and Yantras in the Hindu Traditions,* ed. Gudrun Buhnemann, 251–270. Leiden: Brill, 2003.

Mencher, Joan. "Kerala and Madras: A Comparative Study of Ecology and Social Structure." *Ethnology* 5:2 (1966): 135–171.

Michell, George. "Introduction." In *Temple Towns of Tamil Nadu,* ed. George Michell, 2–17. Bombay: Marg Publications, 1993.

———, ed. *Eternal Kaveri: Historical Sites Along South India's Greatest River.* Mumbai: Marg Publications 51:1 (September 1999).

Michell, John. *The Earth Spirit: Its Ways, Shrines and Mysteries.* New York: Thames and Hudson, 1975.

Miles, William. "Account of the Hill-Fort of Champaner in Guzerat." In *Transactions of the Literary Society of Bombay,* Vol. 1, 150–156. Bombay: Bombay Education Society's Press, 1877 [1819].

Mishra, Ranjani. *Holy Pushkar: A Pilgrim's Journey in Quest of Lord Brahma.* New Delhi: Kanishka Publishers, 1999.

Mitra, Ashok. "Rural House Types and Village Settlement Patterns." In *India: Cultural Patterns and Processes,* ed. Allen Noble and Ashok Dutt, 105–124. Boulder, CO: Westview Press, 1982.

Mitra, Debjani. *Buddhist Monuments.* Calcutta: Sahitya Samsad, 1971.

Moffat, Michael. *An Untouchable Community in South India.* Princeton, NJ: Princeton University Press, 1979.

Mohammed, Sheikh Gulam. "Story of the Tongue and the Text." In *Narrative: A Seminar,* ed. Amiya Dev, 266–267. New Delhi: Sahitya Akademi, 1994.

Morris, Anthony E.J. *History of Urban Form.* London: George Goodwin, 1979.

Mudiraj, G.N.R. "Spatial Differentiation of Castes: Analysis of a Regional Pattern." *Man in India* 53:1 (January–March 1973): 24–37.

Mukerji, A. B. "Jats—A Study in Human Geography." *Geographical Review of India* 16:2 (1984): 12–31.

Nakamura, Hejime. *Gotama Buddha.* Los Angeles: Buddhist Books International, 1977.

Nanda, Vivek. "Urbanism, Tradition, and Continuity in Ahmedabad." *Mimar* (March 1991): 26–36.

Narayanan, Vasudha. "'One Tree Is Equal to Ten Sons': Hindu Responses to the Problems of Ecology, Population, and Consumption." *Journal of American Academy of Religions* 65:2 (June 1997): 291–332.

Nelson, Lance, ed. *Purifying the Earthly Body of God: Religion and Ecology in Hindu India.* Albany: State University of New York Press, 1998.

Neumann, Eric. *The Great Mother,* 2nd ed. Princeton, NJ: Princeton University Press, 1972.

Nitz, Hans-Jurgen. "Planned Temple Towns and Brahmin Villages as Spatial Expressions of the Ritual Politics of Medieval Kingdoms in South India." In *Ideology and Landscape in Historical Perspective: Essays in the Meanings of Some Places in the Past,* ed. Alan Baker and Gideon Biger, 107–124. New York: Cambridge University Press, 1992.

Oldenburg, Hermann. *Buddha: His Life, His Doctrine, His Order,* trans. W. Hoey. Delhi: Indological Book House, 1971.

Olin, Laurie. "Form, Meaning, and Expression in Landscape Architecture." *Landscape Journal* 10:2 (Fall 1991): 149–168.

Otto, Rudolph. *The Idea of the Holy.* New York: Oxford University Press, 1970.

Parry, Eric. "Ritual of the City." *Architectural Review* 181:1081 (1987): 14–23.

Parry, Jonathan. *Death in Banaras.* Cambridge: Cambridge University Press, 1994.

Patel, G. D. *Gujarat State Gazetteers: Panchmahals District.* Ahmedabad: Government of Gujarat, 1972.

Patil, Devendrakumar R. *Kusinagara.* New Delhi: Archaeological Survey of India, 1981.

Paul, Debjani. "Antiquity of the Visnupada at Gaya: Tradition and Archaeology." *East and West* 35:1–3 (September 1985): 103–141.

Pieper, Jan. "Arboreal Art and Architecture in India." In *Concepts of Space—Ancient and Modern,* ed. Kapila Vatsyayan, 333–342. Indira Gandhi National Centre for the Arts, New Delhi: Abhinav Publications, 1991.

Pollock, Sheldon. Introduction, Translation, and Annotation of *The Ramayana of Valmiki—An Epic of Ancient India.* Vol. 2: *Ayodhyakanda,* ed. Robert Goldman, 136–137. Princeton, NJ: Princeton University Press, 1986.

———. Introduction, Translation, and Annotation of *The Ramayana of Valmiki—An Epic of Ancient India.* Vol. 3: *Aranyakanda,* ed. Robert Goldman, 3–84. Princeton, NJ: Princeton University Press, 1991.

Pramar, V. S. *Haveli: Wooden Houses and Mansions of Gujarat.* Ahmedabad: Mapin Publishing, 1989.

Prime, Ranchor. *Hinduism and Ecology: Seeds of Truth.* London: Cassell, 1992.

Rangarajan, L. N., ed. *Kautilya—The Arthashastra.* New Delhi: Penguin Books, 1992.

Ray, Amita. *Villages, Towns and Secular Buildings in Ancient India.* Calcutta: Firma K.L. Mukhopadhyay, 1964.

Raz, Ram. *Essay on the Architecture of the Hindus.* Varanasi: Indological Book House, 1972.

Read, Herbert, Michael Fordham, and Gerhard Adler, eds. *The Collected Works of C. G. Jung.* London: Routledge, 1953–1978.

Rewal, Raj. "The Use of Tradition in Architecture and Urban Form." In *Contemporary Architecture and City Form: The South Asian Paradigm*, ed. Farooq Ameen, 52–63. Mumbai: Marg Publications, 1997.

Rhys Davids, Thomas W. *Buddhist India*. Delhi: Motilal Banarsidas, 1971.

Richman, Paula, ed. *Many Ramayanas—The Diversity of a Narrative Tradition in South Asia*. Berkeley: University of California, 1991.

Rowe, William "Caste, Kinship, and Association in Urban India." In *Urban Anthropology: Cross Cultural Studies of Urbanisation*, ed. Aidan Southall, 211–247. New York: Oxford University Press, 1973.

Roy, Ashim Kumar. "Architecture: The Dream and the Plan." *Marg* 30:4 (1977): 25–26.

Schama, Simon. *Landscape and Memory*. New York: Alfred Knopf, 1995.

Schopen, Gregory. "The Buddha as an Owner of Property and Permanent Resident in Medieval Indian Monasteries." *Journal of Indian Philosophy* 18 (1990): 181–217.

———. "Burial 'Ad Sanctos' and the Physical Presence of the Buddha in Early Indian Buddhism—A Study in the Archaeology of Religions." *Religion* 17 (1987): 193–225.

Sen Gupta, Sankar, ed. *Tree Symbol Worship in India—A New Study of a Pattern of Folk Religion*. Calcutta: India Publications, 1975.

Shaheer, Mohammad. "Landscape Architecture—Where We Are: Where We Should Be." *Architecture + Design* 13:3 (May–June 1996): 17–19.

Shiva, Vandana. *Staying Alive: Women, Ecology, and Development*. London: Zed Books, 1991. Singer, Milton, ed. *Traditional India: Structure and Change*. Philadelphia: American Folklore Society, 1959.

Singh, Jai Pal, and Mumtaz Khan. "Saptadvipa Vasumati: The Mythical Geography of the Hindus." In *Mythical Space, Cosmology, and Landscape: Towards a Cultural Geography of India*, ed. Jai Pal Singh and Mumtaz Khan, 9–29. New Delhi: Manak Publications, 2002.

Singh, Ram Bachan. "Cities and Parks in Ancient India." *Geographical Review of India* 36:1 (March 1974): 62–75.

Singh, Rana P.B. "Rama's Route After Banishment: A Geographic Viewpoint." *Journal of Scientific Research, Banaras Hindu University* 41B (1991): 39–46.

———. "Varanasi: Cosmic Order and Cityscape. Part III: Shiva's Universe and Pilgrimage Journeys." *Architecture and Design* (March–April 1995): 83–85.

Singh, Yogendra. "Chanukhera: Cultural Change in Eastern Uttar Pradesh." In *Change and Continuity in India's Villages*, ed. Kariqoudar Ishwaran, 241–270. New York: Columbia University Press, 1970.

Sinha, Amita. "Architecture and Identity in Colonial Discourse." *Journal of the Indian Institute of Architects* 66:10 (November 2001): 21–25.

———. "Bungalows of Lucknow Cantonment, India." *Open House International* 24:2 (1999): 56–63.

———. "The Conservation of Sacred Sites: Sarnath, a Case Study." *Landscape Research* 16:3 (Winter 1991): 23–30.

———. "Indian Architectural History: A Post-Colonial Perspective." *Journal of the Indian Institute of Architects* 68:7 (December 2003): 46–49.

———. "Introduction: Varieties of Nature Viewing." In *Landscape Perception,* ed. Amita Sinha, 1–10. London: Academic Press, 1995.

———. "On Holy Ground." *Landscape Design* 235 (November 1994): 34–36.

———. "Participant Observation: A Study of State-Aided Self-help Housing in Lucknow, India." In *Housing the Poor in the Developing World,* ed. Graham Tipple and Kenneth Willis, 16–34. New York: Routledge, 1991.

———, and Rajat Kant. "Urban Evolution and Transformation in Lucknow, India: A Comparative Study of Its Streets." *Open House International* 23:1 (1997): 34–42.

Smith, David. "Chidambaram." In *Temple Towns of Tamil Nadu,* ed. George Michell, 58–75. Bombay: Marg Publications, 1993.

Smith, Marion. "Social Structure in the Punjab." In *India's Villages,* ed. M. N. Srinivas, 161–179. Bombay: Asia Publishing House, 1960.

Spink, Walter M. *Krishnamandala: A Devotional Theme in Indian Art.* Ann Arbor: Center for South and Southeast Asian Studies, University of Michigan, 1971.

Spirn, Anne Whiston. "The Authority of Nature." In *Nature and Ideology: Natural Garden Design in the Twentieth Century,* ed. Joachim Wolschke-Bulmahn. Washington, DC: Dumbarton Oaks, 1977.

———. *The Language of Landscape.* New Haven: Yale University Press, 1998.

Srinivisan, Doris. *Mathura—The Cultural Heritage.* New Delhi: American Institute of Indian Studies, 1989.

Staal, Frits. "The Centre of Space: Construction and Discovery." In *Concepts of Space: Ancient and Modern,* ed. Kapila Vatsyayan, 83–100. Indira Gandhi National Centre for the Arts, New Delhi: Abhinav Publications, 1991.

Stevens, Anthony. *Archetypes: A Natural History of the Self.* New York: William Morrow & Co., 1982.

Streep, Peg. *Sanctuaries of the Goddess: The Sacred Landscape and Objects.* New York: Little, Brown and Company, 1994.

Subrahmanyam, K. M. "Four Main House Types in South India." *Journal of Madras Geographical Association* 13:2 (1938): 168–175.

Subramanyam, Y. S. *Social Change in Village India: An Andhra Case Study.* New Delhi: Prithvi Raj Publishers, 1975.

Thakur, Upendranath. *Buddhist Cities in Early India—Buddha Gaya, Rajagriha, and Nalanda.* New Delhi: Sundeep Prakashan, 1995.

Thiis-Evensen, Thomas. *Archetypes in Architecture.* Oslo: Norwegian University Press, 1987.

Thomas, Edward. *The Life of Buddha as Legend and History.* New York: Alfred Knopf, 1927.

Tilakasiri, J. *Kalidasa's Imagery and the Theory of Poetics.* New Delhi: 1988.

Tillotson, Giles H.R. *The Rajput Palaces: The Development of an Architectural Style, 1450–1750.* New Haven: Yale University Press, 1987.

Tiwari, J. N. *Goddess Cults in Ancient India*. Delhi: Sundeep Prakashan, 1985.

Van der Veer, Peter. *Gods on Earth—The Management of Religious Experience and Identity in a North Indian Pilgrimage Centre*. London School of Economics Monographs on Social Anthropology, no. 59, 127–135. London: The Athlone Press, 1988.

Vatsyayan, Kapila. *The Square and the Circle of the Indian Arts*. New Delhi: Roli Books International, 1983.

Vaudeville, Charlotte. "Evolution of Love—Symbolism in Bhagavatism." *Journal of the American Oriental Society* 82 (1982): 31–40.

———. "The Govardhan Myth in Northern India." *Indo-Iranian Journal* 22:1 (January 1980): 1–46.

Venkaramayya, M. *Sravasti*. New Delhi: Archaeological Survey of India, 1981.

Verma, Anil K. "Mishrikh." *Architecture and Design* 11:4 (July–August 1994): 79–85.

Vidyarthi, L. P. "Thinking About a Sacred City." *Eastern Anthropologist* 13:4 (1960): 203–215.

Vogel, Jean Philippe. Ph. *Indian Serpent Lore*. Varanasi: Prithvi Prakashan, 1972.

Wacziarg, Francis, and Aman Nath. *Rajasthan—The Painted Walls of Shekhavati*. New Delhi: Vikas Publishing House, 1982.

Wagoner, Philip. "Architecture and Mythic Space at the Hemakuta Hill: A Preliminary Report." In *Vijayanagara: Progress of Research, 1985–87*, 142–148. Mysore, India: Directorate of Archaeology and Museums, 1985.

———. *Tidings of the King: A Translation and Ethnohistorical Analysis of the* Rayavacakamu. Honolulu: University of Hawaii Press, 1993.

Watson, J. W. "Historical Sketch of the Hill Fortress of Pawagadh in Gujarat." *The Indian Antiquary: A Journal of Oriental Research* 6 (1877): 1–19.

White, Charles. "Krsna as Divine Child." *History of Religions* 10:2 (November 1970): 156–177.

White, Stephen. *Building in the Garden: The Architecture of Joseph Allen Stein in India and California*. Delhi: Oxford University Press, 1993.

Wolschke-Bulmahn, Joachim. "The Nationalisation of Nature and the Naturalisation of the German Nation: 'Teutonic' Trends in the Early Twentieth-Century Landscape Design." In *Nature and Ideology: Natural Garden Design in the Twentieth Century*, ed. Joachim Wolschke-Bulmahn, 187–219. Washington, DC: Dumbarton Oaks Research Library and Collection, 1997.

Index